THE WILD WOMAN

AND OTHER PLAYS

Studies in Austrian Literature, Culture, and Thought

Translation Series

Felix Mitterer

THE WILD WOMAN
AND
OTHER PLAYS

Translated by Todd C. Hanlin and
Heidi Hutchinson

Afterword by
Todd C. Hanlin

ARIADNE PRESS

Ariadne Press would like to express its appreciation to the Austrian Cultural Institute, New York and the Austrian Ministry of Education and Art, Vienna for their assistance in publishing this book.

Translated from the German.
Performance rights for all plays by Felix Mitterer must be acquired from Österreichischer Bühnenverlag Kaiser & Co., Vienna.

Library of Congress Cataloging-in-Publication Data

Mitterer, Felix, 1948-
    [Plays. English. Selections]
    The wild woman and other plays / Felix Mitterer ; translated by Todd C. Hanlin and Heidi Hutchinson ; afterword by Todd C. Hanlin.
        p.   cm. -- (Studies in Austrian literature, culture, and thought. Translation series)
    Contents: The wild woman -- Home -- Children of the devil -- One everyman -- Abraham.
    ISBN 1-57241-002-7
    1. Mitterer, Felix, 1948- --Translations into English.
I. Hanlin, Todd C. II. Hutchinson, Heidi. III. Title. IV. Series
PT2673.I79A25   1995
832'.914--dc20

                                94-43185

Cover design:
Art Director: George McGinnis
Designer, Illustrator: Paul D. Rodriguez

CONTENTS:

The Wild Woman

Translated by
Todd C. Hanlin

Wild Women

According to numerous legends, so-called "wild women," "wild maidens," "blessed women" approach men and establish erotic relationships with them. Usually the man would then marry such a woman who would bring great happiness and many blessings. However, the man must not break a given tabu, for example, he must not ask the woman her name or her origin, must not touch her with the back of his hand, must not strike her, must not undo her hair, must not pull her floor-length hair into bed at night, he must not encourage her to dance and sing, and so on. In all the legends, the man eventually breaks the tabu, the woman leaves him, and he is overwhelmed by unhappiness and misfortune.

CHARACTERS

A WILD WOMAN (between 25 and 35 years old)
JOCK (45)
LEX (35)
ELIAS (70)
MUTT (30)
WENDL (17)

TIME : A winter, long ago

LOCATION: Woodcutters' cabin in the woods

STAGE SETTING: On the wall, stage right, a ladder leads up to a wooden trapdoor into the hayloft. At the left of the ladder a wall cupboard containing shirts, socks, sewing materials and other utensils. On the right rear wall, a slew of hooks and fasteners to hold the woodcutters' tools and chains. Several chains and spare tools are hanging on the wall (axes, picks, pruning hooks, a saw). To the left of the tools is a small, partially frosted window. To the left of the window, the front door. To the left of that, at eye level, a wall cupboard for foodstuffs, beneath that a stool. Further left, stretching to the left corner, is an open brick hearth with an iron tripod which can hold pots and pans. Above the hearth, a movable pivot holding a water kettle. Over the hearth, running its entire length, is a wooden frame for hanging wet clothes to dry. A large slab of bacon is also hanging from the frame. Along the left wall, to the rear, hooks to hang up cooking utensils, and a cupboard for dishes, kitchenware.

Next to that, a board where the men can lay their hats, and below the board, more hooks to hang up clothes. Four knapscks are hanging from the hooks. Downstage left, a narrow hutch with a rustic curtain, barely concealing a rough-hewn bed with straw matting. A stool stands in front of the bed. Downstage right, a long, large table with benches, a kerosene lamp over the table.

INSTRUMENT: Mutt plays an instrument. Possibilities: accordion, harmonica, hand organ, zither, dulcimer, Jew's harp, etc.

1ST SCENE

(*Evening. It is almost completely dark. A growing snow-storm howls outside. WENDL stands at the hearth and warms gruel in a pan. Only the light from the fire illuminates the room. After a while we hear outside the sounds of men approaching, the rattling of their tools and chains. The front door opens, snow blows inside, JOCK appears with his snowshoes in his hand, THE OTHERS are in the process of removing theirs. ALL enter: JOCK, ELIAS, MUTT, and LEX. They are wearing heavy winter clothes, under their hats all are wearing caps or head-bands. LEX has a crow's feather sticking from his hat, MUTT is carrying the knapsack which held their afternoon snack. The men are carrying axes, picks, pruning hooks, chains, and a long two-man saw. As the last to enter, LEX closes the door behind him. They hang up their tools and snowshoes, take off their mittens and hang them over the hearth to dry, remove their hats and caps and lay them on the plank. MUTT hangs up the knapsack. ALL take off their coats and hang them on the pegs. LEX crosses to his knapsack and pulls out a bottle of whiskey, takes a swig. The MEN sit down on the benches, remove their leggings and shoes, place the shoes near the hearth, hang the leggings over the hearth, slip into straw slippers. JOCK lights the kerosene lantern above the table. MUTT and ELIAS warm their hands over the fire. LEX peers into the pan which WENDL is stirring.*)

LEX: Not gruel again!

ELIAS: Hot dumplin's, noodles, women and gruel,
      Make a woodcutter's mouth start to drool.

LEX: I bet our landlord's got pork on his table!

(*ALL but WENDL sit down at the table, where the spoons are already in place.*)

MUTT: Too bad you're not a landlord!

LEX: I still will be, someday!

JOCK (*with scorn*): You... a landlord?

ELIAS: Give a beggar a horse,
And he'll ride it to death.

(*LEX frowns at ELIAS, because the old man's proverbs get on his nerves. WENDL puts down the pan of gruel in the center of the table on a trivet, sits down himself.*)

JOCK (*crosses himself*): In the name of God, the Father, the Son, and the Holy Ghost, amen!

(*THE OTHERS cross themselves and join him in saying grace, then reach for their spoons and start to eat.*)

JOCK (*after a while*): I found a hatchet in a tree today. In a tree that was still standing. (*to LEX*) The hatchet had your mark on it.

LEX: I must of forgot it.

JOCK (*after a while*): Don't ever let it happen again! It's not right! (*after a while*) Besides, I want you to do a better job. You leave half the branches on the tree. And then the trees just get left behind when we haul 'em off. Understand?

LEX (*supressing his rage*): Yeah.

MUTT: Hey, Lex, it's a whole lot easier shootin' deer, ain't it? (*LEX doesn't answer.*)

ELIAS: You can say that again! If our work died, Lex'd be the first one at the funeral!

LEX: Shut up, you old quack! Or I'll break your neck!

ELIAS: Some things never change: The worst dogcart Always makes the most noise!

(*LEX stops eating, looks angrily at ELIAS. It looks as if he's about to hit ELIAS, but he just gives him a dirty look and resumes eating.)*

LEX *(after a while)*: Come springtime, you can kiss my ass goodbye. That's when I'm takin' off.

MUTT: That so? Where you plannin' on goin'?

LEX: 'Cross the border. To the coal mines. I can make ten times as much, minin' coal!

ELIAS: Better to eat gruel at home.
   Than steak abroad!

LEX: At home! To hell with that!
   The only kind of luck I ever had at home was bad luck!

ELIAS: Bad luck is never so bad.
   That something good couldn't have come from it!

MUTT: Well, I can understand why a tenant farmer like you takes off.

LEX: Who the hell do you think you are?

MUTT: We've got a farm! I'm a farmer!

LEX: Come on, don't give me that! You got three cows and a piece of land the size of a handkerchief!

MUTT: So what? That's more 'an you got!

LEX: But you got nothin' to show for it! What kind of farmer has to chop wood for a living?

MUTT: I'll be glad to go home. *(angrily)* Just don't compare me with you!

(LEX grins, contemptuously.)

ELIAS: The world's like a haystack.
   The more you eat off the bottom,
   The more falls in your lap.

LEX: That's the way things are! And I'm gonna eat all I can! Even if I have to take what I want!

JOCK (*after a while*): You can go whenever you want. Nobody's gonna miss you. I'll tell the landlord how you repaid his generosity.

LEX (*bursts out laughing*): Generosity!

JOCK: Yeah, did he give you a job or didn't he? Who else would've given you a job? A convict like you! And you probably committed some crimes on his property, too!

LEX: You bet your ass I did!

JOCK (*after a while*): Let me tell you something—you'd better get out of here right now. (*LEX does not answer.*) You got wax in your ears? I told you to clear out!

LEX: I need the money. Otherwise I can't get out of here.

JOCK: Then sit down and shut up.

(*LEX is furious and embarrassed.*)

ELIAS: If you piss into the wind, you're gonna get your pants wet.

LEX: One more of your stupid sayings, and I'll hit you in the mouth!

ELIAS: Always fear and honor, as you've been told:
God, your superiors, and the old.

LEX (*grabs ELIAS by the shirt collar and pulls the old man toward him*): I told you .. !

(*JOCK looks threateningly at LEX. LEX shoves ELIAS away, gets up, goes over to his knapsack, takes out the bottle of whiskey, takes a big swig, walks over to the window with the bottle in his hand, looks out, takes a couple more sips.*)

JOCK (*crossing himself*): In the name of God the Father, the Son, and the Holy Ghost, amen!

(*The OTHERS—all except LEX—also pray and cross themselves. WENDL gets up and begins to clear the table,*) *then cleans the pan. JOCK stuffs his pipe and lights it, ELIAS pulls out a tin of tree gum, takes a portion and sticks it in his mouth, then crosses to the hearth, picks up a large bowl, dips it into the kettle of hot water to fill it, sits down on the stool next to the hearth, pulls off his socks, rolls up his pantlegs, pulls up the leggings of his long underwear, sets his feet in the water. MUTT picks up an instrument and starts playing, improvising as he goes.)*

JOCK (during the above): Wendl, my coat over there . . . *(points to the clothes rack)* . . . it's about to lose a button! Sew it on for me!

WENDL: Okay.

(ELIAS enjoys wiggling his toes in the warm water.)

ELIAS: Ahhh! If you've got warm feet and a cool head, You'll live a long, long time before you're dead!

(LEX walks away from the window and is about to return the bottle to his knapsack, when suddenly we hear a WOMAN's voice, singing a strange melody that is interrupted from time to time by the howling storm. LEX is the first one to hear her song. He stops and listens.)

LEX: Hold it, Mutt!

MUTT: What?

LEX: Stop playing for a minute!

(MUTT stops playing. Now ALL hear the WOMAN singing, and they listen. LEX goes back to the window, but before he reaches the window, the song stops. LEX looks out the window, sees something outside not far from the cabin, breathes on the partially frosted glass pane, rubs his hand over it, squints out the window to one side.)

LEX: Damn, what the hell's that? *(to THE OTHERS)* Somebody's out there!

(LEX opens the door, snow blows inside. In front of the door

stands a WOMAN, bundled up against the cold. She is wearing boots, a long skirt, a shawl, and a scarf around her head that covers half her face.)

MUTT: Hey, look! A woman!

LEX (*to the WOMAN*): Come on in!

(The WOMAN enters, LEX closes the door. The WOMAN looks at the MEN one by one, then removes her wet scarf. She has black hair and dark skin, as if she came from the south of Europe. The MEN all stare in amazement. The WOMAN walks over to the hearth and warms her hands over the fire. WENDL steps back, out of respect, and stares at her with his mouth wide open.)

LEX (*holds up his bottle*): Want a drink to warm up?

(The WOMAN looks at him and shakes her head.)

JOCK: Where'd you come from? (*The WOMAN just looks at him.*) Where you from?! (*The WOMAN points outside.*) Did you cross the border? (*The WOMAN doesn't answer.*)

MUTT: I bet you she's Italian!

JOCK: Well, what's the matter? You lose your voice in the cold? (*The WOMAN doesn't answer.*)

LEX: Maybe she can't talk. (*to the WOMAN*) Can't you talk? (*The WOMAN doesn't answer.*)

JOCK: Where you headed? (*The WOMAN shakes her head.*)

MUTT: She ain't headed nowhere. You oughta know that!

ELIAS: The more questions you ask,
    The more confused you get!

JOCK: Well, all right, then there's not a whole lot we can do! If she can't talk or doesn't want to talk . . .

WENDL: Maybe she's hungry?

LEX (*pointing to his mouth*): Want something to eat? (*The*

WOMAN nods. LEX to WENDL) Bring her some
bacon and bread! (*to the WOMAN*) Have a seat!

(*The WOMAN removes her shawl, WENDL shyly takes it
and hangs it on a peg over the hearth. The WOMAN hangs
her scarf next to it, walks over to the table and sits down.
MUTT watches her out of curiosity, JOCK looks upset. LEX
approaches the table with the bottle in his hand and also
sits down. ELIAS dries his feet, puts on socks and straw
slippers, carries the bowl over to the door, opens the door
and tosses the water outside, closes the door again, returns
the bowl to the hearth, and sits down at the table as well.
Meanwhile, WENDL brings a cutting board with a chunk
of bacon, some leftover bread, and a sharp knife on it. The
WOMAN takes the knife, looks at it, tries to cut off a chunk
of bacon, but doesn't have much luck. LEX notices.*)

LEX: Here! (*He scoots his chair closer to her, takes the knife,
　　cuts the bacon into slices. The WOMAN begins to
　　eat, while the MEN watch her.*)

JOCK (*to the WOMAN*): I guess where you come from folks
　　don't say grace before they eat, eh?

(*The WOMAN doesn't answer, doesn't even look at him.
MUTT plays a few bars on his instrument. WENDL sits
down on the stool next to the hearth and looks over at the
WOMAN.*)

JOCK (*after a while*): When you're finished, you'd better
　　get going!

LEX: Aw, come on, she's not going anywhere, not in this
　　storm! Not in the middle of the night!

JOCK: I didn't invite her in!

MUTT: You gotta be kidding, Jock! She'll freeze out there!

JOCK: We've got no room for a woman here! I can't just put
　　her up there in the hayloft with you men!

LEX: Why not?

ELIAS: Never take a women up into the hay,
     It'll turn to chaff the very next day!

LEX: You old fool!

ELIAS: What do you mean, old fool? That's what people say! Because that's the absolute truth, that women give off poisonous vapors, you understand? And that'll ruin the hay!

LEX: You're the one who gives off poisonous vapors, you old fart!

(*MUTT bursts out laughing.*)

JOCK: It's not right to have a woman in a woodcutters' cabin! Out!

MUTT: Aw, come on! Just for one night!

JOCK (*after a lengthy pause*): Well, all right! Just for one night! (*to the WOMAN*) You can have my bed over there! And I'll sleep with you men up in the loft.

LEX (*after a while*): Hey, woman! You really can't talk?

(*The WOMAN just looks at LEX.*)

MUTT: But you understand what we're saying?

(*The WOMAN nods.*)

ELIAS: Now there's a blessing! Why, I'd of married a woman who couldn't talk! That reminds me of an old saying!

LEX: Oh, come on, not another one of your old sayings!

ELIAS: When the chicken crows before the rooster,
     When the wife talks before her spouse,
     When the cat runs away from the rat—
     You've got big troubles in your house!

MUTT (*laughs*): Yeah, that's a good one!

LEX: You're right, for once in your life!

(*WENDL just remembers that he is supposed to sew on a*

button. He gets up, takes JOCK's coat, gets needle and thread, sits down at the table to take advantage of the light, threads the needle.)

JOCK: Hold it, Wendl! If there's a woman present, she should do it!

(The WOMAN stops eating, looks at JOCK, looks at WENDL, takes the coat and needle out of WENDL's hands, begins to sew the button on. WENDL watches, then clears away the cutting board, bacon, bread, and knife, sits down on the stool next to the hearth, looks over at the OTHERS. MUTT begins to play a few bars on his instrument, then gets an idea.)

MUTT: You know what? I bet she's a gypsy!

LEX *(looks at the WOMAN)*: Yeah, could be!

ELIAS: Oh, Jesus! Keep an eye on your valuables!

MUTT: Maybe she's a relative of yours, Wendl!

(WENDL lowers his gaze.)

LEX: How come?

MUTT: His father had one of those pushcarts, too! He was a knife sharpener!

LEX: Aha! *(to WENDL)* I guess your momma sharpened his knife for him, eh?

MUTT: You bet! None of the local guys was ever good enough for her, what a stuck-up bitch!

LEX: What happened then?

MUTT: The farmer tossed her out, he did, when she got as big as a house! And by then the dark-skinned guy was long gone! One day we caught her out in the barn, when she had the baby! Two weeks later she jumped into the river, along with her bastard kid! But they fished little Wendl out.

(WENDL starts to cry, tries to hold back his sobs. LEX looks over at him, feels sorry for WENDL.)

ELIAS: When a woman dies, it's no big deal.
    But when a horse dies, your problems are real.

LEX *(to ELIAS)*: Hey, just shut your filthy mouth!

JOCK: She got what she deserved! You should never get involved with a guy with a pushcart!

ELIAS: You can say that again! "I got nobody to blame but myself," the ox said, as he hauled his own dung out to the field!

(WENDL sobs, holds his hand over his mouth, goes to the door and opens it, goes outside, closing the door behind him.)

JOCK: Hey, where's he going?

(The WOMAN also watches WENDL leave. She has now finished sewing on the button, hangs the coat on its peg, puts the sewing gear away in a cupboard, goes over to the door and opens it. WENDL is standing outside with his back to the door, his face in his hands. The WOMAN goes outside, closing the door behind her.)

MUTT: What's she up to?

(LEX gets up, goes over to the door, opens it. The WOMAN and WENDL are facing each other, she has placed her hand on his cheek. He is hiding his face in her hand, sobbing. The WOMAN looks at LEX who then shuts the door, somewhat embarrassed. The OTHERS look at him questioningly. LEX sits down, MUTT starts to play something on his instrument. After a while the door opens, WENDL and the WOMAN enter. WENDL goes to the hearth, jabs a poker around in the ashes out of embarrassment. The WOMAN sits down on a stool near the hutch. A lengthy silence.)

ELIAS: "Where there's smoke, there's fire," the farmer said, and lit his pipe with a fresh horse turd.

JOCK (*gets up*): Well! It's time!

(*JOCK blows out the kerosene lamp over the table, goes over to the ladder, slips out of his straw slippers, climbs the ladder, opens the trapdoor, climbs up into the hayloft. Now the room is illuminated only by the red glow from the hearth. The OTHER MEN also get up, walk over to the ladder, slip out of their straw slippers. Before LEX goes to the ladder, he slips the whiskey bottle in his knapsack.*)

MUTT: Ga' night, woman!

(*MUTT climbs the ladder, WENDL climbs up, looks back at the WOMAN, then disappears into the hayloft. ELIAS climbs up.*)

LEX: Sleep well, woman! Sweet dreams!

ELIAS (*from the ladder*): A good night's sleep brings you
one step closer to the grave!

(*LEX, the last one to climb the ladder, takes one final look back at the WOMAN, then closes the trapdoor behind him. The WOMAN is left sitting alone, scarcely more than a shadow.*)

LEX'S VOICE: That's my place, Jock!

JOCK'S VOICE: Then I'll just sleep over here!

ELIAS' VOICE: Always sleep with your feet toward the
door,
Or you might not live much more!

JOCK'S VOICE: You're not pulling my leg, are you . . . ?

(*The WOMAN looks up at the trapdoor, looks over at the front door, ponders a moment, looks over at the hutch, then stands up, pulls back the curtain to the hutch.*)

(*Blackout*)

2ND SCENE

(Night. Light shines from the glowing hearth. Outside, the storm has abated, everything is completely quiet. The curtain of the hutch is closed, the WOMAN is lying in bed, her clothes are arranged on the stool next to the bed. After a while the trapdoor to the loft silently opens. LEX—in his shirt, pants, and socks—appears on the ladder, carefully closes the trapdoor, climbs down the ladder, glances over at the hutch, crosses to his knapsack, takes out the whiskey bottle, takes a gulp, puts the bottle back, crosses to the hutch, looks at the curtain, notices the clothes on the stool, picks up the clothing, lays it back down, looks at the curtain, pulls it back a bit, sneaks into the hutch. The WOMAN silently tries to fend him off. The audience cannot see the struggle, since the curtain is completely closed.)

LEX'S VOICE: Come on, now! Don't fight! Don't fight, I said!—Listen, don't play games with me or I'll beat the hell out of you!

(We hear the sounds of panting and struggling, and then a blow. It is suddenly quiet. The trapdoor opens a crack, ELIAS peeks out unnoticed, listens.)

LEX'S VOICE: I told you! I warned you! Usually I never hit a woman! Believe you me! Come on now, I'll be good to you from now on! Come on!—Shit, why are you just lying there? Do something! What's the matter? Move! I can't get a hard-on!—Sonofabitch! What's goin' on? That's never happened before!—You slut! What a slut! What're you tryin' to do to me? That's never happened before!

(LEX climbs out of the hutch. ELIAS closes the trapdoor as quick as a wink. LEX pulls up his pants, buttons his fly. He crosses to his knapsack, takes a big gulp of whiskey, looks down at his fly, shakes his fist angrily in front of his fly.)

LEX: Goddamn pecker! Just leave me hanging there! What am I, a capon or somethin'? (*takes another drink*) What a slut! That goddamn witch! Never had that happen to me before! Bitch! (*in the direction of the hutch*) Just you wait, I'll get you, sooner or later! It's just because I haven't had any for so long! Two years in prison, and then straight into the woods! Shit! (*takes a drink*) Just you wait, I'll get you! Never had that happen before! (*He puts the bottle away, climbs back up the ladder, opens the trapdoor, climbs into the loft, closes the door behind him. Momentary silence.*)

JOCK'S VOICE: Hey, Lex!

LEX'S VOICE (*surprised*): Yeah, what's up?

JOCK'S VOICE: Where you been?

LEX'S VOICE: Where you think I've been? To the shit-house, that's where!

JOCK'S VOICE: So that's where you were. You were gone a long time!

LEX'S VOICE: So what? Now you're gonna tell me there're rules about how long I can take a crap?

ELIAS' VOICE: A long crap means a long life!

JOCK'S VOICE: You were with that woman. Weren't you? (*Pause*) Hey, I asked you a question!

LEX'S VOICE: Yeah, I was with that woman! So what?

(*Extended silence.*)

ELIAS' VOICE: When a man sees a hole, he's got to fill it! Most of the time he falls right in!

(*Extended silence.*)

MUTT'S VOICE: And she didn't resist?

LEX'S VOICE: No woman can resist me!

JOCK'S VOICE: She's a whore! And sleeping in my bed, too!

MUTT'S VOICE: She really didn't fight back?

LEX'S VOICE: Not a bit! Jumped right up in the saddle, spread her legs, and away we went!

MUTT'S VOICE: What then? I mean, what was it like?

LEX'S VOICE: A racing stallion! A horny bitch! She'll drive you crazy!

ELIAS' VOICE (*sings*):
> A monk without a frock,
> A woman without a tit,
> A shepherd without a flock—
> These three ain't worth shit!

LEX'S VOICE: What do you mean by that?

ELIAS' VOICE: Nothin'! It's just a proverb!

JOCK'S VOICE: Let me get some sleep, for God's sake!

(*Blackout*)

3RD SCENE

(*Morning. It is snowing and already light outside. The MEN and the WOMAN are dressed, sitting around the table, eating noodles out of the pan. An extended period of silence.*)

LEX (*looks over to the window*): More miserable weather!

ELIAS: If winter doesn't freeze your root,
> Then summer won't be worth a hoot!

(*Silence.*)

JOCK (*to the WOMAN*): Tell me, woman, what are your plans? What's the matter? Don't look at me like that! I just want to know what your plans are!

(*Pause.*)

LEX: Want to stay here a couple of days? You won't get very far, not in that snow!

(*Though the WOMAN looks at LEX, she doesn't react, just continues eating.*)

JOCK: You got any other crazy ideas? The tramp's got to go!

LEX: You know, you've said just about enough!

JOCK: If she's not a tramp, then what is she?

MUTT: Who cares? I mean, it ain't such a bad idea. What'd'ya say?

(*JOCK looks over at MUTT, looks at the WOMAN, continues eating.*)

JOCK: I've got a wife at home, and four kids.

LEX (*grinning*): Good for you!

ELIAS (*sings*):

> A rifle for shootin'
> And an ax for choppin'
> And a girl for smoochin'—
> That's what a young man needs!

(*A long silence.*)

JOCK: All right. (*to the WOMAN*) You can stay a couple of days. Until the weather changes. But you'll have to work for your keep! Cook, clean, mend things! You understand? (*The WOMAN looks at JOCK, nods. JOCK crosses himself.*) In the name of God the Father, the Son, and the Holy Ghost, amen!

(*ALL—except the WOMAN—cross themselves and mumble JOCK's prayer. The MEN all rise, put on their caps and hats, pull on their gloves, take up their tools and snow-shoes. WENDL also shoulders the knapsack with their mid-morning snack. The WOMAN picks up the spoons and the pan and carries them over to the hearth.*)

JOCK (*to the WOMAN*): For lunch, fix us some beans and bacon. The bacon's hanging over here. And the beans are over there! (*The WOMAN nods.*) All right. Let's get going!

(*The MEN exit, with LEX bringing up the rear. He looks back and wants to say something, but doesn't, closes the door behind him. The WOMAN walks over to the window and watches them depart, turns around, ponders for a moment, goes to the hearth, takes her boots, sits down on the stool near the fire, takes off the straw slippers she's been wearing, slips into one boot, stops, stares off into space, lost in thought.*)

(*Blackout*)

4TH SCENE

(*Night. It is snowing heavily outside. Light from the hearthfire. The WOMAN is lying in the hutch, the MEN are up in the hayloft.*)

ELIAS' VOICE: Oh, does that feel good! A tired man enjoys his rest, a lazy man enjoys it even more!

(*Extended silence.*)

JOCK'S VOICE: It's my turn tonight! If you don't like it, Lex, just say so! Then we'll settle it just between the two of us!

LEX'S VOICE (*after a while*): Go ahead and try! If she'll let you . . .

(*The trapdoor opens, JOCK climbs out in his shirt, pants, and socks. He closes the trapdoor, climbs down the ladder, looks over at the hutch, slowly approaches, thinks for a moment, starts to reach for the curtain, but then doesn't. He sits down on the stool where the WOMAN's clothes are lying.*)

JOCK (*after a while*): It's me, woman, Jock! I'd like to come visit you.—I won't force you, it's up to you. I'd really like to join you. It's probably a sin . . . I know it is. I never cheated on my wife. But it really would be nice, just once. To feel a different body. A younger one. You know, my wife . . . she's a decent woman . . . takes good care of the kids . . . she never was a good looking woman. A weather-beaten old rock. A cold oven. The only time I touch her anymore is when I'm good and drunk. But you get me all excited. Every time I look at you, I get hard. (*looks over at the curtain*) If you can put up with Lex, you sure ought'a be able to put up with me. That's what I think. Or did the two of you just hit it off?—If that's the way it is, I'd rather you didn't stay. I been thinkin' about how that'd work out. Men are just men, doing what comes naturally. You really don't want to marry him, don't want to marry Lex, do you? You're not the marrying kind, seems to me. A stranger to these parts, and bein' hot-blooded and all . . . Yeah, woman, I'd really be grateful to you if you'd let me have some, too! (*He looks at the curtain, gets up, opens the curtain slightly, slips inside. The trapdoor opens, LEX peeks out, MUTT appears behind him.*)

MUTT: Did she let him in?

LEX: Looks like it. Damn slut! (*He closes the trapdoor.*)

(*Blackout*)

5TH SCENE

(*Evening. Light from the kerosene lamp and from the hearthfire. It has stopped snowing outside. The WOMAN is washing the dishes. WENDL is sitting on the stool near the hearth watching her, absent-mindedly whittling a piece of wood. JOCK, MUTT, and ELIAS are sitting around the table. JOCK is smoking his pipe, MUTT is playing his instrument, ELIAS has fallen asleep. After a while the door opens: LEX stumbles in, carrying a slaughtered deer, and tosses it on the table. ELIAS wakes up with a start, MUTT stops playing.*)

ELIAS: Oh, our Sunday roast!

JOCK: What? Are you out of your mind?

LEX: What do you mean? Be glad there's meat for a change!

JOCK: I guess being in jail once just wasn't enough for you, eh?

LEX: Go ahead and turn me in, if that's the way you feel!

JOCK: Pack your stuff and get out of here!

LEX: Fine! I'll leave! You won't mind if I just pay a brief visit to your wife? Or, better yet, I'll shout it in the village square: Hey, folks, your good ole woodcutter Jock's got his meat loaf in some other woman's oven! Well, what do you think'll happen! All the gossips in town'll perk up their ears!

JOCK (*angrily*): Get that animal off the table!

(*LEX takes the deer and carries it over to the back wall, lays it down on the floor, gets a hatchet and some nails.*)

LEX: Get over here, Mutt! (*MUTT gets up, crosses to LEX who holds the deer up against the wall like a crucified human.*) Lift it up!

(*MUTT holds the deer up against the wall, LEX nails it up by its front hooves. MUTT notices the wound that runs around the deer's throat.*)

MUTT: So, you caught it with a wire snare!

JOCK (*to LEX*): Did you reset the snare?

LEX: 'Course I did!

JOCK: You're gonna get it for this, you'll see! Next time they catch you, they'll shoot you. Just as sure as the day is long!

LEX: We'll see about that!

(*MUTT sits back down. LEX hangs up his hat, pulls off his coat.*)

LEX (*to the WOMAN*): Well, woman, what do you think of that? Now we can celebrate your new home!

(*The WOMAN looks at LEX, JOCK gets mad. ELIAS looks at LEX and then at the WOMAN, then back at LEX.*)

ELIAS (*sings*):

A poacher sees clearly,
Till love clouds his sight.
The tiniest woman
Can catch a man twice her height!

LEX (*has gone over to his knapsack, pulls out his whiskey bottle, takes a swig*): No woman's gonna catch me! I'm the catcher!

(*Blackout*)

6TH SCENE

(*Night. Light from the hearthfire and from the moon shining in the window. The deer hangs from the wall. The WOMAN is lying in her bed, the MEN are in the hayloft. The trapdoor opens, LEX appears, behind him MUTT, trying to hold LEX back.*)

MUTT: No you don't! It's my turn tonight!

LEX (*shoves him back*): Beat it, you turd! (*He climbs out, pushes the trapdoor closed, MUTT tries to push it open.*)

MUTT: Jock! That's not fair!

JOCK'S VOICE: You two work it out between you!

(*LEX forcefully pushes the trapdoor shut, climbs down the ladder. MUTT opens the trapdoor again, climbs onto the ladder. LEX grabs hold of the ladder, pulls it away from the wall. MUTT is standing at the top of the ladder, off-balance, while JOCK and ELIAS peer out of the loft. LEX shakes the ladder, MUTT holds on desparately. LEX turns the ladder to one side, lets go of it. MUTT leaps off at the last minute, as the ladder comes crashing down. Ignoring MUTT, LEX heads straight for the hutch. MUTT chases after him and tries to pull him back. LEX grabs him, spins him around, shoves him in the direction of the loft, kicks him in the pants, turns around and heads back to the hutch. MUTT spies the tools on the wall, takes down a pick. LEX sees him and stops dead in his tracks.*)

LEX (*grinning*): Come on, put it back, Mutt!

ELIAS: Yeah, yeah, that's the way it is:
        Chickens, children, and gals,
        Come between the best of pals!

(*LEX slowly approaches MUTT. MUTT raises the pick, but at the same time retreats, until his back is against the wall.*)

LEX: Come on, Mutt, hand it over, otherwise you're just gonna hurt yourself!

(*LEX tries to grab the pick, MUTT hits him in the chest with the dull edge. LEX falls backward, gets back up and goes after MUTT again. MUTT raises the pick and strikes. LEX is barely able to dodge the blow.*)

LEX: Hey, what're you doin'? Are you crazy? (*looks over to JOCK*) He's really tryin' to kill me!

JOCK: Fair is fair. It's his turn tonight!

(*LEX looks at MUTT, looks over at the hutch.*)

ELIAS: "The smarter one should always give in," the farmer said to the ox, "so you give in!"

LEX: Okay, fine! But don't you ever try that again! If you do, you're dead! You can count on it!

(*LEX goes over to the ladder, picks it up, leans it against the entrance to the loft, climbs up. JOCK and ELIAS withdraw from the trapdoor opening. MUTT watches LEX go, is shocked at his own behavior.*)

MUTT: Hey, Lex, I didn't mean it that way! I really didn't! My temper just sorta got the best of me!

(*LEX climbs up into the loft and closes the trapdoor. MUTT looks down at the pick in his hand, hangs it back up on the wall, looks over at the hutch, slowly walks over to it. As he passes the hearth, he notices the kettle of water, dips both hands in the water, slicks back his hair with his wet hands, goes to the hutch.*)

MUTT: It's me, Mutt! Can I come in? (*He waits for a moment, then slips into the hutch.*)

(*Blackout*)

7TH SCENE

(Daytime. Outside the blizzard has stopped. The deer hangs on the wall. The WOMAN is standing at the hearth, cooking. The front door flies open, LEX enters. The WOMAN looks at him briefly, then goes back to stirring her bowl. LEX goes over to his knapsack, takes out the whiskey bottle, takes a swig, stows the bottle in the knapsack, looks over at the WOMAN, sits down at the table, looks at the WOMAN.)

LEX *(after a while)*: I don't understand you! Why d'you let 'em all sleep with you? Only a whore'd do that! Well, maybe you're nothin' but a nympho! You get chased out of town somewhere, huh? Or did you run away from your wild animal tamer? Or did he send you here? Maybe he's following you, your pimp? To get the money we owe him? *(The WOMAN is standing with her back to LEX and doesn't react. LEX gets up, walks over to her, stands behind her.)* I like you! I never liked any woman as much as you! Never! *(He grabs her from behind, clasping her breasts.)* I gotta have you! *(The WOMAN doesn't move. LEX spins her around to face him.)* Hey! You hear what I said? *(The WOMAN just looks as him, calmly.)* Don't play games with me! Or you're gonna get it! If you let the others sleep with you, then you gotta let me, too! *(The WOMAN turns back to the hearth. LEX spins her around again.)* I won't hit you! I won't ever hit you again! I only did it 'cause I was so crazy about you! Understand? Now, come on, I don't have much time! I've taken off from work! Snuck off!

(The WOMAN looks at him, then walks over to the hutch, steps inside. LEX pulls off his coat, lays it on the stool, puts

his hat down on top of his coat.)

(*Blackout*)

8TH SCENE

(*Night. Light from the hearthfire and from the moon, shining in the window. The deer hangs on the wall. The WOMAN is in bed, the MEN are in the hayloft.*)

LEX'S VOICE: My turn again, huh?

ELIAS' VOICE: Uh-uh! Tonight's the night I tuck her in!

LEX'S VOICE: Get out'a here! What'a you got in mind, you old fart! You with your rusty pick!

ELIAS' VOICE: Don't kid yourself! The old goats aren't the worst!

(*The trapdoor to the loft opens, ELIAS appears. LEX is right behind him and pulls ELIAS back.*)

JOCK'S VOICE: Let him go! Elias's got just as much right as you do!

ELIAS (*appears in the loft opening, climbs out onto the ladder, closes the trapdoor, climbs down. During the above, he mumbles to himself*):

A strong enemy,
A young woman who's slim,
Both keep an old man fit and trim!

(*He looks at the hutch, goes over, pauses, scratches his head.*)

I'm really not as young as I used to be, and I haven't had a bath since Easter! Damn!

(*He walks right up to the hutch, stops, then walks away. He sees LEX's knapsack, goes over to it, takes out the whiskey bottle, takes a swig.)*

LEX: Who knows if she'll even take an old codger like me?

(He takes another swig, sticks the bottle back in the pack, walks over to the window, looks out, sings quietly.)

> It gets white when it snows,
> And icy when it freezes.
> A sweet girl's lovin'
> Is mighty hard work, by Jesus!

(He turns around, looks over at the hutch.)

> Oh, God, when was it, when was the last time? Let me see. Way back then, at the church fair. The maid from. . . . aw, can't remember anymore. Oh, she was so soft and warm and wet! It's probably been thirty-five years now! Thirty-five years! Yeah, the good old days! Back then I had all I wanted! On all the high holy days I used to have my little sweets! *(sings)*

> That I've never fallen down,
> I thank God for that!
> But I've stumbled quite a lot
> Over the Sixth Commandment!

> After a while your pecker just falls asleep, eh? Just like the priests who pee in their habits. If they don't have a horny housekeeper . . . *(looks over to the hutch)* But lately the sap has been rising in the old tree trunk, something's stirring again! Who'd'a thought it!

(Sings):

> Why shouldn't I love a sweet little girl,
> The birds do it all the time,
> Till the tree branches curl!

(*He looks over at the hutch, walks to his coat, takes out a tin case, opens it, takes out a chunk of tree gum.*)

A chunk of tree gum, so my mouth doesn't stink so bad! (*sticks the tree gum in his mouth, starts to chew it, puts the tin back in his coat, and pulls himself together.*) Well, I guess I'll just give it a try!

(*ELIAS goes over to the hutch, slips inside.*)

(*Blackout*)

9TH SCENE

(*Daytime. Outside the snow has stopped. The deer is no longer hanging on the wall. From the left rear corner, a rope runs from the hearth to the hutch, various items of clothing are strung from it to create a temporary curtain. Through the space between the bottom of the clothes and the floor we can partially see a large wooden tub. The water kettle is hanging over the fire, the water is boiling. The MEN sit around the table, eating. JOCK is listlessly eating gruel out of a pan, the OTHERS have chunks of LEX's venison on wooden plates and are eating it with relish.*)

LEX (*to JOCK*): Well, how's that mush?

(*JOCK doesn't answer. ELIAS is enjoying sucking on a bone.*)

ELIAS: Good is good—but better is better!

(*The WOMAN enters through the front door with a bucket full of water, goes over to the wooden tub, pours in the water.*)

LEX (*to the WOMAN, annoyed*): Why don't you eat some? It's your game! I got it for you!

(*The WOMAN doesn't react.*)

MUTT: Maybe she don't like venison . . .

LEX: You're gonna eat now! Com'ere!

(*The WOMAN shakes her head, goes back outside with the bucket. LEX angrily watches her go, pushes his plate away.*)

MUTT: I can't eat anymore! Christ, I'm so full I could bust.

JOCK (*crosses himself*): In the name of God the Father, the Son, and of the Holy Ghost, amen!

(*LEX, WENDL, and MUTT also cross themselves, mumble the prayer along with JOCK. ELIAS does not—he's still eating. LEX goes over to his knapsack, takes out the whiskey bottle, starts to take a drink, but stops, looks at the bottle.*)

LEX: Somebody been drinking out of my whiskey bottle?

MUTT: Not me!

(*LEX looks over at JOCK who is just stuffing his pipe.*)

JOCK: What're you looking at me for? I don't need any of your illegal swill!

(*The WOMAN re-enters with the newly filled bucket, pours the water into the tub.*)

LEX: Then it must'a been you, Elias!

ELIAS (*still eating*): Leave me out of this! I don't like whiskey! Never did!

MUTT (*to LEX*): You probably drank it all yourself!

(*LEX looks sullen, takes a swig.*)

JOCK (*to the WOMAN*): Woman, clean up the table!

(*The WOMAN comes over to the table, takes the pan from JOCK and the plates from MUTT, LEX, and from WENDL. ELIAS points to the meat platter.*)

ELIAS: But leave that here! I'm not done yet!

JOCK: When I'm done, everybody's done!

(*JOCK hands the meat platter to the WOMAN. ELIAS quickly grabs a bone, sucks on it. The WOMAN carries the plates to the hearth. MUTT picks up his instrument and begins to improvise a tune, LEX sits down at the table with his whiskey bottle, WENDL carries the rest of the plates to the hearth. The WOMAN wipes off the table. MUTT plays, grinning at the WOMAN, she looks at him briefly, continues wiping the table. WENDL takes out his carving block (that is beginning to resemble a miniature Madonna), pulls a little whittling knife out of his pocket, sits down on the stool near the hearth and begins to whittle. ELIAS observes him.*)

ELIAS: Put it down, Wendl! When you carve on Sunday, you cut the Lord's finger!

(*WENDL, ignoring ELIAS, continues whittling.*)

LEX (*to JOCK*): How come you're not goin' home today? (*JOCK doesn't answer him.*) Usually, you go home every Sunday. Your old lady'll be waitin' for you!

JOCK: There's too much snow!

LEX (*grinning*): Oh! So that's what it is!

MUTT (*stops playing*): Better hope your old lady doesn't find out! Or else there'll be all hell to pay!

(*JOCK doesn't answer.*)

ELIAS (*sings*):

Since I've been married
Love has fled,
Now all I get are sermons
And snacks in bed!

(*LEX and MUTT laugh, JOCK looks unhappy. MUTT starts to play again. The WOMAN picks up the bucket*

*again, dunks it in the kettle of hot water, pours the water in
the tub. ALL watch her. LEX gets up, goes over to her.)*

LEX: Here, gimme that! I'll give you a hand!

*(LEX reaches for the bucket. The WOMAN shakes her head
resolutely, dips the bucket back into the kettle. LEX returns
to the table, out of sorts. The WOMAN pours more hot water
into the tub, then goes behind the curtain and undresses.
We can see her bare feet. She climbs into the tub. The MEN
watch her. MUTT continues playing on his instrument.
Suddenly he stops. We can hear the sound of water splashing.)*

ELIAS *(slyly)*:
    If you're born black,
    No use washing you or your clothes!

*(Extended silence. The MEN stare off into space, MUTT
improvises on his instrument.)*

LEX *(suddenly, in the direction of the WOMAN)*: Why you
    hidin' back there? You don't need to hide yourself
    from your men!

*(LEX gets up, walks over to the temporary curtain, pulls
down a few articles of clothing from the line. The WOMAN
is sitting in the tub, her breasts are visible, though she
doesn't try to cover them. She only looks at LEX impassively. ALL look at her, even WENDL who immediately
looks down at the floor in embarrassment. JOCK gets up,
walks over, hangs the clothing back on the line, looks at
LEX grimly, returns to the table, sits down. MUTT starts to
play again. LEX also returns to the table, takes a drink
from his whiskey bottle. A long silence. We can hear the
WOMAN splashing in the tub. JOCK looks over in the direction of the WOMAN.)*

JOCK *(in a hushed voice)*: I've never had a woman like that
    before.

MUTT (*in a hushed voice*): Yeah . . . Has she got tits! . . . And an ass . . . I can't stand it!

JOCK (*in a hushed voice*): A bed of moss . . . It's enough to drive you crazy! (Pause) Her mouth tastes like raspberries . . .

(*LEX is jealous, but tries to hide it. A long silence.*)

MUTT (*in a hushed voice*): What do we do if she gets pregnant?

LEX (*in a normal tone*): What do we care!

JOCK: Well, aren't you men taking precautions?

LEX (*loudly*): What're you talking about! You think I'm gonna climb down out of the saddle just when we're gallopin' along like crazy?

JOCK: It's easy for you men to talk! When you're married, like I am, then you learn to take precautions!

ELIAS (*grinning*): It's all the same to me! You can't make butter out of skim milk!

(*Silence. LEX drinks his whiskey, then notices WENDL carving.*)

LEX: Christ, Wendl, we almost forgot about you! That's not right! If we all get a piece of the action, then you should, too! Okay, Wendl, it'll be your turn tonight!

WENDL: My turn to do what?

LEX: "To do what?" he asks. The idiot! To be with the woman! Tonight you get to nail her!

WENDL (*shaking his head*): I don't want to.

LEX (*bursts out laughing*): "I don't want to," he says! And every time one of us is in bed with her, he lights his sparkler!

WENDL: What sparkler?

MUTT (*grinning, pantomimes masturbation*): When you play your hand organ! You think we didn't notice?

(*WENDL is embarrassed.*)

ELIAS (*comforting WENDL*): That's all right. Every now and then a young man has to tamp his pipe! I've done it too!

LEX: Believe you me, Wendl, your hand is nothin' compared to her furnace!

MUTT: He's not ready for it! Leave him alone!

LEX: Go on! Chicken shit! You don't have to be scared! It's easy, it just happens all by itself! And you won't find anything better than that (*nods in the direction of the WOMAN*) to practice on!

WENDL: I don't want to!

ELIAS: You're right, Wendl!
If you get hurt, you get wise!
If you fall in love, you fall on your face!

(*Blackout*)

10TH SCENE

(*Evening. The kerosene lamp is lit, the hearth glows. It has stopped snowing outside. The tub and temporary curtain are gone. WENDL is sitting on the stool next to the hearth, carving his madonna. The OTHER MEN are sitting around the table, playing cards. JOCK is paired with ELIAS, LEX and MUTT are partners. The WOMAN is sitting nearby, on the stool that usually is next to the hutch. She is mending a sock, sitting near the MEN to take advan-*)

ge of the light. She takes no interest in their card game. In front of LEX are two whiskey bottles; one is empty, the other is still almost full. LEX is already drunk.)

ELIAS (*looks at his cards, with a wily look*): "Well, what do you know," said the fox, when he found himself in the henhouse! (*lays a card on the table*) I'm out! You guys lose!

(*ELIAS collects the cards from the middle of the table, picks up a piece of charcoal from the hearth and makes a mark on the table top beside him.*)

LEX: Aw, shit! (*to MUTT*) Why'd you throw away the jack? You dumb ass!

MUTT: Well, hell, I just made a mistake! Wouldn't'a done us any good anyway! With the crappy cards we got!

JOCK: Whatta you say, you want to play one more hand?

LEX: I don' wanna' play no more! (*He takes a drink from the full bottle.*)

JOCK: Hey! Come on!

LEX: What?

JOCK: That's our whiskey now! That was our bet! Or did you forget already?

(*LEX shoves the bottle over to JOCK, who takes a big gulp, passes the bottle on to ELIAS who also takes a big gulp.*)

ELIAS: Ahhhh! That warms up the old gizzard!

MUTT (*to ELIAS*): Gim'me a drink, too!

ELIAS: Nope! You were one of the losers!

(*ELIAS takes another swig, gives the bottle back to JOCK who also takes another drink.*)

LEX (*to ELIAS*): Didn't one of you guys say he didn't like whiskey?

ELIAS: Well, like it or not . . . You know what I always say: Better to drown in whiskey than in the creek!

LEX: Yeah, yeah . . . Just watch yourself, you old goat! (*LEX gets up, goes over to his knapsack, takes out another bottle of whiskey.*)

MUTT: Now he's got another bottle! What'd you do in prison, run a still, or somethin'?

LEX (*pulls the cork out of the bottle, smells the cork*): Hell, no! This is my inheritance! From my old man! (*takes a drink*) Thirty bottles of whiskey! I hope he rots in hell!

JOCK: It's a miracle that you've got so much left! Your father used to drink like a fish!

LEX (*comes back to the table, sits down*): That's none of your business, Jock! I'm the only one who's allowed to cuss my father!

MUTT: Come on, Lex, gimme something to drink! 'Specially since you've got so much!

LEX: Yeah, sure! 'Specially since you played your cards so damn dumb! (*holds the bottle out toward WENDL*) Here, Wendl, drink! So you can be a man!

(*WENDL hesitates, then walks over, takes the bottle, drinks a tiny sip.*)

LEX: What're you doin'? More!

(*WENDL takes another drink, gives the bottle back to LEX. LEX looks at him disapprovingly. WENDL sits back down on his stool. LEX looks over at the WOMAN, holds the bottle out toward her.*)

LEX: Here, woman, take a drink! (*The WOMAN shakes her head.*) You tryin' to insult me? You won't eat the meat I bring in, and my whiskey ain't good enough for you! Then I'll just have to pour it down your throat!

(*LEX gets up, walks over to her, grabs her by the nape of her neck, yanks her head back, tries to pour the whiskey down her throat. She holds her lips together so tightly that the whiskey runs down her chin and neck.*)

JOCK: Let her alone, if she doesn't want any!

(*With one hand, LEX squeezes her cheeks together until the WOMAN opens her mouth. He shoves the bottle in her mouth.*)

JOCK (*getting up*): That's just about enough!

(*LEX doesn't respond. JOCK shoves LEX away from the WOMAN, looks at LEX threateningly. The WOMAN wipes off her mouth.*)

LEX: Dumb bitch! I'll just have to drink it all myself!

(*LEX drinks, sits down across from MUTT. JOCK sits back down. LEX stares at MUTT, suddenly holds up his middle finger.*)

MUTT: What?

LEX: No guts?

MUTT: I don't want to.

LEX: Chicken shit!

(*MUTT glances over at the WOMAN, looks back at LEX, then readies himself for the finger-wrestling match. LEX, too, takes his position, they hook their middle fingers and begin to tug. The WOMAN goes back to her mending, from time to time glancing over indifferently at the two combatants. LEX suddenly pulls MUTT over the table, lets go of him, sits back to catch his breath, drinks from his whiskey bottle.*)

LEX: You need to eat a few more dumplings, Mutt!

(*MUTT sits back down, rubs his aching finger, is embarrassed.*)

JOCK: Think you can beat me too, Lex?

LEX: No problem! Think I'm afraid of you?

(*JOCK sits down at the table across from LEX, MUTT slides out of the way. JOCK and LEX hook middle fingers and begin to tug. Slowly but surely, JOCK pulls LEX over the table, lets go of him. LEX leans back, exhausted. MUTT grins with satisfaction.*)

ELIAS (*grinning*): The rougher you are, the stronger you are.
The stronger you are, the more you win!

JOCK: You need a little bear grease, Lex! Not just a big mouth!

LEX (*furious, embarrassed*): If I weren't so drunk, I'd'a whipped you!

ELIAS: Sure, sure!
If we didn't have the word "if,"
Then cow manure'd be butter!

(*LEX shoves ELIAS off the bench; ELIAS falls to the floor. The WOMAN stops her mending, watches. LEX walks over to ELIAS, yanks him to his feet.*)

LEX: I've had it up to here with your bullshit! (*He punches ELIAS in the face, knocking ELIAS down, then kicks him in the side.*) Get up! I'm not done with you yet! Get up, I said!

JOCK (*gets up, stands between LEX and ELIAS*): Leave the old man alone, Lex! Why don't you pick on somebody your own size—like me!

(*LEX steps back, gets ready to fight. JOCK also puts up his fists. They circle each other, start to fight. ELIAS gets up off the floor, rubs his aching back and sits down. WENDL doesn't move from his stool. The WOMAN watches the fight, betraying no emotion. JOCK fights according to the rules. LEX fights dirty, kicks JOCK, pulls JOCK's hair, etc. JOCK is able to put a hold on LEX. MUTT jumps up.)*

MUTT: That's it! That'sa way! Grab 'em! Throw 'em down!

(LEX pokes JOCK in the eyes. JOCK has to let him go.)

MUTT: Cut it out, Lex! You fight like a yellow-belly!

(Finally, JOCK is able to throw LEX down on the floor and to pin his shoulders. MUTT leaps over, kneels down, and peers in, like a referee, to see if LEX's shoulders are touching the floor.)

MUTT: That's it! That's a way! *(holds his fingers about an inch apart)* Just this much more! More! . . . More! . . . Yeah! It's all over! Hey, Jock!

(LEX's shoulders touch the floor, MUTT enthusiastically leaps up. JOCK lets go of LEX and gets up. LEX lies on the floor for a while in embarrassment. JOCK sits down, drinks LEX's whiskey.)

ELIAS *(sings in a mocking voice)*:

Is there no one in the land
Who can throw me, who can catch me,
Who can throw me, who can beat me,
And take my crown away!

(LEX gets up off the floor unsteadily, totters toward the door. ALL watch him go. LEX goes outside and closes the door behind him. MUTT goes over to the window and watches LEX.)

MUTT: He's rollin' around in the snow! Like a horse!

(MUTT comes back to the table and sits down. JOCK drinks from the whiskey bottle. MUTT looks at him. JOCK gives MUTT the bottle, MUTT takes a big gulp, hands the bottle back to JOCK.)

MUTT *(to JOCK)*: Now you got an enemy for life!

JOCK: I'm going to make him leave anyway!

ELIAS (*shaking his head*): Never drive your old enemies away—You never know how bad your new enemies'll be!

(*MUTT starts to play his instrument again. JOCK stuffs his pipe and lights it. ELIAS reaches for the whiskey bottle and takes a swig. The WOMAN finishes mending the socks, stands up, puts away the socks and the sewing gear, and sits down on the stool next to the hutch.*)

JOCK (*to the WOMAN*): Well, what's the matter? Why are you sitting way over there?

(*The WOMAN doesn't answer. LEX comes back inside. He has washed his face in the snow, his hair is still wet. He seems to be sober again, but full of hate. He approaches the WOMAN. MUTT stops playing.*)

LEX: From now on, you're mine! All mine! Got it? (*The WOMAN looks at him calmly.*) You understand?

(*The WOMAN nods.*)

JOCK: I think we'll have something to say about that.

MUTT (*to LEX*): You're crazy! She's belongs t' all of us! You think you're better'n we are?

LEX (*slowly turns to face the other MEN*): The woman's mine! Anybody else touches her, I'll kill him!

(*The WOMAN gets up, walks over to her boots, takes off her straw slippers, pulls on her boots, lifts her shawl from the hook on the wall and wraps it around her. She takes her time. Except for WENDL, none of the MEN notice. WENDL stares at her in astonishment, but does nothing. Meanwhile, the MEN continue talking.*)

ELIAS (*sings*):

And the rooster and the hen
Gaze at each other again and again.

But when the capon struts past,
Then all hell breaks loose fast!

LEX (*slowly walks over to the table, looks at ELIAS, speaks calmly, coldly*): What'd you mean by that?

ELIAS (*afraid, but still cocky*): That you can't make it!

LEX (*calmly*): I can't make what?

ELIAS (*becoming frightened*): Oh, nothin'!

LEX: I wanna know, Elias!

ELIAS: All right! It ain't any easier to run away, when your pants are full of shit! (*looks at LEX*) You can't make it with the woman!

LEX: That so?

ELIAS: Yup, that's so! I been watchin' you! From the very first night!

(*LEX approaches ELIAS who slowly gets up so he can get away. JOCK and MUTT also get up, to protect ELIAS. At that moment the WOMAN goes to the door. LEX notices.*)

LEX: Hey! Where you goin'? (*The WOMAN opens the door and walks out. LEX follows her, jerks her back.*) I want to know where you're goin'! (*The WOMAN tries to get out the door. LEX jerks her back inside, slams the door shut.*) No you don't! You're stayin' here! With me! Understand? You're stayin' with me!

(*The WOMAN slowly shakes her head, tries to get out the door. LEX hurls her back inside the cabin so that she falls to the floor. JOCK goes over to her, helps her up.*)

JOCK: You don't belong to him! You belong to all of us!

(*The WOMAN looks at JOCK, frees herself from his grasp, slowly backs over toward the door. As she approaches LEX, he gives her another shove so that she falls back down by JOCK, who catches her.*)

JOCK (*angrily*): Woman, you can't run away now! You came here of your own free will! And stayed of your own free will! And slept with all of us of your own free will! Now you're gonna stay here as long as we're workin' these woods! Then you can go wherever you want!

(*The WOMAN stands motionless. LEX goes over to her, rips her shawl off and throws it on the floor, grabs the WOMAN by the arm, strongarms her back to the table, forces her to sit down on the bench. The WOMAN tries to get back up, but LEX forces her back down on the bench. The MEN all watch her.*)

MUTT: She's not gonna stay! She'll run away soon as we're back out in the woods!

(*LEX looks at MUTT, looks at the WOMAN, looks over to the wall where the tools are hanging. He walks over, hunts for a long chain, examines it, looks over at the door where the padlock to the front door is hanging. He walks over, takes the padlock, and with chain and padlock approaches the WOMAN.*)

MUTT: Hey, Lex, I don't think . . . We can't do that!

LEX: Do what? We don't have any other choice!

(*LEX kneels down, pulls the WOMAN's boots off, wraps one end of the chain around the WOMAN's left ankle. JOCK watches, indecisive. ELIAS doesn't like the idea, WENDL is horrified. The WOMAN has given up and doesn't fight back anymore.*)

ELIAS (*is somehow frightened*): Jock! That's not a good idea. Let her go, if that's what she wants! After three days, fish and guests start to stink!

(*JOCK is undecided and doesn't react. LEX slips the padlock in the chain around the WOMAN's ankle. Suddenly WENDL lurches forward, yanks LEX back so that LEX*) *falls over backwards. WENDL tries to take the padlock off and remove the chain. LEX gets up, grabs WENDL by the collar and hurls him across the room, then kneels back down and slips the padlock through the chain. WENDL scrambles back up, tries to get to LEX again. But as WENDL rushes past, JOCK catches him and holds him tight. LEX snaps the padlock shut and pockets the key.)*

WENDL *(in desperation)*: No, don't chain her up! Please, don't hang her up! Don't hang her up! No, don't!

(WENDL sobs in despair, stops struggling, because JOCK has him in an iron grip. LEX takes the free end of the chain and walks over to the wall, stage left, near the front door. He checks to see if the chain is long enough so that the WOMAN can move around the cabin, puts down the end of the chain, grabs an iron bracket and a hatchet, pounds the bracket into the wall about a foot above the floor, pulls the chain through the bracket, then with all his might he pounds the bracket into the wall so that the end of the chain is secure.)

LEX: There, all done!

(JOCK lets go of WENDL who looks at the WOMAN in desperation, sits down, crying, buries his face in his hands. The WOMAN sits there, motionless. She is not upset, just completely calm.)

JOCK *(somewhat embarrassed)*: You got what was comin' to you, woman!

ELIAS *(ambiguously)*: "Get used to it, Kitty, get used to it!" the baker said as he cleaned out the oven with the cat.

(Blackout)

11TH SCENE

(*Nighttime. Light from the hearthfire and from the moon, shining in the window. The WOMAN's chain leads from the wall over to the hutch and disappears under the curtain. The MEN are up in the hayloft.*)

LEX'S VOICE: Well, it's my turn again tonight!

JOCK'S VOICE: Before you go, we want to know what you've got in mind!

LEX'S VOICE: What do you mean, what I've got in mind?

JOCK'S VOICE: You know damn well! You said she was all yours! Until you take that back, we're not going to let you have your turn!

(*A long silence.*)

LEX'S VOICE (*grimly*): I take it back.

JOCK'S VOICE: Fine, now you can go. Won't be too easy . . . tonight.

LEX'S VOICE: Don't you worry! I'll shape her up in no time!

(*The door to the hayloft opens, LEX appears.*)

JOCK'S VOICE: Lex!

LEX (*turns around*): Yeah?

JOCK'S VOICE: Leave the key here! The key to the pad-lock! Or else she'll take it away from you!

LEX: I'll be careful! Hey, I'm no fool! (*LEX steps onto the ladder, closes the door to the hayloft, climbs down the ladder, goes over to the hutch, looks at the chain, hesitates.*) It's me—Lex! I'm comin' in! (*He climbs into the hutch.*)

ELIAS' VOICE (*cautiously*): We got to keep an eye on Lex!

If you let the devil into church, next thing you know he'll want to sit on the altar!

JOCK'S VOICE: I'll keep an eye out, you can bet on that!

(*A long silence.*)

LEX'S VOICE (*from the hutch*): Yeah, I know. You're mad at me. But what could I do? I can't just let you walk away! I got to have you! It's like a craving!—I wish I had you all to myself! It makes my skin crawl, just to think that the others also . . . Why, you'd think you were with a pack of dogs in heat! But what can I do? There are too many of 'em against me!—In ten more days, woman, we'll be done here! If you want, I'll take you along with me. I'm gettin' out of this damn country! If you want to go with me, if you say yes, then I'll let you loose right now! On the spot!—I know of a cabin farther up the mountain! You can hide there till I come! I'll bring you somethin' to eat, too!—What do you say to that? Don't you know how great it'd be?—I promise you, woman, if you come with me, I won't hurt you anymore! Trust me! Well, what do you think? You want to go away with me?— Well, why not? What do you want, anyway? God- damn bitch!—Okay, fine, then that's it! Then we'll just all screw you as long as we can!—Now, come on! Spread your legs! Come on, you hear! Or do I have to do like I did before?—Goddammit, put out, I said! (*We hear him strike her an audible blow.*)

(*Blackout*)

12TH SCENE

(Daytime. Outside the sun is shining, its light casts a shadow on the floor from the window frame's cross. The chained WOMAN is sitting at the table, staring straight ahead. There is no fire in the hearth. After a while the door flies open, WENDL enters out of breath, wearing snowshoes. He doesn't even take the time to remove them, but rushes over to the tools and takes down a pick.)

WENDL: I told them the handle of my hatchet came loose! They sent me to get a new one!

(WENDL, pick in hand, goes over to the iron bracket which secures the chain to the wall, tries to pull the bracket out, but he can't get a good grip on the bracket.)

WENDL *(growing desperate)*: It won't work! *(tries again, then gives up)* It just won't work! He drove it in too deep! *(The WOMAN stands up, goes over to WENDL, takes his face in her hands, smiles at him as if nothing were wrong, as if she knew that nothing, absolutely nothing could hurt her. WENDL looks at her, confused.)* I'll try it with an axe! *(He grabs an axe, tries to pry out the bracket, but it won't work. Then, using the blade, he tries chopping the wood to loosen the bracket. The door opens, LEX enters, out of breath, also wearing snowshoes, sees what WENDL is trying to do.)*

LEX: Just what I thought! *(takes the axe away from WENDL, grabs him by the collar, shoves him over to the door, kicks him outside)* Get outta here, you little shit!

(Filled with despair, WENDL remains standing outside, not knowing what to do.)

LEX *(to the WOMAN)*: I'll let you loose right now, if you'll come with me! *(The WOMAN shakes her head. Out-*

side, WENDL stomps away in his snowshoes, like a dog with his tail between his legs.) Okay, then, don't come! *(He tests the bracket to see if it is loose, confirms that it's not, returns the axe to the rest of the tools. On his way out the door, he notices that there is no fire in the hearth.)* Oh, so you don't wanna cook for us anymore either! *(calls out, in the direction of the woods)* Wendl! Hey, Wendl! *(whistles through two fingers. WENDL reappears, approaches)* From now on, you're the cook again! But God help you if you let her loose, 'cause I'll kill you! I promise! I swear on my dead father's grave!

(LEX walks past WENDL to the door, closes it, and walks off. WENDL looks at the WOMAN, goes over to the window, watches LEX go off, waits until he can't see LEX anymore, unties his snowshoes, goes over to the tools and hangs up his snowshoes. He picks up the axe again, walks over to the bracket, chops at the wood around the bracket with the axe. The WOMAN watches him, then walks over to him, places her hand on his shoulder. WENDL stops chopping. Gently, the WOMAN takes the axe out of his hands, carries it over and hangs it back up. WENDL watches in amazement.)

WENDL: But why? You don't need to worry about me! I'll just run away from 'em! I'll go someplace else! I got nobody here. Nothing's keeping me here.

(The WOMAN goes over to WENDL, places her hand on his cheek, looks into his eyes, then sits down on the stool beside the hearth. WENDL just stands there, confused, not knowing what to do, finally takes some kindling, lays it on the hearth, lights it, blows on it, the flames rise. The WOMAN sits calmly by and stares off into space. She is there, and yet far away. WENDL puts some more wood on, stares into the fire.)

WENDL *(without looking at the WOMAN)*: Further on down the mountain, where the two roads cross, there's a roadside shrine. With the Madonna that people call "Our Lady in the Forest." (*The WOMAN looks at WENDL. He turns, now standing with his back to the hearth, looking straight ahead.*) She's completely black. Because a long time ago lightning struck, and she started to burn. When I don't know what to do, I always go down and talk to her. First, I talk to her, then I don't say anything, I just look at her. And all of a sudden I feel this sweet ache. A real sweet ache. And I forget everything. Everything. I just want to die. It feels so good. So good. (*Silence for a while. The WOMAN looks at WENDL, he looks straight ahead. Then WENDL says softly*) She looks like you.

(*WENDL begins to cry softly, starts to sob, then he is overcome. He sobs louder and louder, he tries to stifle his sobs, but can't. He shudders, he buries his face in his hands. The WOMAN gets up, goes over to him, takes his face in her hands and puts his head on her shoulder, hugs him. His crying now becomes a great release.*)

(*Blackout*)

13TH SCENE

(*Nighttime. Moonlight streams through the window, the hearth is glowing. The chain leads to the hutch. JOCK is on his way down the ladder, when he pauses in thought.*)

JOCK (*in the direction of the hayloft*): Something I've been wanting to ask you, Lex: Did she give you any trouble?

LEX'S VOICE: Yeah, sure did.

ELIAS' VOICE: Shouldn't surprise you. You can't spit sweet if you got a bitter tongue!

LEX'S VOICE: You just have to belt her one! Then she'll give in!

(*JOCK nods, closes the trapdoor, climbs down the ladder, goes over to the hutch, stops, undecided.*)

ELIAS' VOICE: I think we'd of been better off if we'd a kept our punk in our pants! She's a powderkeg!

LEX'S VOICE: Hell, what do you care! Your punk burned down long time ago!

(*JOCK gets up his courage and climbs into the hutch.*)

JOCK'S VOICE: I'd really wish you'd give in right off. I don't like to hit women. I don't even hit horses. I never have!—My God, don't just lay there like a board! I might as well go home to my wife! Come on, now! Don't play games with me!

(*Blackout*)

14TH SCENE

(*Nighttime. Moonlight streams through the window, the hearth is glowing. The chain leads over to the hutch.*)

MUTT'S VOICE (*from the hutch*): I'd really like to marry you, woman. Sure, the people'll talk about it till the cows come home—if I marry a foreigner—but I don't care! You're a good cook, and you'll have healthy kids, I'm sure of that. I wouldn't be buying a pig in a poke with you, and that's really important. But . . . if you're already pregnant right now, well, I wouldn't like that at all. 'Cause I wouldn't know which one of us is the father. But I know a woman ... works in the stalls on a nearby farm—If you say yes, woman, if you'll marry me, then I'll let you loose! I know a little cabin farther up the mountain—you could hide there for the time being! So, what's your answer? Will you have me?—Well, why not? You won't get anybody better'n me, believe you me! After all, what're you? You're just a woodsmen's whore, that's all! Com'ere, whore!

(*Blackout*)

15TH SCENE

(*Nighttime. The moon isn't shining, the glow from the hearth provides the only illumination. The chain leads over to the hutch.*)

ELIAS' VOICE (*from the hutch*): If you don't want to, woman, then we can forget about it. We don't have to. Not at all. It's really a treat just for me to be able to lie next to you. You're so warm, woman. So toasty warm! When I'm lyin' next to you, my old bones don't hurt anymore, and I feel like a child, lyin' next to his mother. Never would've thought I'd feel this way again. I'm grateful to you for that, woman.— Sorry I don't have the strength to untie you. But I'll see if I can get my hands on the key. Then I'll let you go.

(*Blackout*)

16TH SCENE

(Morning. It is gradually growing lighter outside, and it's snowing again. The curtain to the hutch is open, the WOMAN is sitting on the edge of the bed, dressed. ELIAS is lying in bed under the covers, he is very ill. The WOMAN holds his hand.)

ELIAS: You know, woman, I always say: "If you can tickle yourself, you can laugh whenever you want!" And you know what? This rule's helped me get through life pretty good!

(After a while the trapdoor to the hayloft opens. WENDL appears, closes the trapdoor behind him, climbs down the ladder, sees ELIAS and the WOMAN.)

WENDL: Morning! *(WENDL goes over to the hearth, takes some kindling and lays it on the fire. ELIAS has a coughing fit. WENDL looks over, approaches ELIAS and the WOMAN.)* Is anything wrong, Elias?

ELIAS: Nothin's wrong. I'm dyin', that's all.

WENDL: Go on, you've never been sick a day in your life. You're tougher than all the rest of us!

ELIAS: Don't kid yourself! It happens fast, when you come right down to it! Death wears woolen socks. Lots of times you don't hear him coming.

(The trapdoor opens. JOCK, MUTT, and LEX climb down, look over at the hutch.)

JOCK: What's going on? *(He goes over to the hutch. MUTT and LEX follow.)*

LEX *(looks at ELIAS)*: He's a goner!

MUTT: What's wrong, Elias?

ELIAS: Life! Well, at least I've been able to put off dyin' till the end!

LEX: I told you you couldn't handle her! It's a miracle you didn't have a heart attack the minute you climbed into bed!

ELIAS: The bear can always find an excuse if he wants to eat a sheep!—I feel cold. Cold all over. (*smiles*)
A boozer and a wencher in a storm—
The heaviest overcoat can't keep them warm!
(*seriously*) Let the woman go! Or something bad's gonna happen!

(*His head falls to one side, ELIAS is dead. JOCK feels the pulse on his neck, closes ELIAS' eyes, crosses himself. The OTHERS—except the WOMAN—also cross themselves.*)

JOCK: Lord, grant him eternal rest!

ALL (*except the WOMAN*): And may eternal light shine down upon him!

MUTT: Now what'll we do with him?

JOCK: One of us'll have to take him down to the village. Lex, that'd be you!

LEX: You gotta be kiddin'! We'll only be up here one more week! In the meantime we can bury him outside in the snow!

JOCK (*annoyed*): Well, all right.

(*Blackout*)

17TH SCENE

(*Evening. A snowstorm is raging outside. Light from the kerosene lamp and from the glow of the hearth. JOCK, LEX, and MUTT are sitting around the table. JOCK and ting on the stool beside the hearth, the WOMAN is sitting on the stool next to the hutch. ALL just sit there, a mood of depression predominates. For a long time there is nothing but silence. The storm rages around the cabin.*)

JOCK *(to MUTT)*: Play something!

(MUTT picks up his instrument, starts to play a melancholy melody. JOCK takes a drink of whiskey, looks over to the window, stands up with bottle in hand, goes over to the window, looks out into the blizzard.)

JOCK: Now you've got a nice, soft death-bed, Elias! *(raises the whiskey bottle)* Cheers! Here's to you! *(drinks)*

LEX: Hey, guys, what's the matter? How come you're all so down in the dumps? Cut out that funeral music, Mutt! Play somethin' lively!

(MUTT starts to play some dance music. LEX takes a swig of whiskey, looks over at the WOMAN.)

LEX: Do a little dance for us, woman! You hear? We want you to dance!

(The WOMAN looks at LEX, but doesn't react. LEX gets up, walks over to her, takes the key out of his pocket, kneels down, unlocks the padlock on her left ankle, unchains her, gets back up.)

LEX *(almost tenderly)*: Come on! Dance! Please!

(The WOMAN slowly gets up, looks at LEX, walks around the room, begins to do a few dance steps, gradually dancing faster and faster. MUTT also plays faster and faster. The WOMAN's dance becomes wild and turbulent. LEX starts to clap his hands and stomp his foot in time with the music.)

LEX: Hey! Hey! Hey!

(LEX yelps "whoopee," the WOMAN dances, her hair and skirt flying. The MEN watch with enthusiasm.)

(Blackout)

18TH SCENE

(Nighttime. Light from the hearth. Outside, the snowstorm is raging. The WOMAN is sitting motionless at the table, the chain is once again fastened firmly around her foot.)

LEX'S VOICE *(after a while, from the hayloft)*: It's my turn again!

(The door to the hayloft opens, LEX appears, climbs out onto the ladder. He closes the trapdoor, climbs down, looks at the WOMAN, is surprised that she's not in bed. He looks back up the ladder, places it off to one side of the hayloft opening, quietly fetches his shoes, puts them on, pulls on his leggings over them, puts on his woolen jacket and coat, gets out his knapsack. From the cupbord to the left of the ladder he removes a folded shirt, a pair of long underwear, two pair of socks, and stuffs everything into the knapsack. From the food chest he takes a loaf of bread and packs it away too, then ties up the knapsack. From the tool rack he takes two pairs of snowshoes and hangs them on the knapsack, slings the knapsack onto his shoulders, takes out his headband and hat, puts both of them on, puts his gloves in his coat pockets. The WOMAN calmly watches him the whole time. LEX now approaches the WOMAN, takes the key out of his pants' pocket, unlocks the padlock on the WOMAN's ankle, unchains her. The chain rattles, and LEX freezes, looks up to the hayloft, but there is no response. LEX gets up, gets the WOMAN's boots and her shawl, puts

the boots down in front of her, lays the shawl around her shoulders.)

LEX (*whispering*): Come on, woman, we're leaving!

(*The WOMAN shakes her head. LEX kneels down, pulls off her straw slippers, jams the boots on her feet, and gets back up, buttons his coat, grabs the WOMAN by the arm and pulls her to her feet. She resists, and in the struggle the bench is tipped over. LEX looks up at the hayloft, tugs the WOMAN over to the door, opens it. The trapdoor opens, JOCK and MUTT appear.*)

JOCK: Hold it, you double-crossin' son-of-a-bitch!

(*LEX looks back at them, yanks the WOMAN outside. Snow blows in the open doorway. JOCK and MUTT leap down from the loft, behind them appears WENDL who watches, but remains up in the loft. JOCK yanks a pick from the wall, MUTT takes down a pruning hook. BOTH run out and disappear in the darkness.*)

LEX'S VOICE (*yelling*): Come on now, move it, woman!

JOCK'S VOICE: You dirty bastard, where are you?

MUTT'S VOICE: There they are, Jock!

JOCK'S VOICE: Stop right there, Lex, or I'll kill you!

(*After a while ALL FOUR return. JOCK is holding the WOMAN with his left hand on her arm, in his right hand he is holding the pick over LEX's head, threateningly. MUTT is holding the sharp blade of the pruning hook against LEX's throat. They enter, JOCK lets go of the WOMAN, closes the door, looks at LEX, slowly removes LEX's hat and headband and drops them on the floor. With his left hand he pulls off LEX's knapsack and hurls it into the corner.*)

JOCK (*calmly*): You shouldn't'a done that, Lex!

(*LEX doesn't answer. MUTT is still holding the pruning*

hook to LEX's throat. With the dull edge of the pick, JOCK hits LEX in the stomach. LEX doubles up and falls to his knees with a groan. MUTT hits LEX over the head with the handle of the pruning hook. LEX collapses, unconscious. The WOMAN tries to get to the door, JOCK yanks her back.)

JOCK *(points to the table)*: Sit down! And don't move a muscle! Or the same thing'll happen to you!

(The WOMAN sits down at the table. JOCK looks at LEX lying on the floor, goes over to the kerosene lamp, lights it, goes back to LEX, kicks him in the side.)

JOCK: Wake up, buddy! Hey! Wake up, I said!

MUTT: He's out cold!

(JOCK looks down at LEX, looks at MUTT, notices the pruning hook in MUTT's hand and gets an idea. He lays down his pick, rolls LEX over onto his stomach, spreads LEX's arms out, takes the pruning hook from MUTT and shoves the handle in one of LEX's sleeves, over his shoulders, and out the other sleeve, so that LEX's arms are trapped in a spread-eagle position, as if he were being crucified.)

MUTT *(grinning)*: Great!

(JOCK goes over to the door, opens it, goes outside, returns with a handful of snow, closes the door behind him, goes back to LEX and rubs the snow on LEX's face. LEX comes to, coughing, then discovers that his arms are pinned, looks stupified and desperate, tries to get up, but it takes him several arduous tries before he can stand again. Tottering, he stands there with spread arms. Filled with hatred, he looks at JOCK and MUTT. JOCK picks up his pick, MUTT grins at LEX.)

LEX: Get me loose! Right now!

(JOCK doesn't react. MUTT slowly pulls out his hunting knife, holds it casually in his hand, grinning. LEX stares at

the floor, observing JOCK out of the corner of his eye, then suddenly swings his torso around, trying to hit JOCK with the sharp blade of the pruning hook protruding from his sleeve. JOCK quickly raises the pick, LEX's arm bumps into it. Quickly pivoting in the other direction, LEX tries to hit JOCK with the other arm, but JOCK ducks. The movement causes LEX to lose his balance, he swings halfway around. JOCK hits him in the back with the dull part of the pick. LEX falls back down on his stomach.)

WENDL: Stop! Oh, please, stop!

(No one pays any attention to WENDL. LEX struggles to his feet. MUTT watches him, grinning. JOCK goes over to the WOMAN, jerks her to her feet, hauls her over to LEX.)

JOCK: It's your turn again tonight, Lex! Here, take her! What's the matter, huh? Come on, take her! *(LEX looks at JOCK with hate in his eyes. He's like a trapped animal.)* You don't want to, is that it? Or you can't, you limp dick!

(Suddenly, JOCK reaches over and tears open the front of the WOMAN's dress, so that her breasts are partially exposed. The WOMAN stands there, motionless, completely calm; she doesn't try to cover herself up.)

JOCK: Take a peek, Lex! Maybe that'll help you?

MUTT: Well, what'sa matter, Lex? You're such a wild stud! Show us what you can do! Here, I'll unbutton your fly for you!

(MUTT is holding the knife in his right hand; grinning, he carefully reaches for LEX's fly with his left hand. LEX kicks him in the groin, MUTT doubles up, drops to his knees, moans.)

MUTT: You bastard! Son-of-a-bitch!

(JOCK steps behind LEX, grabs him by both wrists, shoves him over toward the WOMAN.)

JOCK: Take her! Come on, take her! That's what you wanted, wasn't it?

(*JOCK forces LEX up against the WOMAN, she doesn't retreat, stands eye-to-eye with LEX. MUTT gets back up.*)

MUTT: You'll never do that again, you dirty jailbird!

(*Knife in hand, MUTT slowly approaches LEX. Suddenly, LEX wheels around as hard as he can, knocking JOCK backward. JOCK staggers, loses the pick. MUTT leaps at LEX with his knife, but LEX is able to dodge, kicks MUTT in the side. MUTT stumbles over to the wall, LEX in pursuit. LEX stands with one side facing MUTT, grabs the handle of the pruning hook with one hand so that it won't slip, and jams the blade of the pruning hook into MUTT's throat. MUTT makes a gurgling noise, drops the knife, grabs his throat with both hands. With blood streaming from his throat, MUTT collapses. Meanwhile, JOCK has retrieved the pick; he now goes after LEX and strikes him in the back with the pointed edge. LEX falls to his knees, freeing the pick. JOCK rears back to strike again with all his might. Just then, LEX pivots to the side and falls to the floor, holding the handle of the pruning hook. JOCK misses, loses his balance and falls forward. The pick hits the floor while JOCK falls on LEX's pruning hook blade which is pointed upward toward him. BOTH MEN fall to the floor, JOCK is dead upon impact. LEX tries to struggle to his feet, but can't make it. He lies on his stomach, breathing heavily, the circle of blood on the back of his shirt expands. Outside, the storm has passed, though it is still snowing heavily. Everything is completely quiet. LEX looks up, trying to locate the WOMAN.*)

LEX: You win! You've killed us all! Damned whore! Damned whore!

(*LEX stops breathing, is dead. WENDL has watched the entire proceedings in horror.*)

WENDL (*sobbing*): Oh, Mother of God, help! Mother of
  God, help! Mother of God, help!

(*The WOMAN looks at MUTT, at JOCK, at LEX, kneels
down over LEX and strokes his hair, gets back up, pulls the
front of her dress back in place, lays the shawl over her
head and shoulders, looks up at WENDL, smiles gently at
him, walks over to the door, opens it, exits, disappearing
into the darkness and the whirling snow. WENDL watches
her go.*)

WENDL (*cries out*): Woman! Woman! Woman! (*He leaps
  down from the loft, races over to the door, looks out
  after the WOMAN, in despair.*) Stay, woman! Stay,
  woman! Woman! Woman! (*He collapses against the
  doorframe, crying, then sobs more softly.*) Woman!
  Woman! Woman!

(*The WOMAN's voice, singing a strange melody, can be

heard from out of the darkness, growing fainter, till it disappears.*)

(*Blackout*)   THE END

Home

Translated by
Heidi L. Hutchinson

Characters

MIKE (23), a runaway (one who wants to come home)

NINA (29), a North German (a butterfly, a flower)

HERMAN (47), Mike's father, police chief (a man of order, sinking in chaos)

GUNTHER (23), a small town policeman (the kind of son you wish for)

OSSI (35), branch manager of a supermarket (a man the women go for)

HILDE (45), Mike's mother (a woman between two social classes)

MONIKA (23), a hairdresser (one who may or may not save herself)

WALTER (70), Hilde's father, a small–town doctor (from an earlier day when an empire hoped to last 1000 years)

Scene
Near a small town. A half–completed highway bridge, raw concrete, protrudes into the scene. A ladder leads down from the end of the bridge. Under the bridge are piles of construction materials such as wood molding and steel girders. A large billboard containing the construction site data stands with its back to the audience.

If it is not possible to construct a highway bridge, it can be omitted. Alternately, the scene can be a wild–looking garbage dump with an automobile wreck. The wreck is drawn into the action. A sign reads "No garbage dumping!"

Time

The present, autumn, dusk to darkness.

The Prodigal Son

And he said, "A certain man had two sons: And the younger of them said to his father, 'Father, give me the portion of goods that falleth to me.' And he divided unto them his living. And not many days after the younger son gathered all together, and took his journey into a far country, and there wasted his substance with riotous living.

And when he had spent all, there arose a mighty famine in that land; and he began to be in want. And he went and joined himself to a citizen of that country; and he sent him into his fields to feed swine. And he would fain have filled his belly with the husks that the swine did eat; and no man gave unto him.

And when he came to himself, he said, 'How many hired servants of my father's have bread enough and to spare, and I perish with hunger! I will arise and go to my father, and will say unto him, Father, I have sinned against heaven and before thee, and am no more worthy to be called thy son: make me as one of thy hired servants.' And he arose, and came to his father.

But when he was yet a great way off, his father saw him, and had compassion, and ran, and fell on his neck, and kissed him. And the son said unto him, 'Father, I have sinned against heaven, and in thy sight, and am no more worthy to be called thy son.' But the father said to his servants, 'Bring forth the best robe, and put it on him; and put a ring on his hand, and shoes on his feet: and bring hither the fatted calf, and kill it, and let us eat, and be merry: for this my son was dead, and is alive again; he was lost, and is found.' And they began to be merry.

Now his elder son was in the field; and as he came and drew nigh to the house, he heard music and dancing. And he called one of the servants, and asked what these things meant. And he said unto him, 'Thy brother is come; and thy father hath killed the fatted calf, because he hath

received him safe and sound.' And he was angry, and
would not go in: therefore came his father out, and in-
treated him. And he answering said to his father, 'Lo,
these many years do I serve thee, neither transgressed I
at any time thy commandment: and yet thou never gavest
me a kid, that I might make merry with my friends: but as
soon as this thy son was come, which hath devoured thy
living with harlots, thou hast killed for him the fatted
calf.'

And he said unto him, 'Son, thou art ever with me,
and all that I have is thine. It was meet that we should
make merry, and be glad: for this thy brother was dead,
and is alive again; and was lost, and is found.'"

Luke 15, 11–32

(*Dusk. After a while the sound of an old motorcycle can be heard approaching on the highway above. The motorcycle stops. The engine dies. After a while MIKE mounts the ladder at the end of the bridge and looks down at the area below the bridge. He has a band–aid on his cheek and a plastic shopping bag from the supermarket in his hand. He climbs all the way to the ground, walks to the middle of the stage and looks around. He knows this place from earlier. He looks down at his feet, takes one step backward, kneels down, sets down the plastic bag, digs in the dirt with his hands (where his right foot has just been), and lifts out a large shiny glass marble. He holds it up, looks at it, throws it into the air, catches it, puts it in his pocket, picks up the plastic bag, walks over to a pile of lumber, sets down the plastic bag, sits down, rolls a cigarette, lights it. Up above, at the end of the bridge, NINA lies on her stomach, looking down, with a whisky bottle in her hand.*)

NINA: Hey, take a look! I've got something for you!

(*MIKE looks at her briefly, then looks away. He is furious at NINA. NINA disappears, reappears at the top of the ladder, climbs down and approaches. NINA's clothing and hairstyle are a bit bizarre. She looks pregnant. She is a heroin addict suffering from withdrawal symptoms, and is trying to hide her pain from MIKE. She looks at MIKE, opens the whisky bottle and offers it to MIKE. He ignores her. NINA takes a big swallow, closes the bottle, sets it down next to him, pulls a brand new, folded nighty with the price tag still attached out of her clothing (this explains why she looked pregnant), unfolds it, looks at it and smiles, then holds it up against herself. The nighty looks very romantic.*)

NINA (*to MIKE*): Hey! (*MIKE looks at her.*) Isn't this cute?

MIKE: Awful!

NINA: What?

MIKE: Go on, get out of my sight!

NINA: You don't think it's cute? Well, I think it's cute! Lady Di would flip!

MIKE: You know I told you not to take anything! Stupid bitch!

(*NINA looks at him, swats him over the head with the nighty, walks to the other side. Suddenly she doubles over in pain, sits down on a pile of wire mesh with her back to MIKE, gets out a small bottle of lighter fluid from some-where in her clothes, pours the contents on a section of the nighty, drops the bottle, presses the soaked portion of the nighty to her mouth and nose, inhales the lighter fluid fumes, and has to cough. MIKE looks at her, then gets up and walks over to her, sees what she is doing, sees the bottle on the ground, picks it up, reads the label.*)

MIKE: Lighter fluid! (*He throws the bottle away, grabs the nighty out of NINA's hands, tosses it away. She starts to go after it, MIKE pushes her back.*)

NINA: Asshole! Male chauvinist pig! Bastard!

(*MIKE looks at her, picks up the nighty, throws it at her, walks toward the ladder.*)

NINA: Hey, man! Where you goin'? (*runs after him, stops him*) Hey! You can't leave me now! (*MIKE tries to tear himself loose.*) Hey! I need you, man! I can't make it alone!

(*MIKE looks at her, grunts in disdain, walks back to the pile of lumber, throws his cigarette on the ground, climbs up on the pile and sits down, takes a sandwich and a can of beer out of the plastic bag, opens the beer can, drinks, eats the sandwich. NINA stands there with her arms crossed, presses them against the pain in her body, looks around.*)

NINA: Great countryside you got here! The asshole of the world! (*NINA walks over to the whisky bottle, picks it up, turns away from MIKE, takes a big swallow, puts the bottle down, sits down. Suddenly she doubles over in pain, tries to suppress her cries, pounds her fists against one of her thighs to relieve the cramps. MIKE watches impassively for a while and continues to eat. Then he gets up, walks over to her, kneels down and pulls the band–aid off his cheek. NINA watches. Under the band–aid is a tiny packet. He opens it. It contains heroin. NINA sits up and looks at it.)* Oh, man! Thank you! Thanks! You got a needle?

MIKE: 'Course I don't have a needle! *(NINA carefully takes the packet out of his hand, snorts the heroin through her nose, inhales deeply. She feels better immediately. A moment later, she feels wonderful. She hugs MIKE.)*

NINA: I'll keep my promise! Honest! But not until we're down there, you know? I just can't do it here! I can't make it here! But down there, at the ocean, on the beach, in the sunshine, I can make it! Really! *(MIKE pulls away from her.)*

MIKE: Okay! *(MIKE goes back to where he was sitting and continues to eat and drink. NINA lies down and stretches out.)*

NINA: Once I met a guy at the Bahnhof Zoo station in Berlin. I was 'way down at the time. This guy looked at me real funny. But I wasn't scared. Though he did have a rotten nose. I said, "What are you looking at me so funny for?" And he said, "I'm looking funny because I'm Jesus." "Hey, Jesus," I said, "got a little shit for me maybe?" And he handed me a piece of chocolate. I ate it so I wouldn't hurt his feelings, 'cause he was lookin' so funny. And all of a sudden I felt wonderful. I felt real light, real light, like a butterfly. "Hey," I said, "What's in this stuff?" But he was already gone. Probably 'cause of the cops. 'Cause there were suddenly a whole bunch of cops around. Staging a raid. I would've liked to see him again. One time I saw him from a distance at a demonstration. I yelled to him, but he didn't hear me. He disappeared in the crowd. (*She gets up.*) Hey, you really grew up in that little god–forsaken town back there? (*MIKE nods.*) Man oh man! A real cow town! But somehow it seems kinda neat! So tiny. Like a toy. Don't you want to visit your folks?

MIKE: Naw!

NINA: How come? Then what're we doin' here? It was 'way out of our way! (*MIKE doesn't answer.*) C'mon, tell me!

MIKE: Shit! Why can't you quit this shoplifting?

NINA: So what? That wasn't your folks' store, was it? Or do they own the supermarket?

MIKE: Naw! Don't be stupid!

NINA: See! Besides, they didn't catch us!

MIKE: Almost!

NINA: Well, don't piss in your pants, cowboy! Hey, you guys got any cows?

MIKE: Naw!

NINA: No? Too bad! Today I saw real cows for the first time! Did you see 'em, too? They were standing there next to the highway, real quiet ... Neat! They got such beautiful faces. I didn't know that. Sorta like women. So totally gentle. And those things. They just hang there. So unprotected. What do you call 'em?

MIKE: What?

NINA: You know, those things on the breasts! Where you squeeze the milk out!

MIKE: I can't remember!

NINA: Oh, give me a break!

MIKE: Cow tits!

NINA: What?

MIKE: Teats! Those are the teats on the udder!

NINA: Teats! Great! Teats! I wish I was a farmer's daughter! No, really! Squeeze a little milk from the teats, and have a vegetable garden, and everything . . . And at night zip into town, to party! (*MIKE can't help grinning.*) What's the big town like?

MIKE: Which one?

NINA (*points*): Come on, that one over there! The one we just drove past!

MIKE (*shrugs his shoulders*): A couple of peep shows, twelve TV channels and bad air. The people like to dress like country folks.

NINA: Hey, neat, man! If it were warmer, I'd go cold turkey right here!

MIKE: God, no!

NINA: Sure! Your town with its little houses . . . Kinda cute somehow! Smoke rising from the chimneys, the cows eating the sparse autumn grasses . . .

MIKE: Fuck your autumn grasses! I'd rather be lying on a hot sandy beach!

(*NINA has spotted the nighty on the ground, picks it up, removes her shoulder bag, puts it down, puts on the nighty.*)

MIKE: You've got some weird ideas! Why do you think I took off?

NINA (*prances and skips around in the nighty*) Because

Jesus moved from your cowtown to Berlin? Is that it? Because you like concrete better than sparse autumn grasses? Is that it? Because the farmers don't flip for Madonna? Is that it? You don't want to tell me? (*starts to skip around, singing*) Johnny's gone, all alone, far away and wand'ring on; cane and hat don't look bad, he's a merry lad! But his mom sheds tears galore, has no Johnny any more—(*stops*) Aren't you gonna tell me?

MIKE: I left for the same reason you did.

NINA: And why did I leave?

MIKE: Because you were fed up!

NINA: With what?

MIKE: With your folks! Right?

NINA: Naw! My folks are super! Really great! Nothing but super! Understanding to the max! You can do whatever you want, they understand everything! Absolute pushovers! Old softies!

MIKE: So why did you leave?

NINA: 'Cause I'm searching for Jesus.

MIKE: Spare me your Jesus crap! You're out of your mind! Take off that rag! You hear me?

NINA: This is not a rag! What are you talking about? This is the cutest nighty I've ever lifted!

MIKE: I'm gonna puke! My mother's got a crummy nightgown just like that!

NINA: Oh! Oh my God!

MIKE: You always take the most useless crap! That's weird, you know, really!

NINA: You haven't the faintest idea what we women like! (*She tries to sit on his lap, he gets up in disgust.*)

MIKE: Beat it!

NINA (*puts MIKE'S hand on her breast*): I'm your cow, milk me!

MIKE (*pulls his hand away*): Take that off, dammit! You hear me?

NINA (*tries to kiss him, he turns his head away and pulls up on the nighty to get it off of her. NINA resists.*) No! No! Help! (*She runs away from him, then hops around.*) I'm an elf! A light–footed elf! I'm going to find myself a deer and ride through the forest!

MIKE: You can look all you want! All you'll find is a rabid fox—if you're lucky!

NINA: What? Are the deer all gone?

MIKE (*tosses away the beer can*): Come on, let's get back on the road!

NINA: Well, I just can't believe it. Here I am in the country for once, and all of a sudden there aren't any more deer.

(*She walks over to the billboard, gets a spray can of red paint out of her clothes and sprays on the back of the billboard: "Down with the forest ranger, long live the deer!" From above, the sound of a car approaching.*)

MIKE (*listens*): Hey, come on! We've gotta get out of here! (*NINA ignores him and continues to write. MIKE runs to the ladder.*) Nina, come on, dammit!

NINA (*continues spraying; MIKE runs over to her, pulls her away; the car's headlights light up the backdrop; the car stops. NINA resists.*) Hey, man, what's your problem? Can't you see I'm busy?

(*The sound of the car's engine dies, the headlights are turned off, three car doors slam. MIKE quickly pulls the nighty up over NINA's head, runs over to the whisky bottle,*)

*picks it up, runs to the side with both items and disappears.
NINA has gone back to the billboard, finishes her spraying,
looks at her handiwork with satisfaction, puts the spray
can back in her clothes, looks around perplexed for MIKE,
walks to the front.*)

NINA: Hey, Mike, hey! (*At the top of the ladder, the policeman GUNTHER appears, looks around, sees
NINA. NINA continues.*) Just walks away and
leaves his little milk cow! Well, maybe he had to go
tinkle! (*She has turned around and now sees
GUNTHER.*) Oh, a big game hunter! (*GUNTHER
waves to someone up above and climbs down the
ladder. Behind him, OSSI climbs down. He is wearing a white lab coat and chewing gum.*) And a
butcher!

(*Behind OSSI, Police Chief HERMAN appears and also
climbs down. He has had too much to drink, but it isn't obvious, because he is one of those people who turn more and
more to stone the more they drink.*)

NINA: And a ranger! Well, of all the nerve! What do you
want here? There are no more deer! You killed them
all off! What am I supposed to ride through the forest on now, huh? You bad boys! Is that any way to
behave? (*The three men have approached and are
looking at NINA.*)

OSSI: Wow, she must be crazy!

(*It's already fairly dark. GUNTHER looks around, finds a
light switch and turns on the construction site lighting.*)

HERMAN: Where's your beau, huh?

NINA: If only I knew! I assume he's out doing a deed! A gallant deed!

MIKE (*approaches from the side, zipping up his pants*):
Oh, a visit from the authorities! (*HERMAN recog-*

nizes his son MIKE; GUNTHER recognizes him, too.)

GUNTHER: I can't believe it! Is that you? (*He looks over at HERMAN, who looks impenetrable.*)

OSSI: Who is he? (*GUNTHER looks expectantly at HER-MAN, who doesn't react.*)

HERMAN (*to OSSI*): These the ones?

OSSI: You got it!

HERMAN (*walks over to MIKE*): So, what did you two steal? (*MIKE doesn't answer. HERMAN suddenly slaps him. MIKE looks at him coldly.*)

NINA: Why Mr. Ranger! That's my beau! You can't just hit him like that! Gosh!

OSSI (*to NINA*): Are you drunk, or what?

HERMAN (*to MIKE*): What did you two steal?

NINA: Oh, dear Mr. Ranger, sir, what do you want from us? We're harmless tourists! Travelers! Out of the smog of the big cities into nature! (*HERMAN looks at her, sits down on a pile of lumber, lights a cigarette, and observes them with apparent calmness. GUNTHER looks at him, then at NINA.*)

GUNTHER: Okay, Miss, that's enough! Don't give us any lip, alright?

OSSI: A half hour ago you two were in my store! There (*points*), there's the bag! (*GUNTHER walks over and turns the plastic bag upside down. A sandwich and a can of beer fall out.*)

MIKE: So? You tryin' to say we didn't pay for that?

OSSI (*to NINA*): I saw it through the door! You had something in your waistband!

NINA: In my waistband? Of course I have something

there, smart guy! It's my cuddly little white belly!
You wanna have a look, you horny toad? Huh?

OSSI (*to HERMAN*): They stole something, Herman! For
sure! Otherwise they wouldn't have run away
when I tried to stop them!

NINA: Wow, I can't believe this! (*to HERMAN*) Mr. Ranger,
Sir, I wish to make a statement! When we entered
the supermarket, faithful customers that we are,
this man was standing at a shelf and was stacking
tubes of mustard! No! Jars of bouillon! Anyway,
when I walked past him, contemplating the wonderful world of wares, drool, drool, he looked at me
with lustful glances and said to me in a hoarse
voice: Well, you little whore, shall I stick my fat dick
into you—And I said to him: No, you little creep,
why don't you jerk off over your bouillon jars instead!

OSSI: This is unbelievable!

NINA: Of course this gentleman was very upset at that
and therefore he is trying to accuse us of shoplifting! End of transmission, where can I sign the transcript?

(*MIKE is angry with NINA, because he knows these provocations will only bring trouble.*)

OSSI: She's crazy! She's out of her mind! The nerve!

HERMAN (*to NINA*): You call me Ranger one more time
and I'll smash your painted face in!

NINA: But dear Mr. Forester, sir!

MIKE (*to NINA*): Give it a rest, dammit! (*NINA goes off to
the side, pouting, and sits down.*)

OSSI (*impatiently*): So? Now what?

HERMAN (*to OSSI*): You better not have chased us out here for nothing!

OSSI: They stole something! I swear!

HERMAN (*to GUNTHER*) Search 'em!

GUNTHER: Yessir! (*walks over to NINA*) Miss, please stand up, body search! (*NINA gets up slowly, stands there with her legs spread and holds out her arms. GUNTHER searches her quickly, finds her I.D. card, looks at it, looks at her, puts the I.D. card in his pocket, continues to search her, turns to HERMAN.*) Nothing!

HERMAN: Look carefully! Maybe she's got some narcotics on her! (*he sees NINA's handbag on the ground, goes over to it, picks it up, examines it carefully, looks at every makeup utensil, lets each piece fall carelessly to the ground as soon as he has checked it. GUNTHER is now searching NINA's clothing more carefully.*)

OSSI (*meanwhile*): Oh yeah, you're right! (*looks over at NINA*) She's high! That's why she's babbling like that! You've taken something, haven't you?

NINA (*sings*): The answer, my friend, is blowin' in the wind, the answer is blowin' in the wind!

HERMAN: The answer will be determined by the medical examiner.

GUNTHER: Nothing!

OSSI: In her waistband!

(*GUNTHER searches under NINA's waistband. She wriggles with feigned pleasure.*)

NINA: Ooh, you do that well! Ooh, that's nice! Ah! Boy, I could get to like you!

OSSI: A real city bitch! Gentlemen!

GUNTHER (*is somewhat embarrassed, has found nothing, looks at HERMAN*): Nothing! You want to go, Herman?

OSSI: Well, and what about him? (*points to MIKE*)

HERMAN (*to GUNTHER*): Search him! (*He is finished with the handbag, drops it, sits down.*)

GUNTHER: Are you serious?

HERMAN: Go on!

(*GUNTHER walks over to MIKE and searches him. NINA collects her scattered makeup and cosmetics and puts them back into her bag and then sits down. GUNTHER finds the tobacco on MIKE, opens the package, smells it, gives it back to him, finds a pocket knife, puts it in his own pocket, finds his I.D. card, looks at it, gives it back, reaches into MIKE's pants pocket, finds the glass marble, looks at it with surprise, looks at MIKE, looks back at the marble, remembers, looks at the spot where MIKE found it.*)

MIKE: Do you remember?

GUNTHER (*doesn't answer, shoves the marble back into MIKE's pocket, notices a button on MIKE's jacket and reads*): Better to eat pussy than to kiss ass!

OSSI: What?

GUNTHER (*reads*): Better to eat pussy than to kiss ass!

OSSI (*grins*): Sure! No question! Horny and lazy!

GUNTHER (*reads the second button*): "All cops are bastards!" That's an insult to us, Herman! It says all police are bastards!

(*HERMAN looks impassively. GUNTHER continues to search MIKE.*)

MIKE (*to GUNTHER*): Well, Gunther! You still remember how the two of us broke into gumball machines?

GUNTHER: You, maybe!

OSSI: What? What's going on?

MIKE: We were nine years old! And when we were thirteen we even took an entire cigarette machine off the wall. We brought it here, to this very place, and demolished it with great finesse! Then we split the money. Gunther bought himself an air gun and I got a Kodak Instamatic. And we puked like pelicans from smokin' all those cigarettes, huh, Gunther?

OSSI: What? You two know each other?

HERMAN: At least he became a policeman!

MIKE: Yeah, at least one of us! (*OSSI is confused, since he is not privy to the story.*)

GUNTHER (*has finished his search and has found nothing*): Nothing!

HERMAN: Look over by the bike!

GUNTHER: Yessir! (*walks over to the ladder, climbs up and disappears above*)

OSSI (*watches him go*): Well, I can see that I have to take matters into my own hands! (*He looks around, starts to search for his goods, notices the spraypaint on the billboard, reads.*) Down with the forest ranger, long live the deer! —What the hell is this?

HERMAN (*to MIKE and NINA*): You two do this?

NINA: Yes, the handwriting on the wall is mine!

OSSI: What bullshit!

NINA: That is an existential statement, you idiot!

HERMAN: Malicious destruction of property!

OSSI: I've never seen such a crazy broad in all my life! (*looks around further, disappears off to the side*)

HERMAN (*looks at MIKE, who sits down and rolls himself a cigarette and smokes. HERMAN looks at NINA, walks over to her, pushes up her left sleeve to expose the lower arm, sees the needle marks and the bruises*): Bravo! An addict! (*to MIKE*) You've gotten yourself a dope addict! Congratulations! (*walks over to MIKE, pushes up his left sleeve, then his right, but finds nothing, stops and looks at him. MIKE gets up, walks around him to NINA, takes her by the arm and starts to leave with her, but not toward the ladder, since GUNTHER is at the top, but in another direction. HERMAN calmly*): Stop right there!

(*MIKE and NINA keep walking, HERMAN follows them quickly, grabs MIKE from behind with both arms and squeezes. MIKE gasps for air.*)

NINA: What are you doing, you dirty cop? You got a screw loose? Let go of him, man!

(*NINA tries to help MIKE, tugs at one of HERMAN's arms, she is not able to loosen his grip, MIKE nearly faints, HERMAN lets go of him. MIKE slips to the ground, gasping for air.*)

HERMAN (*to MIKE*): What am I gonna do with you? What am I gonna do with you?

GUNTHER (*comes down from above, while NINA helps MIKE up*): Nothing!

OSSI (*reappears from the side, holding in his right hand the whisky bottle and in his left the nighty*): I knew it! They stole these two things! (*HERMAN looks at the things in OSSI's hands, looks at MIKE and NINA, sits down. He is crushed because of his son, but he doesn't show it.*) Well! That's enough, isn't it? Don't you want to arrest them? Come on, what's the matter, do it! My bachelor party's tonight! (*to GUNTHER*) You're coming, aren't you?

GUNTHER: 'Course! The last night before your wedding is an important occasion! (*grins*) After tomorrow you're like this! (*crosses his wrists as if they were tied*)

OSSI (*grins*): Aw, go on! I've got her trained, my little Monika! Don't worry! (*MIKE pricks up his ears. He knows Monika.*)

GUNTHER: You two have sure waited till the last minute! She's almost due!

OSSI: Aw, shit! I didn't really want to get married anyhow! But with her belly! Two old maids wrote to her mother! The new branch manager seduced a town virgin and now he wants to leave her high and dry! Can you imagine! I was summoned to her mother's! Fish or cut bait! The customers don't like that!

GUNTHER: Well, gee, haven't you ever heard of these? (*pulls out a pack of condoms*)

OSSI: She told me she was on the pill! But the slut quit taking 'em.

GUNTHER: Then she really tricked you!

OSSI: What was I s'posed to do? The customers don't like that! Besides, she's got money! That's a consolation prize, isn't it?

HERMAN: Over there, there used to be a hazelnut bush! (*looks at MIKE*) I carved you a whistle from it fifteen years ago! You still remember? (*MIKE doesn't answer, looks down at the ground.*)

OSSI: What?

NINA: I think I'm going to flip out completely in a minute! Hey, is this your old man?

MIKE: Yes.

OSSI: What? (*to HERMAN*) This is your son? The one who ran away? (*HERMAN nods imperceptibly. GUNTHER lights a cigarette.*)

NINA: Wow, I think that's pretty weird! Man oh man! The town cop is your big boss! (*walks over to HERMAN*) Listen! I stole the stuff. Mike had nothing to do with it!

HERMAN (*gets up, walks around slowly and despondently, takes off his cap, runs his hand over his forehead and head, puts his cap back on, sees the whisky bottle in OSSI's hand, hoarsely*) I need a swallow!

OSSI: Huh? Oh, yeah! (*hands HERMAN the bottle*) Here you go!

(*HERMAN reaches into his pocket, gets out his wallet, hands OSSI a five dollar bill; OSSI takes it, somewhat perplexed. The whisky costs more than that, but OSSI doesn't dare say it. HERMAN turns away, opens the bottle and takes a big swig.*)

NINA (*to MIKE*): I'm really sorry I got you in trouble! Really! Please believe me! (*HERMAN sits down and takes another drink.*)

OSSI: Well, listen . . . under these circumstances, I withdraw my charges! You hear me, Herman? (*HERMAN doesn't answer.*) 'Course it's pretty crappy when the son of the police chief is a crook! (*looks at MIKE*) You must smoke pot, too, huh? —Say, where in the world did you net yourself this bird of paradise, huh? (*MIKE doesn't answer.*) Wanted to come back home, did ya?

MIKE: Naw. Just passing through!

OSSI: Would have been better if you hadn't passed through!

HERMAN (*to MIKE*): Do you know what it did to me when you left? Do you know? My whole reputation was ruined! My authority as an executive official! People laughed at me behind my back! The police chief isn't even capable of keeping a tight rein on his own boy! It was a long time before the people respected me again! But I cleaned this place up, you better believe it! Guys like you haven't got a chance here! Our town is purged! Purged! You understand?

NINA (*stands at attention, clicks her heels together, and extends her right arm in a Nazi salute*): Yessir! Purged! Sieg Heil!

HERMAN: Shut up, you Kraut whore!

OSSI: Purged! In the Catholic Youth Hostel they screw around right in front of the Priest! The fourteen–year–olds!

HERMAN (*shouts*): I can't be everywhere! The parents have to be capable of something, too!—I did everything for him! Everything! Bought him a bike and a model airplane and the most expensive skis. Every winter I sent him on a skiing vacation, to skiing lessons! At age seven he was already skiing like the devil! Could have been a racer! I had it all planned out! I would have sent him to the police academy, they would have released him for ski training! And it would have been a secure job! A secure job for all time! But no, he doesn't want to, he refuses!

GUNTHER (*to MIKE*): With our rate of unemployment! I don't understand you, Mike! Really!

MIKE: Man, you keep out of this!

HERMAN: My wife wanted him to become a doctor! An ac-

ademic! An academic! My father–in–law would
have paid for medical school and later would have
transferred his own practice over to him! But no!
He doesn't want to, he refuses!

MIKE: I want to decide what I want for myself! Understand that once and for all!

HERMAN (*gets up*): I see, and what are you doing? Huh?
What are you doing? You're a gypsy! Gypsying
through the world! Don't want to work! Don't want
to accomplish anything! You're a shoplifter!

MIKE (*grinning*): No, no, it's not quite like that! I'm ac-
complishing something! I've got an honorable occu-
pation!

HERMAN: What? What is it?

MIKE: I am a junk dealer!

HERMAN: You're a what?

MIKE: A junk dealer!

OSSI: What's that supposed to be?

MIKE: I get things out of the dump, put them back in
order, and sell them at the flea market! Second
hand!

GUNTHER (*grinning*): And you can make a living from
that?

MIKE: Sure! (*OSSI and GUNTHER think this is hilarious
and begin to laugh.*)

OSSI: A trash rummager is what he is! Wonderful! The son
of the police chief is a trash rummager!

HERMAN (*with despair*): You don't need to rummage
through trash! You had every opportunity! You got
everything from me!

MIKE: Yeah, everything! Including solitary confinement!

(*to NINA*) He used to lock me in the drunk tank at the police station!

NINA: You're kidding!

HERMAN: What was I supposed to do, when you didn't obey? Beat you up?

NINA: He's really a zombie! Man oh man!

HERMAN: I only wanted to make a decent human being out of him! I only wanted what was best for him!

NINA: But that's not what you got, right?

HERMAN (*doesn't listen to her, sits down despondently, takes a swallow, shakes his head*): Naw! I don't deserve this! Really! I don't deserve a son like this!

NINA (*furious*): Now, quit shitting in your pants, you asshole! Keep out of our faces with your damned whining! I can't listen to this any more, understand?

OSSI: He who cannot hear must feel! Go on, Herman, let her have it! Or are you going to put up with this, huh?

HERMAN (*to NINA*): Just you wait, I'll think of something for you yet!

NINA: Oh, man, don't have a cow! You don't need to play the tough guy here! Do you think I'm afraid of you? Country cop! I've marched through streams from water cannons, man! And tear gas! I've been hit in the mug with billy clubs! What else can *you* possibly do to me?

HERMAN: Just you wait!

OSSI: Wow, she sure has a foul mouth!

HERMAN (*takes another swallow, is beginning to feel the effects of the alcohol. To MIKE*): You are now dead as far as I'm concerned! You don't exist any more!

(*points to GUNTHER*) This is my son now! Your school buddy Gunther! He lives with us now! And he will get our house!

MIKE (*looks at GUNTHER*): My pleasure! A shitty house for a shitty cop!

GUNTHER: Careful, Mike! You don't talk to me like that!

NINA: Hey, Mike! Come on, let's get out of here! I can't handle these freaks any more!

HERMAN (*gets up*): Our house is a shitty house, you say?

MIKE: A shitty house with shitty furniture, with shitty wallpaper, with shitty curtains, and with shitty cops in it!

NINA (*pulls MIKE away*): Come on, Mike, let's cut out!

HERMAN (*yells*): I built that shitty house with these hands, with these hands! Shovel by shovel, brick by brick!

MIKE: Not to mention *my* hands!

NINA: Come on! (*NINA pulls MIKE toward the ladder.*)

HERMAN (*calm again*): The interrogation is not over!

(*MIKE and NINA continue toward the ladder. GUNTHER follows them and steps in front of them, pulling his billy club.*)

GUNTHER (*shouts*): The interrogation is not over! (*MIKE tries to pass, GUNTHER pushes him back, MIKE tries to shove GUNTHER aside, GUNTHER lifts his club threateningly.*)

NINA: C'mon, cop, let us go!

(*NINA tries to get past GUNTHER, he hits her hard on the upper arm with his club, NINA screams, MIKE lunges at GUNTHER, GUNTHER hits him with the club, NINA throws herself at GUNTHER, knocks the cap off his head and pulls his hair, OSSI runs over to them, pulls NINA back and holds her tight from behind, with one hand on her breast. NINA struggles vainly, GUNTHER clubs MIKE, not stopping until MIKE is lying on the ground.*)

GUNTHER: Give up?

MIKE: Okay! (*GUNTHER stows the club and puts his cap back on.*)

NINA: You bastards! You miserable assholes! (*to GUN-THER*) Jerk! (*She tears herself away from OSSI, kneels down to MIKE and helps him up. MIKE holds his bruised head in his hands. NINA leads him over to a pile of iron girders and helps him sit down.*)

GUNTHER (*to MIKE*): I'm sorry!

OSSI: The big dope apologizes! (*to HERMAN*) So? What now?

HERMAN (*takes a big swallow and sits back down. He is quite drunk by now. To GUNTHER*): Put the hand-cuffs on him!

GUNTHER: What?

HERMAN: Put the handcuffs on him and lock him to some-thing!

GUNTHER: Come on, Herman! What're you tryin' to do?

HERMAN: Are you going to do what I tell you, or not?

GUNTHER: I'm holding you responsible.

(*GUNTHER gets out his handcuffs, walks over to MIKE, takes one of his hands, NINA tries to get the handcuffs away from GUNTHER, GUNTHER pushes her away, OSSI catches her and holds her again, grinning, GUNTHER puts one handcuff on the wrist of the dazed MIKE.*)

NINA: Stop it! That's against the law!

OSSI: Oh, come on, since when are you concerned with the law, huh?

(*GUNTHER fastens the second handcuff to several layers of the iron girders that MIKE is sitting on. OSSI lets go of NINA; she walks over to MIKE, who is staring at the handcuffs in disbelief.*)

MIKE (*to HERMAN*): Tell him to let me loose! You hear? (*OSSI and GUNTHER look expectantly at HERMAN, who continues to drink.*)

HERMAN (*after a while*): My father always shook my hand after he had beaten me. And everything was okay again. Mother never understood that. She never understood much of anything. Women don't understand us men. They force themselves between us, tear us apart, pit us against one another. (*pause*) How should we punish her? (*looks at NINA*) How should we punish you?

NINA (*with resignation, to HERMAN*): Let us go, old man! Please!

OSSI (*to HERMAN*): I've got an idea, Herman! (*looks at NINA; HERMAN looks from OSSI to NINA; OSSI looks at GUNTHER*) What do you say, Gunther?

GUNTHER: What?

OSSI (*looks at NINA, GUNTHER understands, looks terrified at HERMAN. OSSI approaches NINA, suddenly serious*) Whoever steals from me is my enemy, you understand? Whoever makes fun of my bouillon jars is my enemy. My supermarket is the world, understand? It has everything a person needs in life. I know every shelf, every product, every price. If a jar is taken away, five minutes later there's a new one in its place. There are no gaps. If a jar sticks out in front of the others by two centimeters, I go crazy. My employees know that. I write the signs advertising the specials myself, in my wonderful handwriting. The floor is clean and shiny, none of the shopping carts squeaks. The customer is always right.

(*OSSI looks at NINA, grabs her hair with one hand, pulls her head close to him, kisses her on the mouth, she pulls away and runs, GUNTHER catches her, she kicks him in the groin, GUNTHER falls to his knees, groaning. OSSI catches NINA, pulls her back, throws her down.*)

MIKE (*shouts*): I'll kill you all! (*he pulls on his shackle, but it's no use. NINA gets up.*)

OSSI: All right, Sexy Hexy! This is where my bachelor party begins! What shall we do, huh? (*He remembers the nighty, which he had hung over his shoulder some time back, takes it in his hand and grins. GUNTHER gets up, holding his groin.*)

GUNTHER (*to NINA*): Just you wait! You won't do that ever again!

OSSI (*grinning*): Well, I'm afraid you may be out of commission now, right?

GUNTHER (*groaning*): What? Why?

OSSI (*throws NINA the nighty*): Put this on! 'Course, you'll have to take that other filthy stuff off first! (*NINA doesn't move; GUNTHER looks with shock at OSSI, then looks at HERMAN.*) Hurry up! Or do *I* have to undress you?

(*NINA slowly takes off her jacket and T-shirt, puts on the nighty, then takes off her shoes and pants. She leaves the rest of her clothes on.*)

GUNTHER (*meanwhile to HERMAN*): Herman, I think we should be going, don't you?

MIKE (*to GUNTHER*): Get the cuffs off me, Gunther!

OSSI (*to GUNTHER*): That's what I thought, that you'd shit in your pants!

GUNTHER: Herman!

HERMAN (*looks up; to GUNTHER*): She needs to be punished, understand?

OSSI (*looks at NINA*): Everything, I said! (*NINA takes off her socks and pantyhose.*) There's still something missing, isn't there? (*NINA looks at OSSI, OSSI approaches her, NINA takes off her panties, OSSI stops.*)

MIKE (*pulling on the handcuffs*): I can't believe this! I can't believe this! (*to HERMAN*) Papa! Papa! Look at me! Papa!

HERMAN (*staring straight ahead*): There's no Papa here!

MIKE: Gunther! If you stand by and let this happen, you're really in for it!

GUNTHER (*to OSSI*): Mr. Leitner, I ask you to step back!

OSSI (*to HERMAN*): Herman, do I have free rein? Will this stay just between us?

HERMAN: Just between us! Everything will stay just between us!

OSSI (*eyes NINA from head to toe, walks around her, grinning*): Very nice! Very attractive! By the way, it's only $19.95 on sale!

GUNTHER: What are you going to do, Ossi?

OSSI: What do you think, you big dope? (*looks at NINA, looks at GUNTHER, walks over to him and takes the pack of condoms out of his pocket*) You can't be too careful! She might have something! You never know with these filthy pigs!—You'll get 'em back tomorrow! (*GUNTHER looks shocked, OSSI puts the condoms in his pocket and walks back to NINA*)

NINA: What are you trying to prove with this? Tell me.

OSSI: The police chief just said it! We need to punish you women!

NINA: And I've just said it to the cop, too. There's nothing you can do to me that hasn't been done to me before!

OSSI: Don't be so sure, little girl!

NINA: Oh, but my boy! I've walked the streets to earn money for drugs! You wouldn't believe the shit I've seen! I can't imagine that some idiot branch manager could come up with anything new!

(*OSSI looks at NINA with cold fury in his eyes.*)

GUNTHER: Herman, as a police officer, I refuse to be a party to this!

(*OSSI suddenly knocks NINA down with a single blow.*)

MIKE (*screams*): No!

GUNTHER (*to OSSI*): Mr. Leitner, I am warning you! I'm going to have to place you under arrest!

OSSI (*to GUNTHER*): Get lost!

GUNTHER (*to HERMAN*): Herman, we can't do this! We are here in the name of the law!

HERMAN (*to GUNTHER*): Go back to the car!

GUNTHER: But Herman!

HERMAN: Go to the car or I'll throw you out! (*GUNTHER is perplexed. NINA starts to move again.*)

MIKE: I'll report you all! All of you!

OSSI: Go on, no one believes you anyway!

HERMAN (*to GUNTHER*): Beat it, man! (*GUNTHER walks uncertainly toward the ladder, climbs up, hesitates, looks back.*) Go on, I tell you!

(*GUNTHER continues to climb and then disappears from

view. HERMAN drinks from the bottle as if he wanted to drown himself. The whisky runs down the front of his uniform. OSSI pulls NINA up by her hair.)

OSSI: You think nothing else can happen to you, since you've seen it all? Every obscenity! Well, you'll be amazed, girl! (*He drags NINA by the hair to the back and disappears with her.*)

MIKE: Papa, please! Please! You can't let this happen! You can't do this! You want respectable people! Is that respectable what they're doing? Is that respectable, huh? Is that respectable?

(HERMAN shows no reaction, but withdraws into himself.)

NINA (*screaming from offstage*): No! No! Please don't! Please don't! (*GUNTHER climbs back down the ladder with his pistol in his hand. NINA continues.*) Stop it! Go away, you pig! Mike! Mike! Mike, help me! Help m—

(NINA's voice breaks off. HERMAN stares straight ahead. MIKE looks desperately in the direction the cries are coming from.)

MIKE: Nina! Nina! (*GUNTHER runs offstage to the back.*)

VOICE OF GUNTHER: Get off her, you bastard!

(GUNTHER appears with OSSI who now looks panicky, pulls him over to MIKE, takes off MIKE's handcuffs. MIKE runs offstage to the back.)

OSSI: Herman, I didn't mean to! Really I didn't! (*GUNTHER puts a handcuff on OSSI, locks him to the iron girders, and also runs offstage to the back. Meanwhile OSSI continues.*) Y'know, I've had a little too much today, too! People kept coming into the store and wanting me to drink a toast to my wedding! (*HERMAN shows no reaction, just stares straight ahead. Only now does OSSI notice that he is handcuffed)* Whoa, is this for real? *(looks around for GUNTHER)* Hey, Gunther, you out of your mind?

(GUNTHER and MIKE appear, carrying NINA. She has a head wound and blood is running down her face. They set her down.)

MIKE: Nina! Hey! Nina! *(to OSSI)* What did you do to her, you bastard?

(GUNTHER kneels down next to NINA, pulls out a handkerchief, wipes the blood off her face, strokes her cheek, looks around, sees her clothes, goes and gets them and places them under her head like a pillow, and continues to stroke her.)

MIKE: Nina! *(he looks over at OSSI, runs over to him, punches him, OSSI defends himself with his free hand and kicks at MIKE with his feet. HERMAN sinks over on his side as if he has fainted. GUNTHER has laid his ear on NINA's heart.)*

GUNTHER: She's alive!

MIKE *(goes back to NINA, kneels down next to her, looks at her, looks at GUNTHER)*: Call an ambulance! Go on! *(GUNTHER walks to the ladder.)*

OSSI: No! Gunther! No ambulance! *(GUNTHER climbs up the ladder.)* Herman! Herman! *(HERMAN doesn't move.)* Gunther! Then there'll have to be a police report!

GUNTHER *(pauses on the ladder)*: Yeah, sure! So what?

OSSI: Then I'm in for it!

GUNTHER: You sure are in for it! *(continues up the ladder)*

OSSI: But so are you!

GUNTHER (*pauses*) Why?

OSSI: You let it happen!

GUNTHER: I didn't either! I intervened!

OSSI: Yeah—but when?

GUNTHER (*points to HERMAN*): But *he* sent me away!

MIKE (*furious, to GUNTHER*): Well, are you his slave, or something?

OSSI: Herman's in trouble, too! He provoked me! Do you think I would have had the guts otherwise?

(*GUNTHER reconsiders, comes down, walks over to HER-MAN.*)

GUNTHER: Herman! Hey!

(*HERMAN doesn't react.*)

OSSI: He's drunk!

GUNTHER: Herman! (*shakes HERMAN, HERMAN doesn't move*) Shit! Why do you have to drink like this? (*walks over to MIKE and NINA*) He's always getting drunk! (*to MIKE*) How often do you think I've pulled duty for him?

MIKE: That's why you're getting his house! Now, go and call an ambulance, dammit!

(*GUNTHER looks at HERMAN, looks at NINA, goes back to the ladder.*)

OSSI: Gunther! Wait a minute! We at least have to get our stories straight!

GUNTHER (*stops*): What stories?

OSSI: Two shoplifters! Two drug addict shoplifters! Attempted escape! She stumbles, hits her head! The two of them want to get even with us, and so they start babbling something about an attempted rape!

MIKE: You bastard!

GUNTHER: We can't do that!

OSSI: Of course we can! No one'll believe those two! Just look at 'em! Anyone who looks like that, no one believes anything they say!

GUNTHER: Naw, I can't do it! (*walks to the ladder*)

OSSI: Gunther! I'm your friend! I'm supposed to get married tomorrow! (*GUNTHER climbs up.*) We go to the sauna together! We play poker together! I lose to you all the time! (*GUNTHER is almost at the top.*) Gunther! No ambulance! Call Herman's father–in–law! He won't tell! (*GUNTHER disappears.*) Gunther! (*HERMAN sits up slowly, looks around, sees MIKE and stares at him. In the distance, we can hear GUNTHER speaking, and an answer coming from the two–way radio. To HERMAN*) Take these cuffs off, Herman! You hear? You're in this thing, too! You're heading for deep water, too! (*HERMAN doesn't answer, gets up slowly, walks toward MIKE as if in a trance. GUNTHER comes back down the ladder.*) Who did you call?

GUNTHER (*points to HERMAN*): His father–in–law!

OSSI: Well, thank God! Unlock me, Gunther!

(*HERMAN is standing in front of MIKE, looks at him silently, ignores NINA. GUNTHER unlocks the handcuffs from OSSI and puts them in his pocket.*)

GUNTHER: But only for his sake! (*points to HERMAN*)

OSSI (*grinning*): And a little for your sake, right? (*rubs his wrist where the handcuff was attached*) You still want a few more gold stars, don't you? (*GUNTHER walks sullenly away from OSSI. OSSI follows him.*) Come on, give me a cigarette, please!

(*GUNTHER reluctantly gets out his cigarette pack. OSSI throws away his chewing gum and takes a cigarette. GUNTHER starts to walk away from him.*) I don't have a light, either! (*GUNTHER stops and gives him a light.*) You know, I really don't smoke anymore! But right now I need one! (*GUNTHER walks away from him.*)

HERMAN (*to MIKE*): You've got to ask my forgiveness, Mikey!

MIKE: Aw, leave me alone!

HERMAN (*pulls MIKE up*): You've got to ask my forgiveness, Mikey!

MIKE: Never! (*pulls away; HERMAN draws a pistol and points it at MIKE.*)

GUNTHER: Hey, what are you doing?

(*MIKE looks at HERMAN, sees the pistol, turns away and kneels down next to NINA. HERMAN walks over to him, holds the pistol to the back of MIKE's head. MIKE turns around, gets up slowly, looks at his father.*)

HERMAN: You've got to ask my forgiveness, Mikey!

(*MIKE sees in his father's eyes that he is serious, and that he is prepared to pull the trigger.*)

GUNTHER: Come on, Herman, cut it out! (*walks over to HERMAN, moves to take the pistol away from him. HERMAN points the pistol at him, GUNTHER backs away.*)

OSSI: That drunken son–of–a–bitch is gonna spoil everything! Cut it out, man!

HERMAN (*turns back to MIKE*): Say: "Forgive me, Papa!" Then everything will be okay! (*MIKE doesn't move, doesn't answer. HERMAN holds the pistol close to MIKE'S forehead.*) "Forgive me, Papa!"

MIKE (*softly*): Forgive me, Papa!

HERMAN: "Papa, I love you so!"

MIKE: Papa, I love you so!

HERMAN: "Papa, I want to be just like you!"

(*MIKE says nothing. HERMAN holds the pistol against MIKE'S forehead.*)

GUNTHER (*screams*): Cut it out, dammit!

HERMAN: "Papa, I want to be just like you!"

MIKE: Papa, I want to be just like you!

HERMAN (*lowers the pistol, puts his arms around MIKE, strokes his hair. MIKE tolerates it with a stony face*): I like you, too, Mikey. We're gonna be all right. We'll get back together. You're my son, after all. (*turns away slowly, puts the pistol away, sits down on one side with a distant, distraught look on his face. Later he slips to the ground and falls asleep; his cap falls off.*)

GUNTHER (*looks full of emotion at HERMAN, whom he loves like his own father*): Mikey, Mikey, Mikey! You've lost him, don't you see that?

(*MIKE watches his father walk away, feels sorry for him, hates and loves him at the same time, turns to NINA, kneels down next to her, lays her head in his lap, takes off his jacket and covers her with it.*)

OSSI: What a sorry drunken sap! I can't believe it! But nothing surprises me anymore!

(*The sound of a motorscooter approaches up on the highway. Everyone listens. The motorscooter comes to a stop, the engine dies. OSSI looks at GUNTHER questioningly, both look over toward the ladder. MONIKA appears at the top, then climbs down. She is eight months pregnant and can't stop smiling. OSSI walks toward her.*)

OSSI: What are *you* doing here?

MONIKA: I heard you'd come out here with the police!

OSSI: So what? Man, get out of here! Go back home! (*MONIKA looks ahead into the site, tries to walk forward. OSSI blocks her view and forces her back.*) I said go home!

MONIKA: Ow! You're hurting me! You're hurting our little boy! (*OSSI releases her instantly. MONIKA walks toward the front, one hand over her belly.*) Hi, Gunther!

GUNTHER: Hello, Moni!

MONIKA (*sees NINA on the ground and MIKE next to her. She acts as if NINA didn't exist*): Hi, Mikey!

MIKE: Hello!

MONIKA (*sees NINA's panties on the ground, nudges them with her toe as if by accident, notices the sleeping HERMAN*): Good evening, Mr. Police Chief, sir! (*sits down slowly and carefully, clasps her hands on top of her belly, and smiles. She speaks without looking at NINA.*) Who is that?

OSSI: Man, Moni, please go home!

MONIKA (*to OSSI*): I was worried about you, you know!

OSSI: Well, what for?

MONIKA: You said you'd be by at six! Before you went to the bachelor party!

OSSI: You know, I've got other stuff to worry about right now!

MONIKA (*smiling*): Like what?

OSSI (*screams*): Go home, I tell you! You don't belong here!

(*MONIKA does nothing of the kind. Embarrassed silence. NINA wakes up, moves, and reaches up to touch her head.*)

MIKE: Hey! Nina!

NINA (*distantly*): Yeah?

MIKE: How are you?

NINA: What?

MIKE: Nina!

NINA (*disoriented*): May I please go home?

MIKE (*shakes her*): Nina!

NINA (*tries to sit up, MIKE supports her, NINA looks at OSSI, groans, buries her face in MIKE's chest, crying*) Mama! Mama! Mama! Mama!

MIKE (*strokes her*): Calm down! Calm down! It's all over! All over!

NINA (*crying*): I want to go! Please, I want to go!

MIKE: We have to wait for the doctor, Nina! You're hurt!

NINA: No, I don't want to stay here anymore! I want to go! Please, Mike!

MIKE: The doctor'll be here soon! It's important! We can't just leave!

(*NINA looks around nervously, looks at everyone, her glance hesitates for a moment at OSSI. While she looks at him, she reaches between her legs, suddenly fearful.*)

MIKE: It's nothing, Nina! He didn't do anything to you!

OSSI: Exactly! No one did anything to you!

NINA (*buries her head again*) How come everyone is still here? I want them to leave! Please!

OSSI: Yeah, um, that may be the best thing anyway! Except . . . it kind of depends . . .

MONIKA: What happened? What's the matter with her? (*No one says a word. She smiles.*) Why doesn't anyone tell me anything?

GUNTHER: Miss Monika, this is official business, please go home!

MONIKA (*smiling*): I'm not supposed to get excited. Because of the baby, you know!

GUNTHER: Exactly!

MONIKA: Where have you been all this time, Mikey? (*MIKE doesn't hear her.*) Where have you been all this time, Mikey?

MIKE: What?

MONIKA: Where have you been all this time?

MIKE: Berlin. Amsterdam.

NINA (*softly*): Mama! Jesus!

MONIKA: You left back then without saying a word to me!

MIKE: Yeah. Sorry. I didn't tell anyone.

MONIKA: That wasn't very nice of you!

MIKE: I'm sorry.

MONIKA: I had my whole trousseau ready, all the dishes and everything. Bedding, the best comforters. Nine months ago I finished beauty school. I've got my hairdresser's license now.

MIKE (*would never have gone through with it, but he likes MONIKA*): Great!

OSSI: Oh, come on! Were you going steady with this guy?

(*NINA looks at MONIKA.*)

MONIKA: Yeah, I was going with him. We used to come here a lot, right, Mikey? It used to be nice. Like Tahiti. (*to MIKE*) Used to play your guitar for me. (*sings*) We enjoyed, we had fun, we had seasons in the sun, la, la, la, lalala.—Then suddenly you were gone. And he came along. (*looks at OSSI*) The new branch manager. An attractive guy. Tomorrow is our wedding day. Wanna come, Mikey?

OSSI: Boy, just what I needed! Great! Thanks a lot! This bum as my predecessor! Well, great! Cheezus!

MONIKA: Not a bad predecessor, Mikey! We got along really well! Right, Mikey?

MIKE: Sure.

OSSI: Cheezus, Cheezus! This guy screwed her before me!

MIKE: What are you so upset about? It can't be all that bad! Just a little while ago you tried the same thing again!

MONIKA (*smiling*): Oh, really? How's that?

OSSI: Bullshit!

MONIKA: Oh, my little boy is moving! (*to her belly*) You're kicking again with your little feetsies, aren't you? You little devil! Kicking your Mama in the belly! Getting an early start, are we? (*to MIKE*) Wanna touch, Mikey? You can really feel his little feetsies! Don't you wanna?

MIKE: Naw, thanks!

MONIKA (*smiling innocently, to OSSI*): What did you do to her?

OSSI: Nothing! We didn't do nothing! They're shoplifters, both of them! We were chasing them! And she hurt herself! That's all!

MIKE (*to OSSI*): That's a good story! Now all you have to do is tell it to my father, when he's finished sleeping it off!

NINA (*sits up*): Man, you guys are bastards! Y'know, I really can't believe this! (*to MONIKA*) Your sweetie pie was horny as hell for me! Was going to rape me!

OSSI (*furious*): I was going to punish her! Anyone who steals from me is in for it! I'll crush 'em!

(*MONIKA looks at GUNTHER.*)

GUNTHER: Attempted escape. Like Ossi said!

MIKE: Why are you playing along with this, Gunther?

GUNTHER (*points to HERMAN and shouts*): He cares about me, don't you understand? He cares about me!

MIKE: He's finished, Gunther! I don't understand it! How can you stand it?

GUNTHER: He cares about me! Nobody ever cared about me before! I was always the fool! You betrayed him! It's your fault that he's like this!—We have to stick together! What else is there?

(*Silence.*)

NINA (*to MONIKA*): Well, then, congratulations, young woman! You don't find a husband like this every day!

(*Silence for a while.*)

OSSI: People, where's the doctor?

MONIKA: Yeah, yeah, Mikey! I'm going to open my own hair salon! Inherited a nice sum of money! I'll take care of my little boy for a year, and then I'm going to open a salon! Right on the main square! "Hair By Monika!" The newest cuts, the latest craze!

OSSI: Go on home! Please! What do you want here? (*looks in desperation at GUNTHER*)

GUNTHER: I'm asking you to leave the scene, Miss Monika!

MONIKA: I think I'll wait for the doctor, too.

(*The sound of a car approaching.*)

MONIKA: Ah, there he is!

(*Headlights approach, light up the background, the car stops, the engine dies, the lights go out, two doors slam. Everyone except for NINA looks over toward the ladder. HILDE appears, climbs down the ladder. She is followed by WALTER, with his doctor bag in his hand.*)

GUNTHER: I can't believe it! Now *she's* here, too!

(*HILDE stops at the foot of the ladder, looks around, sees MIKE, runs to him, kneels down, hugs him, weeping, pulls him to his feet. While she is starting her monologue, WALTER looks around, GUNTHER points to NINA, WALTER walks over to her, examines her, cleans her wound, applies a gauze bandage to it, and wraps her head. He looks into her eyes, sees that she has taken drugs, examines her arms, and sees the needle marks. One can tell that he is reluctant to help her. WALTER hates people like NINA. While HILDE is speaking, MIKE makes several attempts to pull away from her, but he doesn't succeed. She is clutching him tightly.*)

HILDE: My God, Mikey! My God, Mikey! You're really back! Oh, Mikey! (*kisses him*) My God! You can't imagine what I've been through since you left! Terrible! Terrible, I tell you! It was simply awful! Your letter! Horrible! I broke down immediately! Nervous breakdown! Ask your grandfather! Horrible! He thought he'd have to take me to a mental hospital! Convulsive sobbing, high blood pressure, headaches, terrible headaches! For weeks at a time I couldn't leave my room! Always in bed! Always with the curtains drawn! Fever! Fever attacks! I called your name! My dearest Mikey! My dearest Mikey! Again and again! Ask your grandfather! He sat at my bedside night after night! Shots! Shots again and again! Sleeping pills! I couldn't sleep a wink!

Always your letter on my mind! I had to read it!
Again and again! That horrible letter! I've never
read such a horrible letter! So full of accusations!
So full of pointless accusations! Even against me!
Why against me? Why did you write that letter to
me? Why not to your father? You left because of
your father, didn't you? That's what you wrote! Because he's such a ruthless person! A policeman! And
a drunk! Since you left, he's a lost cause! Every day
he gets drunk! Every day! Sits in his office, on duty,
and drinks and drinks! Sits in the drunk tank and
drinks! Imagine that! Sits in the drunk tank and
drinks! Doesn't come home anymore! Can you imagine that? Can you imagine how I'm suffering? I
shouldn't have married him, no, I shouldn't have
married him! Your grandfather told me, your
grandfather warned me, ask him! Don't marry this
policeman, he said! The daughter of a doctor should
not be marrying a policeman, he said! Maybe an academic, he said, but not someone from down there,
he said, not some country bumpkin who puts on a
uniform and then thinks he's God knows who, he
said! Policemen always have to associate with
criminals, with thieves, with lowlifes, he said! The
low life must rub off, he said, there's no other way!
Don't marry him, he said! I'll disinherit you, he
said! But I didn't listen to him, I didn't listen to him!
Was simply in love with this brute, this ruffian! It
was his strength, you know, his strength! And his
smile, so self-assured! He wasn't as low as my father believed, no, certainly not! Even though he always burps and breaks wind, I can't stand that!
He's constantly burping or breaking wind! Go out
in the garden, I said, you can burp and break wind
there! Go out in the garden! But he doesn't do it! He
doesn't do it! He wants to drive me crazy! He simply

wants to drive me crazy! And yet, he had every opportunity, before he started to drink! He could have gone to night school and become an officer, he could have become state chief of police, but that's all over now, because he drinks so much! Why does he drink so much, tell me, Mikey, I don't understand it! When we were engaged, he didn't drink at all, or was he just taking a break in order to get me, I don't know! But he built the house, he wasn't drinking then, he was working hard, you have to give him credit for that, Mikey! It was for you that he built the house, for you! And my father didn't help us, didn't give us a dime, I'll never forgive him for that, never, I don't care if he hears this! I'll never forgive him for that! Oh, Mikey! Why did you leave? Why did you leave? I was always there for you! Always! But you also have to show a little consideration! Did you do that? Did you do that? No, you didn't! You never did! You tortured us with your disregard! At sixteen you were going into town, staying all night! And your haircut! Your haircut! I begged you on my knees! I am the daughter of a doctor, the wife of a policeman! You can't do that! You can't have a hairstyle like that! No one in this town ever had a hairstyle like you! With colors in it! You can do that in the city, but not here! I see you don't have colors in it any more, I thank you! You'll be able to fit in! The main thing is that you're back! Did you know that Gunther is living with us now? Did you know? He's got your room, imagine! Your father acts as if Gunther were his son! Imagine! That's treachery! Treachery! I won't betray you, Mikey, Gunther isn't even allowed to call me by my first name, that's out of the question, I'm standing by you, firm as a rock! Oh, my dearest son, I've suffered so! I have suffered so! All those things you accused me of! Terrible!

Horrible! That I was smothering you! That you
were suffocating here! How can anyone write something like that? How can anyone ever write something like that? That was love, Mikey, just love!
Love!

MIKE (*pulls away and screams*): Stop it!

(*MIKE walks away from HILDE. She suddenly stops talking, looks confused, smiles nervously and self-consciously,
looks at NINA, looks at the others, sees MONIKA.*)

HILDE: Oh, Miss Monika, you're here, too?

MONIKA (*smiling*): Good evening, Madam Police Chief!

HILDE: Where is my husband?

OSSI (*points*): He's lying over there!

HILDE (*looks at the sleeping HERMAN but doesn't move*):
   What's the matter with him?

OSSI: He's drunk!

HILDE: Oh! (*looks at NINA*) And what happened here?

GUNTHER: Shoplifting! Injured while trying to escape!

HILDE: I see. (*to MIKE*) And what have *you* got to do with
   it?

MIKE: I'm with the girl!

HILDE: Oh? And were you also shoplifting?

NINA: No, he wasn't! I was the only one who stole anything!

HILDE: Oh? And why? No money?

NINA: Naw, I've got enough dough! I always steal! There's
   no supermarket where I don't steal something!

HILDE: Well, then, whatever for?

NINA: Why not? There's enough stuff!

HILDE: Strange point of view! (*to MIKE*) And you're traveling with her?

MIKE: That's right!

HILDE: Miss Monika would have been much nicer! More respectable! Now it's too late!

MIKE (*doesn't answer. WALTER gets up, picks up his bag. MIKE walks over to him.*) So? How does it look?

WALTER: That's: Good evening, Grandfather!

MIKE: Good evening, Grandfather! What's your diagnosis?

WALTER: Laceration and contusion, suspected concussion! In addition, she has a heroin addiction! (*to GUNTHER*) Call an ambulance!

GUNTHER: Is that really necessary, Doctor?

WALTER: The laceration must be sewn! And a head x–ray is necessary! (*to NINA*) And afterwards it's off to the psychiatric ward!

NINA (*gets up, falters. MIKE supports her, lays his jacket, which had slipped off, around her shoulders.*) Psychiatric ward? You must be off your rocker, man!

MIKE: She doesn't need to go to the psychiatric ward! She's already in a drug treatment program!

WALTER (*sets down his bag, takes a pad and fountain pen out of his jacket pocket. To NINA*) Name?

NINA: I don't want to shoot up any more! Honest! I'm trying to stop!

WALTER (*unruffled*): Name?

NINA: Man, invent one, Doctor Mabuse! (*hands MIKE his jacket, bends to pick up her clothes, falters, MIKE supports her, she picks up her clothes, puts on pantyhose, socks, pants, and shoes under the nighty, then takes off the nighty and throws it to*

      OSSI, who ignores it. She puts the rest of her clothes
      on, the conversation continues meanwhile.)

OSSI: Um, Doctor?

WALTER: Yes?

OSSI: You know, we would all prefer, including the Police
      Chief, if the hospital could be avoided!

WALTER: Why?

OSSI: Well, it would just be better, according to the Police
      Chief, your son–in–law. There could be complica-
      tions!

WALTER: Express yourself more plainly!

OSSI: Well, the Police Chief is an accomplice in the injury!
      It could be bad for him!

GUNTHER: Don't push it, Ossi!

NINA: Come on, Mike, let's get out of here! (*takes MIKE by*
      the arm, pulls him away. He looks at HERMAN.)
      Man, I can tell you, I'd rather fight for my life in the
      cities! This is Transylvania here!

MIKE (*stops, furious*): Oh, all of a sudden? An hour ago you
      were still full of enthusiasm! Everything was cute!
      Neat! (*NINA bows her head, feeling guilty. MIKE*
      looks over at HERMAN, walks toward him, looks at
      him. He is sleeping as if unconscious.) Sure, I can
      remember how you carved me that whistle. (*slowly*)
      I really wanted to come back home.—Someday. But
      now everything is worse than before.

(*HERMAN shows no reaction. MIKE goes to NINA and*
then past her to the ladder.)

NINA (*crushed*): I'm sorry, Mike! Forgive me! I know, I
      caused all of this!

(*MIKE climbs up the ladder. NINA follows him.*
GUNTHER remembers the I.D. card and the pocket knife,

he gets both out of his pocket, walks over to NINA and hands her MIKE's I.D. and pocket knife. She puts both in her pocket and slowly climbs the ladder behind MIKE.)

WALTER (*in NINA's direction*): I wash my hands of any responsibility!

MIKE (*stops*): You do that, Commissioner! You always have!

HILDE: Mikey! I beg you! Don't leave! Stay with me! What am I supposed to do without you? (*MIKE continues to climb. WALTER puts away his pen and notepad.*) Mikey!

WALTER: Let him go! (*picks up his bag*) They should all be euthanized! All of them! (*looks at HERMAN*) Including him! All the losers!

HILDE: What? What do you mean, euthanized?

MIKE (*from the ladder*): Killed, Mother! Killed!

HILDE (*doesn't understand*): What?

(*MIKE and NINA climb out of sight. WALTER walks over to the ladder. HILDE walks over to HERMAN and looks at him.*)

HILDE: Hey! You! (*nudges him with her foot*) I'm getting a divorce! Do you hear? (*HERMAN does not hear.*)

WALTER: Yes, do it, at last! You've been talking about it for ten years!

(*From above, the sound of the motorcycle starting, then driving off. WALTER climbs up the ladder.*)

HILDE (*in a friendly tone to the others*): Good night! (*She walks to the ladder.*)

GUNTHER: Good night, Madam Police Chief!

MONIKA: Good night!

(*HILDE climbs up the ladder, disappears. Car doors slam, the doctor's car drives away.*)

OSSI: Thank God! Now we can forget this whole stupid incident! We did okay, nothing happened! (*looks at his watch*) Oh my God, looks like I'm late to my own bachelor party! The guys'll wonder where I am! (*grinning, to GUNTHER*) Hey, maybe they think I ran away! Scared to death of marriage! Right? But we're already together! Right, Moni? I'm not getting away from you.

MONIKA: You know what, Ossi? I think I'll be having this baby out of wedlock!

OSSI: What? What did you say? (*MONIKA gets up carefully and walks slowly to the ladder. OSSI watches her go, bewildered.*) Hey! Wait a minute! (*He follows her. MONIKA climbs up the ladder slowly and carefully.*) Moni! What's wrong? (*MONIKA disappears from sight.*) Now I'm totally confused! (*climbs up*) But I love you, Moni! (*The motorscooter starts up. OSSI disappears from sight. The motorscooter drives away. GUNTHER walks over to HERMAN. Voice of OSSI*) Moni! Wait up! . . . Aw, shit!

GUNTHER: Herman, wake up! (*pulls him up, shakes him*) Hey, you! (*shouts*) Wake up!

HERMAN (*slowly awakes, looks around, looks at GUNTHER*) What's going on?

GUNTHER: Nothing's going on! (*pulls HERMAN into a standing position, sets the cap that had fallen to the ground back on his head*) Come on now! (*leads HERMAN toward the ladder. HERMAN stops, looks around, appears to be trying to remember.*) Come on! (*tries to pull him along*)

HERMAN (*stops, stares straight ahead, slowly begins to

remember, looks at GUNTHER) Where is Mikey? Where is my boy?

GUNTHER: He's gone!

HERMAN: I want him to stay! I want him to stay!

GUNTHER: Forget him, man! He's through with you! *(pulls HERMAN onward)*

(HERMAN pushes GUNTHER away violently, looks around, breathing heavily, takes out his billy club, removes his cap, beats himself over the head with his club several times. GUNTHER tries to get the club away from him, they wrestle, HERMAN drops his cap, swings at GUNTHER, GUNTHER dodges. HERMAN stands frozen for a moment with his club raised, then puts it back in his belt.)

HERMAN: I'm turning myself in!

GUNTHER: You'll do nothing of the kind! *(picks the cap up off the ground, puts it on HERMAN and grabs him by the arm)* Come on, Herman, let's go home! Please! *(leads HERMAN to the ladder, pushes him up, returns one more time to turn off the construction site lighting. Total darkness onstage.)*

HERMAN *(stops on the ladder)*: I've made a mess of everything! Everything!

GUNTHER *(gets a flashlight out of his belt, turns it on, walks to the ladder, shines the flashlight upward, climbs up to HERMAN, pushes him onward)* Go on now!

(They disappear from sight.)

VOICE OF OSSI: Can I get a ride with you?

VOICE OF GUNTHER: Get lost! You can walk! *(sound of car door opening)* Get in, Herman!

VOICE OF HERMAN *(shouting)*: Mikey!

VOICE OF GUNTHER: Get in, dammit!

(*A car door closes, a second one opens.*)

VOICE OF OSSI: Come on, let me go with you!

(*The car door slams shut, the engine starts, headlights come on.*)

VOICE OF OSSI: Stupid ass!

(*The police car turns around, then drives away.*)

THE END

Children of the Devil

Translated by
Todd C. Hanlin

The confessions of the accused are authentic and on display in the Hauptstaatsarchiv in Munich as well as in the Landesarchiv Salzburg.

Characters

The Court:

COMMISSIONER (Counselor Dr. Sebastian Zillner)
SCRIBE (High Court Deputy Tax Appraiser Gregori Finsterwalder)
EXECUTIONER (Master Moritz Ehegartner)
TWO HENCHMEN

The Miscreants:

DIONYSUS FELDNER, The "Shitspotter" (age 12)
LISL FELDNER, "Little Lisl" (age 8)
VEIT LINDNER, "Crooked Veit" (age 14)
MICHAEL N., "Blindbat Michael" (age 10)
JOHNNY N., "Mow Catcher" (age 6)
DOFFER N., "Dumb Doffer" (age 13)
ANDREE MAYER, "City Reject" (age 18)
MAGDALENA PICHLER, "Raggedy Leni" (age 17)

The children or youths are to be played by young actors and actresses, the members of the Court by actors of the appropriate age.

STAGE SETTING: Office of the Commissioner; below that, the Prison Cell

TIME AND PLACE: 1678 in Salzburg

1. Barbara Koller is burned at the stake

2. Office of the commissioner

(*Sitting behind his desk, the COMMISSIONER OF WITCHERY, Counselor Dr. Sebastian Zillner. In front of him, a crucifix, writing utensils, a few files and blank sheets of paper for his notes. At a second desk, the SCRIBE is sitting between stacks of files which grow from scene to scene, so that by the end of the play he is almost completely hidden by the mountain of paperwork. In the floor, several trap doors that lead to the cells below. On one side of the stage is an exit door; the door to the torture chamber can be located upstage in the center. Beside that door, a bench where the EXECUTIONER Moritz Ehegartner—wearing a black leather half-mask on his face and a white apron—, as well as the FIRST and SECOND HENCHMEN, sits. A large basin filled with holy water, in it an aspergillum and a sprayer similar to an enema bag. Somewhere a chair. In front of the COMMISSIONER'S desk stands the beggar child DIONYSUS FELDNER, alias Shitspotter (age 12), his head constantly drooping to one side—a deformity; nevertheless, he is in good spirits. He is barefooted, wearing tattered, filthy clothes on his filthy body, mange on his scalp—though not yet in chains. The SCRIBE writes at an astonishing speed and copies down everything that is said, as well as how each miscreant reacts. The COMMISSIONER has a list of prepared questions on his desk, though he doesn't usually rely on them, since he adapts naturally to each specific situation and tries to deal with each miscreant in a different way. During the accuseds' responses, he jots down brief notes, for example, when something new comes up that he would like to ask the other children at a later date, or when he wants to come back to something later, but does not want to interrupt the present discussion, or when a new question occurs to him that he would like to ask later.*)

COMMISSIONER: Are you absolutely certain that Jackie the Sorcerer is still alive?

DIONYSUS (*astonished*): 'Course he's still alive!

COMMISSIONER (*in a friendly tone*): Hold your head up.

DIONYSUS: Can't. Sorry, Sir.

COMMISSIONER: You cannot?

DIONYSUS: No, Sir. It hangs down all by itself.

(*The COMMISSIONER gazes calmly at DIONYSUS, then looks at his files.*)

COMMISSIONER: Well, all right. Let us begin the interrogation. (*crosses himself*) In nomine domini! (*to DIONYSUS*) What is your name?

DIONYSUS: Dionysus Feldner.

COMMISSIONER: Nickname?

DIONYSUS: The Shitspotter.

COMMISSIONER: Why?

DIONYSUS: 'Cause my head hangs down. So I always look down at the ground when I walk.

COMMISSIONER: Age?

DIONYSUS: Don't know. Fourteen, I guess.

COMMISSIONER (*smiles*): I would not have guessed a day over twelve!—Birthplace?

DIONYSUS: Schellenberg.

COMMISSIONER: Your parents?

DIONYSUS: Don't know nothin' about my mother. She's dead. My father used to be a hired hand in Schellenberg.—But I haven't been able to find him.

COMMISSIONER (*to the SCRIBE*): Send an inquiry to the parish office in Schellenberg. Verify the boy's age from the baptismal records in the church.

(*The SCRIBE nods, makes a note.*)

COMMISSIONER (*to DIONYSUS*): Do you live on charity?

DIONYSUS: In the summer I help the farmers. When they'll hire me.

COMMISSIONER: Come closer.

(*DIONYSUS steps right up to the desk.*)

COMMISSIONER (*in a friendly tone, though slightly repulsed*): Not so close! Take one step back.

(*DIONYSUS readily takes one step back, the COMMISSIONER examines him from head to toe.*)

COMMISSIONER: Do you feel healthy?

DIONYSUS: Sometimes I fall down. But other than that . . . (*smiles*) I can't exactly lift an ox with my bare hands!

COMMISSIONER (*to the SCRIBE*): The subject is sick, fragile. Mange on his scalp.

(*The COMMISSIONER looks at DIONYSUS for a while.*)

DIONYSUS: I already told the official in Grossarl all I know. They wrote it all down too.

COMMISSIONER: I know.—Why were you arrested?

DIONYSUS: Don't know.

COMMISSIONER: What happened? Tell me.

DIONYSUS: I was standin' on a hill, watchin' a buzzard. He could really fly.

COMMISSIONER: You were looking up at the sky . . . ?
How could you do that with your neck?

DIONYSUS: It was flyin' down below me. Lookin' for
fieldmice.

COMMISSIONER: Continue.

DIONYSUS: So I was just wishin' I could fly too. So I
spread my arms, flapped 'em up and down, just
like the buzzard. All of a sudden, the court bailiff
from Grossarl was standin' there, right behind me!
Wanted to know what I was doin'. So I told 'em. He
asked me if I knew Jackie the Skinner. I said yeah.
So he took me in.

COMMISSIONER (*looks at a piece of paper on the desk*):
You told him "Yes" right away?

DIONYSUS: No.

COMMISSIONER: What changed your mind?

DIONYSUS: The bailiff beat me.

COMMISSIONER: What does Jackie look like?

DIONYSUS: Pretty tall and skinny. He's got light-colored
hair, pretty long. Light-colored mustache under
his nose. A crooked nose.

(*The COMMISSIONER looks over to the SCRIBE who is
frantically searching among his papers, finds the page he
is looking for.*)

SCRIBE (*reads excerpts*): Barbara Koller describes her
son, dated January 17, 1675: Jackie is about
twenty years old; a thin face; straight, long, black,
hair, no beard. Testimony of Paul Kaltenpacher,
dated January 17, 1675: long red hair. Testimony
of Hans Tanhauser, June 30, 1675: Jackie is tall,

has a thin face, gray eyes, a crooked nose; straight, long black hair, no beard.

COMMISSIONER: Do you stand by your statement?

DIONYSUS: Uh-huh. It's the truth.

COMMISSIONER: How do you know it was really Jackie?

DIONYSUS: He told me so.

COMMISSIONER: You are aware that his mother was burned at the stake?

DIONYSUS: Uh-huh. He told me so.

COMMISSIONER: What did he tell you?

DIONYSUS: That she was burned at the stake.

COMMISSIONER: What else?

DIONYSUS: That people want to burn him at the stake too.

COMMISSIONER: And . . . ?

DIONYSUS: That they won't catch him.

COMMISSIONER: Why not?

DIONYSUS: 'Cause he can make himself invisible. That's what he said.

COMMISSIONER: Do you believe that?

DIONYSUS: Well . . .

COMMISSIONER: Well, what?

DIONYSUS: Maybe he was just braggin'!

COMMISSIONER (*smiling*): What you don't know can't hurt you, is that it?

DIONYSUS (*laughs*): Right!

COMMISSIONER: Where did you meet Jackie? And when?

DIONYSUS: In Golling. Beginning of May.

(The COMMISSIONER looks over to the SCRIBE who frantically searches for a document, finds it.)

SCRIBE: Report from the official in St. Wolfgang: Jacob Koller, alias Jackie the Skinner or Jackie the Sorcerer, died here on Good Friday, April 16, 1677, from unknown causes and was buried on the dung heap.

(The COMMISSIONER looks at DIONYSUS.)

DIONYSUS *(after a while)*: He said that's who he was.

COMMISSIONER: How long were you with him?

DIONYSUS: Eight days.

COMMISSIONER: Was there anyone else present?

DIONYSUS: Crooked Veit, when we started out.

COMMISSIONER: His family name?

DIONYSUS: Don't know.

COMMISSIONER: His age?

DIONYSUS: Fourteen? Sixteen? Don't know for sure.

COMMISSIONER: Where was he from?

DIONYSUS: Seekirchen. That's what he said.

COMMISSIONER: Does he have a hunchback?

DIONYSUS: His left foot is bent in.

COMMISSIONER: According to reports, Jackie is always on the move, accompanied by several boys.

DIONYSUS: Uh-huh . . .

COMMISSIONER: But not this time?

DIONYSUS: No.

COMMISSIONER: Where did you go?

DIONYSUS: Golling, Werfen, Bischofshofen, Grossarl.

(*The COMMISSIONER looks at DIONYSUS, looks over to the EXECUTIONER who stands up.*)

COMMISSIONER: Twenty lashes with the consecrated rod!

(*The TWO HENCHMEN rise, walk over and grasp the unsuspecting DIONYSUS under the arms, carry him over to the door of the torture chamber. The EXECUTIONER opens it, and the HENCHMEN carry DIONYSUS inside; the EXECUTIONER follows, leaving the door open. We can see some of the equipment: a rack, a hoist—with weights next to it—, a riding horse; along the wall are thumb screws, two leg screws (Spanish boots), an iron maiden, a basin with holy water, holding an aspergillum and a rod. The EXECUTIONER goes over to the basin, takes out the rod, whips it through the air, disappears in the room. The sounds of the blows can be heard. DIONYSUS does not cry out.*)

COMMISSIONER (*to the SCRIBE*): The subject does not cry out during the lashing.

(*The SCRIBE writes it down; he has a moment free, so he exercises the fingers on his writing hand. The twenty lashes are over. The EXECUTIONER places the rod back in the basin. The HENCHMEN bring DIONYSUS back out, lead him before the COMMISSIONER and return to their seats. The EXECUTIONER comes out of the torture chamber, closes the door, sits down on the bench. The COMMISSIONER calmly looks at DIONYSUS.*)

COMMISSIONER: You actually did meet Jackie?

DIONYSUS: Uh-huh.

COMMISSIONER: Are you in pain?

DIONYSUS: 'Course I am.

COMMISSIONER: But you do not cry out when someone beats you?

DIONYSUS: The farmers don't like it when you do.

COMMISSIONER: Why is that?

DIONYSUS: The farmers beat me all the time. If I yell, then they get mad. And beat me some more.

COMMISSIONER: That is not the way this court operates.

(*Lengthy silence.*)

COMMISSIONER: Did you learn anything from Jackie?

DIONYSUS: No.

COMMISSIONER: Did he do anything unusual during the time you were with him?

DIONYSUS: No.

COMMISSIONER: Why did you accompany him?

DIONYSUS: It's tough to be on the road, alone! Then you're more likely to get beat up.

COMMISSIONER: What did he say when you met him for the first time?

DIONYSUS: Where you goin', buddy?

COMMISSIONER: And what did you say?

DIONYSUS: Lookin' for a little somethin' to eat, that's what I said.

COMMISSIONER: What did he say then?

DIONYSUS: Come on along with me, you'll do all right.

COMMISSIONER: Were you not afraid of him?

DIONYSUS: Why should I be?

COMMISSIONER: He is a sorcerer! Just like his mother! You know that!

DIONYSUS: You hear lots of things these days—

(*Lengthy silence.*)

COMMISSIONER (*to the EXECUTIONER*): Strip him, shave off his hair, search him, give him a shirt, put him in irons. Determine whether he has been through puberty. Do it immediately, if you please.

(*The EXECUTIONER and his TWO HENCHMEN rise, the EXECUTIONER opens the door to the torture chamber and enters, the HENCHMEN walk over to DIONYSUS, lift him up, carry him into the torture chamber.*)

COMMISSIONER (*calls after them*): Search his old clothes thoroughly for hidden nostrums. Then burn them.

(*The FIRST HENCHMAN nods, the three disappear into the chamber. Later we hear the clicking of the shears, then the rattling of the chains.*)

COMMISSIONER (*to the SCRIBE*): Contact Seekirchen for information regarding this so-called Crooked Veit.

(*The SCRIBE makes a notation.*)

COMMISSIONER: Make out an arrest warrant for Crooked Veit. Send one to Golling, Werfen, Bischofshofen, Grossarl. Along with Feldner's description. The complete name to follow.

(*The SCRIBE makes a notation.*)

COMMISSIONER: Send an order to the bailiff in Hüttenstein: Exhume and examine the corpse of the reputed Jacob Koller in St. Wolfgang. Compare

it with the descriptions given by Koller,
Kaltenpacher, Tanhauser, and Feldner.

(*The SCRIBE makes a notation.*)

COMMISSIONER: Did they find anything on Feldner in
Grossarl?

SCRIBE (*frantically checking*): Not a thing! Not a thing!
Oh, yes! He had the paw of some animal on a
string around his neck! According to Feldner's de-
position, it was a mole's paw. (*reads*) He stated it
was a remedy for epilepsy.

COMMISSIONER: Where is the paw?

SCRIBE (*searches*): Gone! Gone! Gone!

COMMISSIONER: Send an advisory to all district
courts—In the future every suspicious person is to
be immediately and thoroughly searched at the
time of arrest. Also search their last-known where-
abouts. Possible items of interest: salves, powders,
jars of vermin, human bones, pictures pierced with
needles, mirrors for telling fortunes, letters from
accomplices, books about black magic, and the
like. Forward everything to this court.

SCRIBE: Yes, Sir, Counselor! (*makes a note*)

COMMISSIONER: Those courts and their abysmal re-
cord-keeping!

(*DIONYSUS comes out of the torture chamber, followed by
the EXECUTIONER and his TWO HENCHMEN.
DIONYSUS, now shaved bald, is also naked, holding a
crumpled, long, black short-sleeved shirt in front of his gen-
itals; heavy chains with bells on his hands and feet. The
EXECUTIONER leads him before the COMMISSIONER,
the HENCHMEN sit down on the bench. In his hand the*

EXECUTIONER is holding a long needle with a wooden handle.)

EXECUTIONER: Hasn't been through puberty. Eight marks. Nothing hidden in his clothes or on his body.

COMMISSIONER: You also searched his bodily cavities thoroughly?

EXECUTIONER: Naturally, Counselor! (*looks down at his hands, wipes them off on his apron.*)

COMMISSIONER: Did you wash your hands?

EXECUTIONER: Huh? 'Course not!

COMMISSIONER (*annoyed*): Please do!

(*The EXECUTIONER enters the torture chamber, returns after washing his hands, positions himself behind DIONYSUS and waits.*)

COMMISSIONER (*during the above, to DIONYSUS*): What can Jackie do?

(*DIONYSUS is totally disoriented by the treatment he has received.*)

DIONYSUS: Everything!

COMMISSIONER: What? Tell me.

DIONYSUS: He can make himself invisible with a little black cape!

COMMISSIONER: We already know about that.

DIONYSUS: He walks into court and listens to what people are sayin' about him.

COMMISSIONER: Invisible.

DIONYSUS: Uh-huh.

COMMISSIONER: Could he possibly be here right now? Here, in this courtroom?

DIONYSUS (*between hope and fear, suddenly sobs*): Yes!

(*The COMMISSIONER watches DIONYSUS silently, looks at the EXECUTIONER who runs his index finger across DIONYSUS' cheek. DIONYSUS recoils. The EXECUTIONER licks off the tear-stained finger.*)

EXECUTIONER (*to the COMMISSIONER*): They're real! (*lifts the needle by its handle*) Should I use this now?

COMMISSIONER (*gently, to DIONYSUS*): You have eight marks on your body . . . Where did you get them? Think back. It is important.

(*DIONYSUS looks down at his body, helplessly.*)

EXECUTIONER: We can eliminate three marks.—Here (*pointing to DIONYSUS' back*), this birthmark—here (*pointing to a finger on the right hand*) an inflamed wart—here (*lifts up DIONYSUS' left leg and points to the sole of his foot*) an infected wound that must have come from a nail.

DIONYSUS: Uh-huh, I stepped on a nail.

COMMISSIONER (*angrily*): Just look at him! How are we supposed to carry out a visual examination? He has dirt all over him, an inch thick!—In the future, all miscreants are to be washed prior to being searched!

EXECUTIONER (*to his HENCHMEN*): You heard the Counselor!

COMMISSIONER: This is just abominable! He smells like ten skinners!

EXECUTIONER (*himself a former skinner*): He's afraid! When you're afraid, you stink!

COMMISSIONER: Wash him! In the future, wash them all!

EXECUTIONER: Yes, sir, Counselor!—To continue: this long scar is suspicious (*points to the right cheek*); this one here (*pointing to DIONYSUS' left side*); this one on the left thumb (*points it out*); this one here (*pulling DIONYSUS' shirt aside, points to a scar on the right hip, near his groin*); and—(*forcing DIONYSUS' mouth open*)—stick out your tongue!

(*DIONYSUS sticks out his tongue, the EXECUTIONER points to a spot.*)

EXECUTIONER: Here! Another scar!

COMMISSIONER (*to DIONYSUS*): Well?

DIONYSUS: I fell down and bit my tongue.

COMMISSIONER: Continue.

DIONYSUS (*points to his cheek*): A horse bit me here!

COMMISSIONER: Go on.

DIONYSUS (*looks at his thumb*): Here's where I cut myself with a knife, cuttin' bacon. (*points to his left side*) That's where Crooked Veit stabbed me, 'cause I got to a farmhouse before he did, and the farmer gave me somethin', but he chased Veit away. That made Veit really mad.

COMMISSIONER: Go on.

DIONYSUS (*points to the scar on his hip*): That's where I ran into a scythe last summer.

COMMISSIONER: Listen to me, Dionysus! One of these five marks is the mark of the devil! Tell us which one!

(*DIONYSUS is silent for a while.*)

COMMISSIONER (*gently*): Tell us.

DIONYSUS (*giving up*): I don't have any mark of the devil.

(*The COMMISSIONER looks at the EXECUTIONER who signals his HENCHMEN, and they approach DIONYSUS. With his left hand ONE HENCHMAN holds DIONYSUS from behind, while putting his right hand over DIONYSUS' eyes, pressing his head to the HENCHMAN'S chest. The SECOND HENCHMAN kneels down and wraps his arms around DIONYSUS' legs. The EXECUTIONER pulls DIONYSUS' shirt aside and sticks the needle into the scar in his side. DIONYSUS yells out in pain. The SCRIBE can barely stand to watch, turns his head away, writes down DIONYSUS' reaction. The EXECUTIONER takes DIONYSUS' left hand away from the shirt he's holding, sticks the needle into his thumb. DIONYSUS doesn't cry out, just shudders. The EXECUTIONER looks at the COMMISSIONER who nods ("That's the spot!"), looks at the SCRIBE who raises his eyebrows, notes this conclusion. The EXECUTIONER raises the needle up to DIONYSUS' left side.*)

COMMISSIONER: Be careful! His heart!

EXECUTIONER (*upset*): Mr. Counselor, I know where his heart's located!

(*The EXECUTIONER sticks the needle into the scar at an angle. DIONYSUS cries out. The EXECUTIONER sticks the needle into DIONYSUS' cheek. DIONYSUS screams.*)

EXECUTIONER: Stick out your tongue!

(*DIONYSUS doesn't do it, so the EXECUTIONER presses his cheeks together, forcing DIONYSUS to open his mouth. The EXECUTIONER pulls out DIONYSUS' tongue, sticks the needle in. DIONYSUS lets out a gargled scream. The*

EXECUTIONER wipes the needle on his apron, looks at the COMMISSIONER.)

COMMISSIONER: Thank you.

(The HENCHMEN let DIONYSUS go, return to their places. The EXECUTIONER looks at the COMMIS-SIONER expectanty, proud that he has found the mark of the devil.)

COMMISSIONER: Thank you, Executioner. You may sit down.

(The EXECUTIONER sits down with his HENCHMEN. Trembling, DIONYSUS can barely stand up.)

COMMISSIONER *(to the SCRIBE)*: The mark of the devil is located on the subject's left thumb.

SCRIBE: I already have it, Mr. Counselor!

(The COMMISSIONER looks at DIONYSUS.)

COMMISSIONER: You can put on your shirt.

(DIONYSUS turns his back, pulls the long black shirt over his head, turns back to face the COMMISSIONER.)

COMMISSIONER: This insensitive spot on your thumb proves that you made a pact with the devil. How did it happen?

(DIONYSUS doesn't answer.)

COMMISSIONER: Jackie introduced you to the devil, did he not? How did it happen?

DIONYSUS *(sobbing)*: I cut myself with a knife!

COMMISSIONER: That is what happened to Jackie's mother, if I remember correctly . . . Scribe!

(The SCRIBE searches frantically among his files, finds the one he is after.)

SCRIBE *(reads)*: Twelve years ago, not far from Werfen,

she surrendered to the wretched devil on a public street in the presence of a beggar woman by the name of Gretel. The devil pinched the spot on her right palm, took blood from the wound, and wrote her name in blood on a slip of paper. (*He looks up from the file.*)

COMMISSIONER (*gently*): Dionysus.

(*DIONYSUS suddenly collapses on the floor, suffering from an epileptic fit. The EXECUTIONER leaps up.*)

EXECUTIONER (*angrily*): What a goddamn mess!

COMMISSIONER: Calm yourself, Executioner!

EXECUTIONER: Just turn him over to me, just turn him over to me! In five minutes I'll have a confession! I'll stretch him till he's so thin you can see right through him!

COMMISSIONER: He has not reached the age of puberty.

EXECUTIONER: According to his own testimony, he's fourteen!

COMMISSIONER: Why, he is not fourteen!

EXECUTIONER: Well, so what! We're not gonna get anywhere at this rate!

COMMISSIONER (*stands up*): Listen to me, Executioner! I am the Commissioner here, not you! I am the lawyer, not you! And I am telling you, you cannot torture someone under the age of fourteen! At least not in this country! This is a civilized nation!

EXECUTIONER: Okay! It was just a suggestion! (*sits down*) You can see how the devil keeps him from talking.

COMMISSIONER (*sits down*): Sprinkle him with holy water.

(*The EXECUTIONER stands up, walks over to the basin.*)

EXECUTIONER: Besides, I've still got to clip off three fingers from a woman who was caught stealing. I don't have all day! (*takes the aspergillum out of the holy water basin, walks over to DIONYSUS, sprinkles him with the water.*)

COMMISSIONER: That must be changed as well! If we remove their limbs, people simply cannot do any work. And consequently they become a burden on society. That is simply irreconcilable with modern legislation!

EXECUTIONER (*sprinkling holy water*): Well, Mr. Counselor, you're the lawyer! I'm not responsible for the laws! I'm only the arm of the law! (*stops sprinkling, enraged*) And I don't get any respect, Mr. Counselor! No respect at all! You know that yourself! (*sprinkles one last time*)

(*DIONYSUS' epileptic fit is over. He begins to stir, rises to his knees. The EXECUTIONER walks over to the holy water basin, throws the aspergillum in, sits down.*)

COMMISSIONER: Bring the chair.

(*The FIRST HENCHMAN gets up, walks over to the chair. DIONYSUS looks around, looks at the COMMISSIONER and moans. The FIRST HENCHMAN brings the chair, picks DIONYSUS up and sets him down on it, then returns to the bench.*)

COMMISSIONER (*to the SCRIBE*): Copy the shape of the mark.

(*The SCRIBE goes over to DIONYSUS, takes his thumb, observes the mark, makes a sketch in the air, returns to his desk, makes a drawing in his file.*)

COMMISSIONER (*to DIONYSUS*): Now confess, Dionysus.

DIONYSUS (*softly*): It's true.

SCRIBE (*speaks up*): What's that?

COMMISSIONER: You will have to speak louder, Dionysus.

DIONYSUS: It's true! He made his mark on me!

COMMISSIONER: Who?

DIONYSUS: Jackie!

COMMISSIONER (*surprised*): Jackie? Not the devil?

DIONYSUS: Jackie did it!

COMMISSIONER: How did he do it?

DIONYSUS: With his knife.

COMMISSIONER: And did he say why he did it?

(*DIONYSUS is silent for a moment. In the background, the
EXECUTIONER impatiently stretches his arms.*)

DIONYSUS: So that nothin'd happen to me if I ever got
locked up.

COMMISSIONER: What is that supposed to mean?

DIONYSUS (*sobbing*): So that nothin'd happen to me!

EXECUTIONER (*furious*): So that you'd keep your mouth
shut!

(*The COMMISSIONER looks over at the EXECUTIONER
with displeasure.*)

COMMISSIONER (*to DIONYSUS*): You mean, so that
you would not confess?

(*DIONYSUS doesn't answer.*)

COMMISSIONER (*loudly*): Say it! Say it!

DIONYSUS: Yes!

COMMISSIONER (*gently*): Say it. Say it out loud.

DIONYSUS: So I wouldn't confess!

EXECUTIONER: Well, finally! (*chortles*) The devil's really underestimated the power of justice this time!

COMMISSIONER: And the power of God!—Hang a breve around his neck!

(*The EXECUTIONER reaches into his pants' pocket and pulls out a breve, tied to a string. He takes it over to DIONYSUS and ties it so tightly around his neck that it chokes him. DIONYSUS fights for air.*)

EXECUTIONER: Just look at him! Like a fish out of water! Uh-huh, the old devil can't stand these consecrated things! (*goes back to the bench*)

COMMISSIONER: Dionysus, you must not confuse things! The devil makes his mark, not man!

DIONYSUS: It was Jackie!

(*The COMMISSIONER looks at him, threateningly.*)

DIONYSUS: But the devil was there too!

COMMISSIONER: I see!—What else? Continue!

DIONYSUS: The devil dipped his finger in my blood and wrote my name in a book.

COMMISSIONER: What did the book look like?

DIONYSUS: Red on the outside, white on the inside.

COMMISSIONER: What did the devil look like?

DIONYSUS: A hunter, dressed in green.

COMMISSIONER: Did he come with Jackie?

DIONYSUS: No! He flew through the air! On a black horse! (*smiles*)

COMMISSIONER: Did he say anything?

DIONYSUS (*smiles*): Hey, Jackie! Did you find another one for me?

COMMISSIONER: Those were his words . . .

DIONYSUS: Yes!

COMMISSIONER: Go on. The oath? Were you required to take an oath?

(*DIONYSUS nods, holds up the index and middle fingers of his left hand.*)

COMMISSIONER: Were you required to renounce God, the Saints, the Sacraments, and the Virgin Mary?

DIONYSUS: Yes!

COMMISSIONER: How? What were the exact words?

DIONYSUS: I had to mock them!

COMMISSIONER: Yes?

DIONYSUS (*his face starts to glow*): A hundred thousand sacrileges on our Lord! Sorcerer, son-of-a-bitch, hooligan, grave robber!

COMMISSIONER: The Virgin Mary?

DIONYSUS: Toad, lunatic, whore!

COMMISSIONER: What did the devil promise you in return?

DIONYSUS (*proudly*): His power and protection!

COMMISSIONER: What else?

DIONYSUS: Anything I want!

COMMISSIONER: And what do you want?

DIONYSUS: Somethin' to eat! Somethin' to drink! A big soft bed! A hundred thousand guilders!

COMMISSIONER: Did he also give you a new name?

DIONYSUS (*nods*): Stargazer!

COMMISSIONER: And he disappeared again after the pact?

DIONYSUS: Yeah! He took off on his black horse!

COMMISSIONER: And Jackie? What did he teach you?

DIONYSUS: How to read, write, and shoot!

(*The COMMISSIONER just stares at him in amazement.*)

EXECUTIONER (*laughs*): How to read, write, and shoot!

COMMISSIONER: Stick to the facts, Dionysus! What did he really teach you?

DIONYSUS: How to make mouses!

COMMISSIONER: Mice?

DIONYSUS: Uh-huh.

COMMISSIONER: How? With a salve?

DIONYSUS: Uh-huh, with a salve! And rats! I made mouses with a red salve and rats with a green one!

COMMISSIONER: How many?

DIONYSUS: A hundred thousand!

COMMISSIONER: Why would you do that?

DIONYSUS: So they'd eat up all the farmers' grain!

COMMISSIONER: Why?

DIONYSUS: We did it to the ones who wouldn't give us anything! The skinflints! (*laughs*)

COMMISSIONER (*to the SCRIBE*): Admission of guilt, regarding malicious destruction.

EXECUTIONER (*gets up*): Counselor, unfortunately I have other obligations!

COMMISSIONER: Just one more minute. (*growing short-tempered*) If you wouldn't mind!

(*The EXECUTIONER sits back down.*)

COMMISSIONER (*to DIONYSUS*): Did you meet anyone else when you were with Jackie? Tell me. Then we will be finished for today.

DIONYSUS: He had a woman with him, her name was Rosina!

COMMISSIONER: What does she look like?

DIONYSUS: She's got big boobs! (*laughs*) That's why everybody called her Little Rosina with the Big Boobies!

COMMISSIONER: What is her full name, and where does she come from?

DIONYSUS: No idea!—They were doin' it, sleepin' next to us in the haybarn! (*laughs*)

COMMISSIONER: Who else was there?

DIONYSUS: Blindbat Michael, his brother the Mow Catcher, and a couple of other guys! But I don't know their names!

COMMISSIONER: Describe the first two. Their ages, appearance, hometown.

DIONYSUS: Blindbat Michael's ten or eleven and he's blind. His brother, the Mow Catcher, he's a lot younger, maybe seven. But I don't know where they come from.

COMMISSIONER: Did they all make a pact with the devil, too?

DIONYSUS: Yeah, and lots more did too!

COMMISSIONER (*thinking out loud*): A conspiracy . . . ! I knew it! Ever since the Koller woman burned at the stake! (*to DIONYSUS*) Why did you say at the beginning that there was only one person with Jackie?

DIONYSUS: The devil made me do it!

COMMISSIONER: Why did you only report this one?

DIONYSUS: Well, 'cause he stabbed me, Crooked Veit did!

COMMISSIONER: I see! Of course!—How long did you say you were on the road with them?

DIONYSUS: Must've been at least three Sundays!

(*The COMMISSIONER looks at the SCRIBE who furiously thumbs through his papers.*)

EXECUTIONER: Before, he said it was eight days!

SCRIBE (*reads from his records*): Eight days!

EXECUTIONER (*meaning the SCRIBE*): A mind like a sieve!

(*Infuriated, the SCRIBE looks at the EXECUTIONER. The COMMISSIONER looks at DIONYSUS with a piercing stare.*)

DIONYSUS (*smiling*): You should always lie, that's what the devil said!

EXECUTIONER: And he took away your pain, eh? That's why you didn't scream during the whipping!

DIONYSUS (*laughs*): Yeah!

COMMISSIONER (*to the SCRIBE*): Send arrest warrants to all the courts regarding the above-mentioned persons!

SCRIBE: Yes, Sir!

COMMISSIONER: Detain all youthful beggars, record their personal histories, and inquire about the above-mentioned persons!

(*The SCRIBE writes it all down.*)

DIONYSUS: I've got a whole lot more to tell you!

COMMISSIONER: Some other time, Dionysus.

(*The COMMISSIONER looks at the EXECUTIONER, nods toward the nearest trapdoor. The EXECUTIONER gives a signal to the FIRST HENCHMAN who stands up, leads DIONYSUS to the trapdoor, unbolts it, opens it.*)

COMMISSIONER (*during the above, to the SCRIBE*): Concluding observation: The inquisition took place "extra locum torturae" and was concluded without incident. Fortunately, the miscreant proved to be most cooperative.

(*The FIRST HENCHMAN pushes DIONYSUS down into the cell, lets the trapdoor slam shut.*)

(*Blackout*)

3. The cell

(The cell is located beneath the Commissioner's office. It is the same length as the office, but only one-fourth as deep, since there are other cells behind it. The ceiling of the cell is so low that the children can't stand upright; they can only crouch. In the ceiling is the trapdoor to the office above. On the floor we see damp, rotting straw, in the corner a kettle for bodily wastes, elsewhere a pile of dirty blankets. A low door that leads to the corridor. No windows. Rats. Semidarkness. DIONYSUS, who has just been shoved down through the trapdoor, is sitting on the floor, looking up at the trapdoor. Then he looks around. He is shivering, so he crawls over to the pile of blankets, takes one, piles up some straw against the back wall, leans back in a half-sitting position, covers himself with the blanket, stares off into space. After a while, a rat scurries across the blanket, stops on DIONYSUS' chest, looks at him. DIONYSUS, who hasn't noticed the rat until now, is paralyzed.)

DIONYSUS *(after a while)*: Why, I know you! I know who you are!—It's all your fault! Why didn't you help me?! Just see if you can stand it! They beat me! And stabbed me!—*Now* you show up! Why don't you go up there and chew off their pricks?

(DIONYSUS rips the breve from around his neck, throws it away. The rat comes up to his chin.)

DIONYSUS: Sure, sure, you flatterer! *(takes the rat in his hands, sits up, looks at the rat)* Ah, old pardner! You and me, we can't fight back! You and me, we can only write our names, that's all we can do! The guys upstairs can write and write till they fill a hundred thousand books! With a hundred thousand letters and a hundred thousand numbers! They write and they write—and bury us under their records! There's nothin' we can do to fight back. They conjure up language! And during broad daylight! (*lays down with the rat by his side*) Come sleep with me! (*pulls the blanket up over himself*) The night belongs to us!

(*Blackout*)

4. The office

(*The COMMISSIONER and the SCRIBE, at their desks. The Commissioner for Witchery also functions as the Commissioner for Charity.*)

SCRIBE (*glances at a letter*): A dispatch from the Inner Austrian government in Graz! (*reads aloud*) To the honorably deputized Commissioner for Charity, Counselor Dr. Sebastian Zillner! Most honorable, highly respected Dr. Zillner—

COMMISSIONER (*impatient*): Yes, yes, enough! Get to the point! Be succinct!

SCRIBE (*reads excerpts*): Encamped at the present time in the vicinity of Aussee are a large number of wretched types, such as vagabonds, riff-raff beggars, gypsy rabble, itinerant soldiers, all in all a highly unsavory group . . .

COMMISSIONER: Go on! Go on! Be succinct!

SCRIBE: . . . that is pillaging and marauding throughout the countryside. For example, just a few days ago in Admont, a woman with her throat slashed and two men, beaten and completely undressed, were found on a public street. (*skips over a few lines*) etc., etc., etc . . . . Therefore we most sincerely request a decree to keep this harmful riff-raff from entering the Archdiocese of Salzburg, and, if possible, to drive them back where they came from. (*looks up*)

COMMISSIONER: The nerve! They should take care of their own problems!

SCRIBE: Your reply?

COMMISSIONER: The usual! We will do our best! And they themselves . . . we respectfully submit . . . should drive back the riff-raff coming from the south via Styria toward Salzburg!—Continue!

(*The SCRIBE has made a notation, picks up a new letter.*)

SCRIBE: A dispatch from the Upper Austrian government in Innsbruck! (*quickly skims the letter, looks up*) Basically the same subject! They are asking your Honor to disolve or disburse the troublesome beggars, just as the Upper Austrian government does.

(*The COMMISSIONER raises his arms to indicate his helplessness.*)

SCRIBE: I'll take care of the reply! (*picks up the next letter*) Report from the caretaker in Tittmoning. (*reads quickly, laughs out loud*)

COMMISSIONER: What is it?

SCRIBE: If you remember, four weeks ago the Bavarian government deported two wagonloads of gypsies to Tittmoning, which is under Salzburg's jurisdiction. The caretaker in Tittmoning sent them right back, labeled "Return to Sender!"

COMMISSIONER: And?

SCRIBE: The Bavarians deported them to Tittmoning again. The caretaker wants to know what he should do now!

COMMISSIONER (*after a moment's thought*): Send the grown men to the Mönchsberg for a year's work as penance. Send the women to the pillory and then deport them via different routes. Have the children brought up in good families. The Counselor will cover all costs.

(*The SCRIBE finishes writing, takes a new document, reads it, reports.*)

SCRIBE: The bailiff in Fügen writes that hoards of well-armed rabble are on the loose in his district; when confronted by the authorities, they respond with a fusillade!

COMMISSIONER: He should call out the militia stationed in Zillertal. Request permission from the commander of the national guard.

(*The SCRIBE finishes writing, takes new dispatches, reads through them.*)

SCRIBE: A couple of complaints about discharged soldiers wandering around.

COMMISSIONER: Arrest them, lock them up for a few days on minimal rations, and then deport them.

(*The SCRIBE writes, picks up a new dispatch, skims over it.*)

SCRIBE: A plague of beggars at the pilgrimage site of Maria Plain. The caretaker in Neuhaus is asking for your advice.

COMMISSIONER: Select two qualified beggars to stand on either side of the main entrance to the church, and let them collect money. They are to deliver the money to a priest who, in turn, distributes it to all trustworthy beggars every Saturday after they have heard mass. Expel foreign beggars, and make the local beggars wear visible badges.

(The SCRIBE writes, picks up a new document, quickly skims it.)

SCRIBE: The lieutenant in Henndorf, George Engelhardt, and his dragoons have arrested and interrogated forty-nine vagabonds. All were foreigners. No crimes reported.

COMMISSIONER: Deport them! But from different border locations. Otherwise they will be sent right back to us.

(The SCRIBE writes, takes a new letter.)

SCRIBE: The caretaker in Abtenau writes: *(reads)* As a result of the present inflation, many recent newlyweds can no longer support themselves; the husbands and wives, along with their children, have taken to begging.—He inquires as to whether such marriages can be prevented.

COMMISSIONER: Then they will live in sin, without the blessing of the sacrament!—Before the wedding they should be informed that they will have to leave the country if they cannot support themselves without being a burden to their neighbors!

(The SCRIBE writes, picks up a new dispatch.)

SCRIBE: The caretaker in Werfen reports that the people there are angry because they are frequently accosted by beggars who threaten to harm the citizens if they don't give the beggars whatever they want!

COMMISSIONER *(leaps up)*: Arrest them! Arrest them immediately! This is precisely the group of beggars where we will find the sorcerers! *(sits down)*

SCRIBE: Yes, Sir! (*writes, reads a new dispatch*) Ah! The results of the nationwide manhunt.

COMMISSIONER (*stands up*): Yes?

SCRIBE: Only a few suspicious individuals taken into custody.

COMMISSIONER (*incredulous*): We organize a manhunt throughout the entire country—and this is the result?

SCRIBE: The caretakers report that the men on patrol go to the brandyhouses and have a few drinks to get their courage up. Then they comb the woods, singing and making noise, as if they were hunting wild animals.

COMMISSIONER: Fifty guilders fine for every man who fails to fulfill his service obligation! Organize new patrols! Arrest every suspicious person! (*sits down*) This just cannot continue! We need trained law officers! How else can we protect outselves? — And we need workhouses like they have in France! It doesn't do any good to simply move the vagabonds back and forth between countries! Either we eliminate them, or we create workhouses! We will take care of the elderly and the infirm, and rigorously require the remainder to work! (*stands up*) They are killing us, Scribe! They are killing us! The plague is rampant in Vienna! And who brings us the plague? Who carries it on? The nomadic riffraff!—Now, start writing! An advisory to the watchmen at the city gates: soldiers, gypsies, beggars, and similar homeless rabble will be refused entry to the city! Whosoever takes bribes and lets this mob into the city will be fired on the spot and jailed!—During the next regular fire inspection, a comprehensive list of the inhabitants of every house is to be drawn up! In the future, homeowners must fill out a room card for every person who stays in their home, and they must be prepared to show said card upon demand!—Have you got that?

(*The SCRIBE writes like a demon.*)

(*Blackout*)

5. The cell

(*DIONYSUS is lying under the blanket. The trapdoor opens, light falls through the opening. DIONYSUS sits up and looks. VEIT LINDNER, alias Crooked Veit (age 14), falls into the cell. He is already washed, shorn, and dressed in a black shirt with chains on his hands and feet. The trapdoor is slammed shut and bolted. VEIT looks around, sees DIONYSUS.*)

DIONYSUS (*happily*): Crooked Veit! Welcome to my humble abode! Hey, how old're you now?

VEIT: Probably around fourteen! What for?

DIONYSUS: Then you'll be tortured! Fourteen and over get tortured! I'm only twelve, that's what they said!

VEIT: I'll just lie!

DIONYSUS: But they'll find out, from the church records in your hometown!

VEIT: Doesn't matter, I told them the wrong one!—What do they want from us, anyhow?

DIONYSUS: They want to know about Jackie!

VEIT: Things still haven't quieted down? They'll never

catch him! He knows his way around better than his mother did!

DIONYSUS: But she was a major witch, too!

VEIT: She was a mean woman!

DIONYSUS: Boy, you wouldn't dare say that to Jackie!

VEIT: She was a mean woman! When we were in Golling, going through the offeratory boxes, she paid me off with a couple of lousy farthings! Jackie wanted to give me more, but she wouldn't let him! She sicked her dog on me!

DIONYSUS: But, boy, could she do stuff!

VEIT: What kind of stuff?

DIONYSUS: She could make weather! And she crippled people! And made cattle die!

VEIT: Where'd you hear that?

DIONYSUS: I was there when they burned her at the stake! They read off the charges against her! With all her crimes!

(*The trapdoor opens, down tumble DUMB DOFFER (13), the blind MICHAEL N., alias Blindbat Michael (10) and his brother JOHNNY N., alias The Mow Catcher (6)—all freshly washed, shorn, in black shirts and chains. The trapdoor is slammed shut. DOFFER stands up, parades around in a crouch, holding his shirt gathered up in front.*)

MICHAEL: Where are we, Johnny?

JOHNNY: I don't know! Looks like a sheep pen!

(*MICHAEL takes a handful of straw, smells it.*)

MICHAEL: They oughta clean this place out!

DOFFER (*parading around*): Such a lovely gown! Such a lovely gown! Such a lovely gown!

MICHAEL (*loudly*): Anybody else in here?

DOFFER: I'm here! I'm here! Do you fellows have a lovely gown like this, too?

MICHAEL: Shut your trap, Doffer!

VEIT: Veit Lindner and the Shitspotter!

MICHAEL: Oh, it's Crooked Veit!

VEIT: Did they get you guys because of Jackie, too?

DOFFER: Jackie, Jackie, he's such a lackey!

MICHAEL: We don't know him at all! Right, Johnny?

DOFFER: I know him really well! Who doesn't know him, he's such a famous man!

VEIT: Of course you know him, Michael! At the Cake House in Hallein, you were there with the rest of us!

MICHAEL: I'm blind! I don't know nothin' about it! (*reaches out for his brother JOHNNY*) Johnny, I'm beggin' you—If they ask you somethin', don't tell 'em nothin'!

JOHNNY: What kinds of stuff do they ask about?

MICHAEL: I dunno! But it can't be nothin' good! You're only six years old, Johnny, and you don't know nothin'! You're just a little kid! They gotta understand that!

JOHNNY: I don't know from nothin'! What could I know?

DOFFER: I know everything! They ought to ask me! I'll tell 'em everything! They won't find anybody better than me! (*sits down*)

VEIT: The Shitspotter says they torture you if you're over fourteen!

MICHAEL: D'ja hear that, Johnny? They can't do nothin' to us! I'm only ten, and you're six!

JOHNNY: What's that mean—torture?

DOFFER: They rip your limbs out of your body so it makes a crunching sound!

MICHAEL: Shut your trap, Doffer!

DOFFER: Just let 'em come! My limbs are made out of Styrian steel! But if they rip my lovely gown, I'll bite their noses off!

JOHNNY: I just wanna leave, Michael!

MICHAEL: We can't, Johnny! (*puts his arm around JOHNNY*)

DOFFER: If I wanted to, I'd just walk right out of here, easy as pie! But I don't want to!

VEIT: Did they already question you, Shitspotter?

DIONYSUS: A little, yeah!

VEIT: What kinds of stuff do they ask?

DIONYSUS: About Jackie!

DOFFER: Jackie is a lackey!

VEIT: What did you tell 'em?

DIONYSUS: Not much.

VEIT: What do they want to know? Come on, tell me!

DIONYSUS: I already told you!

(*VEIT crawls over to DIONYSUS, wraps his chain around DIONYSUS' throat, chokes him.*)

VEIT: Tell me!

DOFFER: If you need my help, Dionys, then just call on

me! I'll rip his limbs out of his body so it makes a crunching sound!

VEIT: You gonna talk?

DIONYSUS: Yeah!

(*VEIT loosens the chain.*)

DIONYSUS: If you tell 'em what Jackie can do, they leave you alone!

DOFFER: I can do lots more than he can! That'll make 'em happy! (*stands up, pounds on the trapdoor*) Hey! I want to testify! I know everything!

VEIT: What else? (*tightens the chain*) What else?

DIONYSUS: The pact with the devil! They wanna hear about the pact with the devil!

VEIT: Is that all?

DOFFER (*pounding on the trapdoor*): Hey, you gentlemen up there! I'm ninety-nine years old and admit everything!

(*The trapdoor opens. Quick as a flash VEIT lets go of DIONYSUS and acts as if nothing had happened. Down from above falls LISL FELDNER, alias "Little Lisl" (8), scrubbed, shorn, in black shirt and chains. She lands on DOFFER, and they both crash to the floor. The trapdoor is slammed shut and bolted.*)

DOFFER (*scrambling to his feet*): Now even the angels are falling from Heaven! (*to LISL*) Did you get bumped by a comet?

(*DIONYSUS crawls over to his sister LISL.*)

DIONYSUS: Lisl!

(*LISL, sobbing, hugs DIONYSUS.*)

DIONYSUS: Where's dad?

LISL: Don't know!

DIONYSUS: Did they get him, too?

LISL: Yes!

MICHAEL: Who's that?

DIONYSUS: Little Lisl! My sister! (*in desparation*) Holy shit! Holy shit! Now they've got us all!

DOFFER: Lisl's not an angel! Lisl's a weasel!

DIONYSUS: Oh, holy shit!

(*Blackout*)

6. The office

(*The COMMISSIONER and the SCRIBE are sitting at their desks. Upstage, the EXECUTIONER and the FIRST HENCHMAN are sitting on the bench. VEIT (age 14) is standing before the COMMISSIONER in chains, with a bent left foot, and talking readily.*)

VEIT: Then he taught me everything he knew! He smeared my skull with a salve, and then I became invisible! That was a riot! In Mittersill I'd walk up to people on the street and box their ears till they cried!

COMMISSIONER (*smiling*): Of course, of course, you can do all kinds of things when you are invisible. —Did you also frequent any establishments? Wine cellars, for example?

VEIT: Everybody piled into the wine cellar and got so drunk that we were all happy as larks!

COMMISSIONER: And you ruined whatever wine you didn't drink?

VEIT: Jackie tossed in something round and green, and the rest of us stomped around in the cask and pissed in it! And of course we stuffed ourselves and got drunk for free in all the restaurants. You can imagine what that was like!

COMMISSIONER: Of course. Did you also change yourself into animals and objects?

(*The SECOND HENCHMAN enters with a letter, gives it to the SCRIBE, sits down on the bench.*)

VEIT: Oh, yeah! Just like . . .

SCRIBE: Excuse me, please! A letter from Hüttenstein! (*opens the envelope, reads, looks at the COMMIS-SIONER*) The caretaker in Hüttenstein reports that they exhumed and examined the aforementioned corpse in St. Wolfgang. No similarity to the descriptions of Jackie!

COMMISSIONER: Then he really is still alive! Send out a warrant for his arrest. Immediately! Include the descriptions! A reward! Twenty gold pieces! Anonymity of the informant will be guaranteed! Publicize it in every courtroom!

(*The SCRIBE has written everything down, gives a sign to the SECOND HENCHMAN, who approaches him, takes the sheet of paper, exits. The COMMISSIONER looks at VEIT, looks at VEIT'S malformed foot.*)

COMMISSIONER: Would you like a chair, Veit?

VEIT: Oh, that's all right, I can stand up!

(*The COMMISSIONER gives a sign to the SECOND HENCHMAN who brings the chair over. VEIT sits down on it, smiling with embarrassment.*)

COMMISSIONER: The animals and objects!

VEIT: Yeah! While the deputies were out patrolling, five times I changed myself into a stick of wood! One time a woman came along and sat on me and broke me in two, and the woman fell on her butt!

(*VEIT laughs, the COMMISSIONER also smiles.*)

VEIT: And one time I was a mushroom! And a sow came along and almost ate me!—Lots of times we'd change into cattle! Most of the time I was a really fast dog. Naturally, I used to bite people's legs! (*laughs*)

COMMISSIONER: And what about the other boys?

VEIT: Dionys, the Shitspotter, turned himself into a buzzard and his sister Lisl into a weasel! Blindbat Michael was always a stag, his brother Johnny a little kitty, that idiot Doffer was a toad!

COMMISSIONER: And did you also manufacture animals?

VEIT: Oh, of course! Mice, rats, bats! The mice ran under the skirts of those old ladies who wouldn't give me a handout and bit 'em really good, so that they swelled up really big! (*laughs*) Of course I also made some pigs! Last year in Aibling, near Rosenheim, I sold a farmer pigs for five guilders! When he drove 'em through the creek, they dissolved into straw and floated away downstream! (*laughs*) The Shitspotter made some pigs, too, but he did dirty things with 'em!

COMMISSIONER: Is that so? Very interesting!

VEIT: He even made some little fellers with a white salve!

COMMISSIONER: Fellers? Little fellows?

(*VEIT nods.*)

COMMISSIONER: How little were they?

VEIT (*points to the crucifix*): About that big! As big as the Lord there! These fellers were having sex with each other!

COMMISSIONER: What?

VEIT: Uh-huh!—They looked so funny! (*laughs*) That Shitspotter, he's really crazy about sex!

(*The EXECUTIONER nods grimly, referring to DIONYSUS, and the COMMISSIONER'S earlier remark that "He hasn't reached the age of puberty." The COMMISSIONER makes a note of VEIT'S remarks, then looks back up at VEIT.*)

COMMISSIONER: I would ask you to keep your ears open when you are down in the cell. If you tell us what you hear, it will be to your advantage later on.

VEIT: You bet, Mr. Commissioner!

(*The COMMISSIONER looks down at his papers, then back up at VEIT.*)

COMMISSIONER: Tell me about the salves and powders. What were they made of?

VEIT: Oh, out of lots of things, I'm not really sure! Herbs and animal fat! The powder for making mice came from the ashes of people who had been condemned and burned at the stake, I think! One thing I know for sure: In Gmünden Jackie grabbed a six-year-old boy right out of the window of his house, boiled him alive, ate his flesh, and made magic powder out of his bones.

COMMISSIONER: Where was that, exactly?

VEIT: In Fürstau. I don't know the name of the house.

COMMISSIONER (*to the SCRIBE*): Request information from Fürstau.

SCRIBE: Yes, Sir! (*makes a note on another piece of paper*)

COMMISSIONER (*to VEIT*): You also used the powders and salves for malicious magic, did you not?

VEIT: Not me! It was the other guys!

COMMISSIONER: Don't make things difficult for me, Veit. You want to cooperate with me, don't you? Or do you want to be taken inside the chamber back there? (*points to the torture chamber*)

(*VEIT looks over at the door to the torture chamber. The EXECUTIONER gets up, opens the door, steps to one side so that VEIT can get a good look. VEIT sees the torture devices, is frightened, looks back at the COMMISSIONER.*)

SCRIBE: Before that, we would have to have certification from the barber! On account of his foot!

COMMISSIONER: Of course!

VEIT: Ah, now I remember! One time I spread some powder in front of a barn door!

(*The EXECUTIONER grins, closes the torture chamber door, sits back down.*)

COMMISSIONER: What happened then?

VEIT: The cattle died!

COMMISSIONER: Why did you do that?

VEIT: Because the farmer chased me away! And cussed at me! "Goddamn cripple! Go to hell!"

COMMISSIONER: Where was that?

VEIT: In Froschheim! The Klausner farm!

COMMISSIONER (*to the SCRIBE*): Request information from Froschheim. *(to VEIT)* You must have done that more than once.—Veit! Talk!

VEIT: One other time. In Siezenheim. But that time I only crippled the cattle! They didn't die! I swear!

COMMISSIONER: The farmer's name?

VEIT: Feldinger, I think.

(*The COMMISSIONER looks at the SCRIBE.*)

SCRIBE: Request information from Siezenheim.

COMMISSIONER: Did you ever cripple people?

VEIT: I crippled a few!

COMMISSIONER: Why did you do that?

VEIT: If somebody calls me a crippled dog, he oughta be crippled himself!

COMMISSIONER: Their names?

VEIT: Can't remember!

COMMISSIONER: Where?

VEIT: I crippled a farmer's wife in Zell! But she recovered a long time ago!

COMMISSIONER: How do you know that?

VEIT: Jackie told me! She had the priest bless an egg. Then she put it in boiling lard, ate the egg, and smeared the lard on her leg!

COMMISSIONER: Where else?

VEIT: In Hallein! I sprinkled a white powder on a farmer's path. He was crippled on the spot and fell down on his knees! (*satisfied*) Today he'd have to have a wooden brace on his knee, otherwise he couldn't walk! His whole foot is paralyzed!

COMMISSIONER: Go on.

VEIT: That's all! I swear on a stack of bibles! (*raises his index and middle fingers*)

COMMISSIONER: All right, we will leave it at that. —It would help us a great deal if you could name a few of the other boys who roam around with Jackie!

VEIT: That's not so easy! I never knew most of the guys' names! And you forget a lot of things, too!

COMMISSIONER: You have told us a great deal, Veit. We shall not forget it. It will be reflected in your sentence, I promise you.

VEIT: Let me think a minute, Sir!—Andree Mayer, they call him the "City Reject"! Magdalena Pichler, "Raggedy Leni"! That's his woman!—Matthias Grebler, "Gypsy Matty"! He cuts open pregnant women! Jakob Tripacher, they call him "Bigfoot"! Christian Fleis, the "Donkey Shepard"; Abraham Halbminger, the "Stick"; Hans Steingastinger . . .

(*Blackout*)

7. The office

(*The COMMISSIONER and the SCRIBE, as before. LISL FELDNER (age 8), in chains, is sitting in the chair in front of the COMMIS- SIONER. She is wearing a breve around her neck. The FIRST HENCHMAN is on his knees, holding her arms tightly behind the back of the chair; the SECOND HENCHMAN uses both hands to hold her head back. The EXECUTIONER is holding a funnel that is sticking out of LISL'S mouth, pouring so-called "holy soup"—made from*) *herbs and holy water—from a pitcher into the funnel. LISL swallows in spasmodic gulps.*)

COMMISSIONER (*extremely cordial*): Now, now, it's almost over. The "holy soup" will help you. It will protect you from the devil and ease your confession. (*after a while, to the EXECUTIONER*) That is enough. (*The EXECUTIONER takes the funnel out of LISL'S mouth. The HENCHMEN let LISL go, return to their bench, and sit down. The EXECUTIONER joins them, after he has put the pitcher and funnel away. LISL coughs and wipes off her mouth.*)

COMMISSIONER (*gently*): Stand up, Little Lisl.

(*LISL stands up.*)

COMMISSIONER: You have already helped us a great deal, Lisl. We now come to the part that may be difficult for you, but we must talk about it; we cannot leave anything unresolved. You were examined by the midwife, were you not? To find the sign of the devil?

LISL: Yes.

COMMISSIONER: Now that is all over. You have showed it to us; we do not need to do the needle test. But the midwife found something else. (*looks at the SCRIBE*)

SCRIBE (*looks at a piece of paper*): A tumor in an unmentionable place. The hymen stretched. Probably no longer intact.

COMMISSIONER: Our inquiry in Schellenberg has shown that you are eight years old. Still so young. And yet—it seems as if you are quite knowledgable about certain promiscuous acts.

(*LISL looks confused, does not answer.*)

COMMISSIONER: The tumor is in an unmentionable place.—How did you get it, Lisl?

LISL (*softly*): Don't know.

SCRIBE: Louder!

LISL: Don't know!

COMMISSIONER: Did someone do something to you?

LISL: Don't know. Must've been the lice. They're miserable!

COMMISSIONER: You did not get that tumor from lice bites. Think back, Lisl! Did someone have carnal knowledge of you?—The devil, perhaps?

(*LISL does not answer, is growing desparate.*)

COMMISSIONER: The consecrated rod! Thirty lashes!

(*The EXECUTIONER and the TWO HENCHMEN leap up. LISL sees them.*)

LISL (*screams*): I'll tell!

(*The EXECUTIONER and the HENCHMEN grin at each other, sit back down. LISL looks at the COMMISSIONER; suddenly her eyes grow wide.*)

LISL: Oh, no!

COMMISSIONER: What is the matter?

LISL: Behind you!

COMMISSIONER (*turns around*): What?

LISL: The black man!

(*ALL look at the COMMISSIONER.*)

COMMISSIONER: Which black man?

LISL (*staring behind the COMMISSIONER*): Oh, no!

Leave me alone! I won't tell! (*listens*) No, don't stab me! I won't tell! (*listens*) No, please don't!

(*The COMMISSIONER stands up, looks around behind him.*)

COMMISSIONER: Who is it?

LISL (*withdrawing*): He's coming! Help me! Help me!— No! I won't tell! I won't tell! (*lifts her hands to protect herself, throws herself on the floor, screams, her hands flail the air, she rips off the breve, suddenly stops, listens, answers*) Oh, thank you! Thank you! God bless! (*is kicked, falls down*) Sorry! Sorry! I'll never say that again! I'll never say that word again! God-bastard! I said, God-bastard! (*listens*) Uh-huh! Uh-huh! I'll do it!

COMMISSIONER: Holy water! Quick!

(*The EXECUTIONER leaps up, grabs the aspergillum, shakes it at LISL, sprinkling her and her surroundings. LISL looks around.*)

COMMISSIONER: Is he gone?

LISL: Yes, he's gone! (*gets up*)

(*The EXECUTIONER puts the aspergillum back, sits down.*)

COMMISSIONER (*to the EXECUTIONER*): Are you sure you used holy water for the soup?

EXECUTIONER: Of course!

COMMISSIONER (*shakes his head, then looks at LISL*): Come over here, Little Lisl.

(*LISL goes over to him.*)

COMMISSIONER: Who was it?

LISL: The black man!

COMMISSIONER: What did he say?

LISL: If I admit anything, he's gonna stab me in the neck with a knife!

COMMISSIONER: What else?

LISL: If I admit anything, he'll tear me to pieces during the night!

COMMISSIONER: What else?

LISL: I should tear off that consecrated thing!

COMMISSIONER: Put it on her again!

(*The FIRST HENCHMAN approaches, ties the breve around LISL'S neck again, returns to his seat.*)

COMMISSIONER: Tell me more, Lisl.

LISL: Then I made him mad. He said he'd protect me! He said I don't need to worry, nothing's gonna happen to me! All I gotta do is believe in him!

COMMISSIONER: What else?

LISL: At night he'll come to me and treat me right!

COMMISSIONER (*to the EXECUTIONER*): Sprinkle down the whole room! Including the cell! Before night falls!

(*The EXECUTIONER looks at the FIRST HENCHMAN, who goes over to the basin filled with holy water, picks up the aspergillum, sprinkles around the room, lackadaisically.*)

COMMISSIONER: In all the corners!

(*The HENCHMAN does as ordered, then sits back down.*)

COMMISSIONER: Lisl! Don't trust him! Don't trust him when he threatens you, and don't trust him when he is nice to you! He is the snake! The Prince of

Hell! He wants to cast all of us into perdition!—
You must pray a great deal! Can you pray?

LISL: Uh-huh! I can pray good!

COMMISSIONER: Then do it! Call on our Holy Mother!
She will spread her cloak over you! And you will
never see the Prince of Hell again! Do not be
afraid! God is with you!—And now, tell us about
the tumor. How did you get it?

(*LISL looks around, cautiously, comes a bit closer to the
COMMISSIONER'S desk.*)

LISL (*softly*): A black man . . .

SCRIBE: Louder!

LISL (*haltingly*): A black man . . . with long claws on his
hands . . . squeezed me hard . . . down there . . .
and it hurt a lot!

(*The COMMISSIONER is silent for a while.*)

COMMISSIONER: Was anyone else present?

(*LISL doesn't answer.*)

COMMISSIONER: Lisl, was anyone else present?

LISL: A boy!

COMMISSIONER: What did he do?

LISL: He squeezed me too.

COMMISSIONER: Both at the same time?

LISL: Yes. Or they took turns. They held me down. Both of
'em held me down.

COMMISSIONER: Who was the boy?

LISL: Don't know. It was at night. In a barn.

COMMISSIONER (*yells*): Tell me this instant who it was,

or I will have you lashed until your skin is in shreds!

(*In the background, the EXECUTIONER grins at the FIRST HENCHMAN.*)

LISL (*sobbing*): Dionys! Dionys!

COMMISSIONER *(calmly)*: I am not angry at you, Lisl. Only at the devil.—So, it was your brother?

LISL: Yes!

COMMISSIONER: How many times?

LISL (*sobbing*): Lots of times! Lots of times!

COMMISSIONER (*in the direction of the EXECU-TIONER*): Get him up here!

(*The EXECUTIONER and the TWO HENCHMEN get up, walk over to the trapdoor, the FIRST HENCHMAN opens it.*)

EXECUTIONER (*yelling down*): Dionysus Feldner!— Hey! D' you hear me?

COMMISSIONER: You do not have to cry anymore, Lisl. We are looking for the truth, and sometimes that can be painful. But when the truth is out, that is good. Sit down.

(*LISL sits down on the chair. The TWO HENCHMEN reach down into the cell below, pull DIONYSUS up by his arms, take him over to the COMMISSIONER'S desk, then sit down. The EXECUTIONER closes the trapdoor, also sits down. DIONYSUS looks at his sister anxiously, looks at the COMMISSIONER who is observing him calmly.*)

COMMISSIONER: Where is your breve, Dionysus?

DIONYSUS (*grasping at his neck*): Don't know. Must've lost it!

COMMISSIONER (*to LISL*): Tell it to his face.

LISL: No!

COMMISSIONER: Tell him!

LISL: He did it to me!

COMMISSIONER (*loudly*): Stand up and tell it to his face!

LISL (*stands up*): You did it to me! You and the devil! You and the devil! (*angrily*) You hurt me! You know it!

(*The COMMISSIONER looks at DIONYSUS. DIONYSUS is terribly frightened, wants to say something, opens his mouth, but cannot speak; he is on the verge of a seizure.*)

COMMISSIONER: Spray holy water in his mouth!

(*The EXECUTIONER goes over to the basin, picks up the spray bag, fills it with holy water.*)

COMMISSIONER (*to DIONYSUS*): Calm down, we can help you!

(*The EXECUTIONER approaches, sprays holy water in DIONYSUS' mouth. DIONYSUS begins to cough, his spasms subside. The EXECUTIONER lays down the spray bag, sits back down.*)

COMMISSIONER: Well?

DIONYSUS: Yeah, it's true!

COMMISSIONER (*after a while*): And your father?

(*DIONYSUS looks at him uncomprehendingly, then realizes what the COMMISSIONER is implying.*)

DIONYSUS (*groans*): No!

COMMISSIONER: You and your sister roamed around with him! Until he found a job, and you all joined Jackie's mob!

DIONYSUS: No! He went alone! Beggin' doesn't work too good when there's more than two!

(*The COMMISSIONER looks at LISL.*)

LISL: Don't lie, Dionys! There were times when all three of us traveled together!

COMMISSIONER: Veit Lindner confirmed it! What are you trying to hide, Dionysus? Lisl has already admitted everything! That your father also made a pact with the devil!

DIONYSUS: Where is he?

COMMISSIONER: Also down below! (*points to the floor*) But deeper!

DIONYSUS (*accusingly*): Do you know what you're doin', Lisl?

LISL: What's true is true!

COMMISSIONER (*to DIONYSUS*): Your father was there when you slept with your sister, was he not?

DIONYSUS: No!

COMMISSIONER: Lisl?

LISL: No! He wasn't there! The devil was there!

COMMISSIONER (*to LISL*): You confessed that he was with you two at the dance!

LISL (*sobbing*): I don't know! I can't remember!

COMMISSIONER (*to the EXECUTIONER*): Sharp lashes! Fifty for Lisl, one hundred for Dionysus! No, two hundred!

(*The EXECUTIONER gets up.*)

LISL: No, don't beat me anymore! Please, don't!

COMMISSIONER (*to DIONYSUS*): Do you confess? Was your father present?

DIONYSUS (*enraged*): Yes! Yes! He was present!

COMMISSIONER: And he also slept with her! Say it!

DIONYSUS: Yes! He did! He did!

(*The EXECUTIONER sits back down.*)

COMMISSIONER (*to LISL*): Is that true, Lisl?

LISL: I don't know! Oh, Mother of God!

(*The COMMISSIONER looks at the bewildered LISL, decides to leave her alone for now, looks at DIONYSUS.*)

COMMISSIONER: Let us talk about animals, Dionysus.—Do you understand me?

DIONYSUS: No.

COMMISSIONER: We are talking about animals.

(*DIONYSUS is silent.*)

COMMISSIONER: Can you tell me something about them?

DIONYSUS (*after a while*): Jackie . . .

COMMISSIONER: Yes? I am listening!

DIONYSUS: Jackie—did it with a red cow!

COMMISSIONER: Did what?

DIONYSUS: Slept with it . . .

COMMISSIONER: Committed promiscuous acts?

DIONYSUS: Yes!

SCRIBE: Oh, the sordid things we have to hear!

COMMISSIONER: Where was that?

DIONYSUS: Between Golling and Kuchl. In a pasture.

COMMISSIONER: Why did the animal not run away?

DIONYSUS: Two guys held it by its horns.

COMMISSIONER: Who?

DIONYSUS: Can't remember!

COMMISSIONER: You! It was you, was it not?

DIONYSUS: Yes.

COMMISSIONER: Who else?

DIONYSUS: Crooked Veit!

COMMISSIONER: Who else was there? Talk, talk!

DIONYSUS: Christian Fleis and Tripacher!

COMMISSIONER: And all of you had your way with that cow, did you not?

DIONYSUS: I didn't want to! Jackie lifted me up and said I was s'posed to make a baby!

SCRIBE: Revolting!

COMMISSIONER: What other animals?—Open your mouth, Dionysus! I know everything! There are witnesses!

DIONYSUS: With a sow!

COMMISSIONER: With several! That you manufactured yourself!

DIONYSUS: No! No!

COMMISSIONER: I will order them to put the thumb-screws on!

SCRIBE: But, Mr. Counselor, you can't do that! You know, according to the report from Schellenberg, he's only twelve years old!

EXECUTIONER: Shut up, Scribe! (*stands up*) I'll go get the thumbscrews, Doctor!

(*The COMMISSIONER hesitates.*)

EXECUTIONER: Eleven, twelve, fourteen! What's the difference! He's reached the age of puberty! When he does it with his sister and with animals, then he's of age! Wouldn't you say so?

COMMISSIONER: Why would you do things like that, Dionysus? You are a human being! Not an animal!

DIONYSUS: Jackie said they'd have a miscarriage!

COMMISSIONER: Oh, so you were trying to cause damage to somebody? Ah, so that is why you did it! Now I understand!

EXECUTIONER: Well, now should I . . . ?

(*The COMMISSIONER dismisses him with a wave of the hand, the EXECUTIONER sits back down.*)

DIONYSUS: But most of the time I was an animal!

COMMISSIONER: What?

DIONYSUS: Jackie held a velvet cape over my head, and I changed into a bull! Or into a giant bear!

LISL: I know something else!

COMMISSIONER: You do? What is it?

LISL: Crooked Veit and Bigfoot held me down, and Jackie put a dog on top of me!

(*The COMMISSIONER looks at DIONYSUS.*)

DIONYSUS: Yeah, that's right!

LISL: You didn't help me!

DIONYSUS: What could I do? Veit pulled his knife on me!

COMMISSIONER: Go on, Lisl!

LISL: They let the dog mount me twice! But it didn't come inside me!—They all laughed! (*to DIONYSUS*) You, too!

(*DIONYSUS is ashamed of himself.*)

COMMISSIONER: That is all for today! (*to the SCRIBE*) An amicable interrogation, no incidents! Send the following dispatch to our colleagues: Since the examination in progress indicates the commission of sodomy with an animal, they should revise their questionnaires accordingly!

SCRIBE: Yes, Sir!

(*The EXECUTIONER and the TWO HENCHMEN rise, the FIRST HENCHMAN leads LISL and DIONYSUS to the trapdoor, opens it. LISL and DIONYSUS jump down into the cell below, the HENCHMAN closes the trapdoor.*)

COMMISSIONER: The henchmen may go now! But you, Executioner, stay where you are!

(*The EXECUTIONER looks surprised, the HENCHMEN leave the room, the EXECUTIONER sits back down.*)

COMMISSIONER (*to the SCRIBE*): Have the results of our inquiries arrived?

SCRIBE: Yes! (*picks up one sheet of paper after the other and reports*): Regarding the malicious magic of Veit Lindner.—Report from Froschheim: on the Klausner farm two cows actually did die.—Report from Siezenheim: the farmer Christoph Feldinger claims that three of his horses died. At about that time Crooked Veit was on his farm!—Report from Hallein: the caretaker searched for a farmer with a crippled leg and a wooden kneebrace, but couldn't find one; he complains that our inquiries frequently mention no names; he has better things to do than tramp around the district all day long and stop at every farm.—Report from Zell: several farmers' wives were crippled and have since recovered; not one of them had put a consecrated egg in lard; the caretaker also complained that we gave no specific names.—Report from Fürstenau: two years ago, a six-year-old boy fell out of a window and broke his neck; however, he was buried in accordance with regulations.

COMMISSIONER: Exhume the boy's body! Maybe Jackie dug him back up!

SCRIBE (*making a note*): Got it!

COMMISSIONER: Is that all?

SCRIBE: That's it for today!

COMMISSIONER: Anything regarding the manhunt for Jackie?

SCRIBE: Reports are arriving daily. It's been a success, as far as locating his accomplices, but as far as Jackie is concerned—unfortunately we've had no results at all! (*glances at a report*) He is supposed to have a pregnant whore in Golling, the aforementioned Rosina, but they haven't come across her yet. (*glances at another report*) A report from Abtenau that Jackie is supposed to hide out there at night sometimes; but there are also rumors that he migrated to Bavaria or Styria! (*glances at a letter*) The county judge in Grossarl is pleading for a replacement for his bailiff who is out searching for Jackie day and night. In addition, his court budget is strained to the limit; he asks if we would be so good as to pick up meal and travel expenses of one-half guilder per day for the bailiff while he's conducting our manhunt!

COMMISSIONER: Denied!

SCRIBE (*glances at a report*): According to testimony from the skinner in Gastein, Jackie sometimes stays with the skinner in Saalfelden who has huge watchdogs that don't let anyone come near. Nevertheless, he was kept under surveillance: Jackie was nowhere to be seen, one of the deputies got bit by a dog.—(*leafs through several letters*) Time and again we find out that people claim to have no knowledge of Jackie, have never heard of him. Apparently these are just excuses, because the people are afraid of him. (*picks up a new page*)—Report from Lungau: according to rumor, Christoph Moser, the skinner from Mauterndorf, was also supposed to have harbored Jackie.

COMMISSIONER: Mauterndorf? Why, that is where Jackie was born!

SCRIBE: Exactly! His grandfather owned the skinnery there! (*looks at the piece of paper*) According to rumor, Moser could change himself into a wolf! (*reads*) Moser's statement: It was true that he frequently took off his coat and rolled around on the ground, but he did that on account of his mange.

COMMISSIONER: Arrange for his transfer to Salzburg!

SCRIBE: Yes, Sir! (*makes a note*)

COMMISSIONER: Aren't they colleagues of yours, Executioner?

EXECUTIONER: How come?

COMMISSIONER: Well, you were formerly the skinner in Laufen, or am I mistaken?

EXECUTIONER: Are you trying to blame me for something?

COMMISSIONER: Oh, no, definitely not.

EXECUTIONER: Somebody's got to get rid of the sick animals!

COMMISSIONER: Certainly.

EXECUTIONER: My grandfather was a skinner! And my father, too! What else can the son of a skinner do? Become another skinner!

COMMISSIONER: Or an executioner.

EXECUTIONER: Yeah, if he's lucky! Every citizen can be whatever he wants to be! A skinner'll be a skinner forever! Somebody who gets rid of the filth! That's all an executioner does! We're on the bottom rung of the social ladder, the lowest of the low! Scum! When I go into the inn, everybody moves away from my table! Nobody'll shake my hand! I'm not even allowed in the public baths!

SCRIBE: Well, you obviously haven't felt the need for one all that often, Executioner! You know, you smell worse than your deliquents!

EXECUTIONER (*to the COMMISSIONER*): He's insulting me! Why's he insulting me? Is he allowed to do that?

COMMISSIONER: Stop whining, Executioner. I am familiar with your tirades. You earn a good living, and the work is not hard. Expect no sympathy from me.

(*The EXECUTIONER is insulted.*)

SCRIBE (*glances at a report*): The skinner in Wagrain, Hans Hamperger, has been arrested. He was caught boiling lungs and liver from diseased animals, resulting in him identifying the man who had made the animals sick.

COMMISSIONER: Let us have a look at him! Start the extradition process!

(*The SCRIBE makes a note.*)

SCRIBE: It might be a good idea to examine all the skinners, Mr. Counselor! Some of them are most certainly conspiring with Jackie!

COMMISSIONER: A good idea! Do it!—And send out a new arrest warrant for Jackie! I have underestimated him! I have really underestimated the rascal! Write the following: Since it is the responsibility of this high office to cleanse the country as thoroughly as possible from evil persons, and since Jakob Koller is a proven sorcerer and warlock and also a seducer of youth, thus for the betterment of the commonweal we declare Jackie an outlaw. Whosoever kills or eliminates this despicable villain shall receive a reward of 100 gold pieces, but whosoever delivers him alive to this court shall receive 200 gold pieces as a reward. —Send it to the Prince for his approval!

SCRIBE (*having written it all down*): Yes, Sir!

COMMISSIONER: Send the arrest warrant to all district courts and also to foreign governments. And specifically to the governor in Carinthia, to the Inner Austrian government in Styria, to the Upper Austrian government in Tyrol, to the electoral councilor in Munich, to the government in Berchtesgaden. Include Jackie's description—Did you get that?

SCRIBE (*writing furiously*): Yes, Sir! Almost! Almost! . . . to the government in Berchtesgaden, include a description!

EXECUTIONER: Dr. Zillner! Do you mind me asking if you still need me?

COMMISSIONER: Oh, yes, I am sorry. I almost forgot about you. (*turning to the SCRIBE*) The report from Laufen.

SCRIBE (*searches for the document, finds it, reads*) According to rumors that are circulating hereabouts, the former skinner here in Laufen, presently the executioner in Salzburg, Moritz Ehegartner, is said to be related to Jackie the Sorcerer.

(*The SCRIBE looks at the EXECUTIONER, as does the COMMISSIONER. The EXECUTIONER is extremely embarrassed by this issue. A long silence.*)

COMMISSIONER: Well, what is wrong, my man! Cat got your tongue? Shall I wash your mouth out with holy water?

EXECUTIONER (*in a monotone*): I can't deny that he's a distant relative.

COMMISSIONER: Is that so? Then you knew Jackie's mother, Barbara Koller?

EXECUTIONER: You can't blame me for anything, Mr. Counselor! I tortured her, just like I was ordered, and, like I was ordered, I carried out the verdict!

COMMISSIONER: I am not blaming you for anything, Executioner. I just find it interesting.—So, you know Jackie, too?—Well, what is wrong? Shall I call the henchmen and have you lashed with the rod?

EXECUTIONER (*leaps up*): Well, I don't have to sit here and take that, Mr. Counselor! I'm a conscientious executioner! I would burn my own mother at the stake! If I had to!

COMMISSIONER (*smiling*): Calm yourself. It was just a joke. What would I do without you? I know you are an expert at your craft.

EXECUTIONER: I beg your pardon! I'm sensitive about my professional reputation! (*sits back down*)—I knew him ... knew Jackie ... saw him a few times. But back then he was just a boy! Eight or nine years old! That's when his father died. He'd been an executioner's henchman. The widow Koller went begging for charity with Jackie.

SCRIBE: And went stealing, too! Six verifiable thefts of offertory boxes! And she was a witch to boot!

EXECUTIONER (*furious*): You don't have to tell me that! I already know all that! After all, who burned her at the stake? You? (*then to the COMMISSIONER*) Do you want me to go on with my story, or not?

COMMISSIONER: Please do.—Be so good as to come a little closer.

(*The EXECUTIONER gets up, walks over to the desk, and now stands before the COMMISSIONER, like an accused person himself.*)

COMMISSIONER: Please. Go on.

EXECUTIONER: Then Barbara Koller applied for work at the skinnery in Mauterndorf—the one that had belonged to her father for thirty-one years. I used my connections to try and help her out! That's all there was to it!

COMMISSIONER: But she did not get the position ...

EXECUTIONER: No, she got in a fight with the skinner and got thrown out! That's all, Mr. Counselor! There's nothing more to it! Never saw Barbara Koller and Jackie again in my life!

SCRIBE: Of course you saw her again!

EXECUTIONER: When? Where?

SCRIBE: Well, here! Right here in this room! That's where you saw her! Didn't you?

EXECUTIONER: Yes, sure! But not before that! Not up to that point! Say, what do you want from me? Just shut up and write! Are you the examining judge here?

SCRIBE: No, I'm not! I'm the Court Reporter! And in that capacity I put great store in accurate statements!

COMMISSIONER: Apparently Barbara Koller did not recognize you, did she? Here, during the interrogation.

EXECUTIONER: Probably not, because of my mask! Thank God! That would have been very painful for me! Especially in the torture chamber!

SCRIBE: How's that? You just said you'd burn your own mother at the stake!

EXECUTIONER: Mr. Counselor, I don't have to put up with that! Not from this pencil-pusher! Why's he always stirring up trouble?

COMMISSIONER: He is right, Mr. Finsterwalder. You can leave the questions to me. I, too, am an expert at my craft.

SCRIBE: I beg your pardon, Mr. Counselor! I exceeded my authority! I beg your pardon!

(*The COMMISSIONER looks at the EXECUTIONER who stands there, upset, and avoids the COMMISSIONER'S gaze.*)

EXECUTIONER: I should have told you, Mr. Counselor, I know! But it was just too embarrassing for me!

*(With a questioning look in his eye, the COMMISSIONER
continues to gaze at the EXECUTIONER.)*

COMMISSIONER *(abruptly)*: Well, fine. Let us leave it at
that.

EXECUTIONER *(bows down, relieved)*: Thank you, Mr.
Counselor! I'm very grateful!

(Blackout)

8. The cell

*(DIONYSUS (12), LISL (8), VEIT (14), DOFFER (13), MI-
CHAEL (10), JOHNNY (6), and FOUR other imprisoned
BOYS—all with shaved heads, in black shirts and chains.
Through the open trapdoor fall ANDREE MAYER, alias
"City Reject" (18), MAGDALENA PICHLER, alias "Rag-
gedy Leni" (17), and three other BOYS—all shorn, in shirts
and chains.)*

DOFFER: Hey, up there, gentlemen, you better get me
outta' here soon, or I'll forget everything I know!

*(The trapdoor closes, the new ARRIVALS look around, re-
main lying on the ground just where they landed, except
ANDREE who gets up into a crouch, looks around, walks
around among the youths lying on the ground.)*

DOFFER: They've subjected the "City Reject" to the de-
jected! Did the "City Reject" get ejected with
Jackie? If the Reject gets rejected, then the world'll
be protected!

*(ANDREE ignores DOFFER, looks at the blind MICHAEL
and his brother JOHNNY, looks at DIONYSUS and his*

sister LISL, suddenly sees VEIT, stares at him for a while. VEIT becomes frightened.)

VEIT *(grinning)*: Hey, City Reject!

(ANDREE looks at him calmly, then motions to VEIT with his finger. VEIT slowly crawls over to him. ANDREE is squatting on his heels, looking at VEIT. MAGDALENA comes over to ANDREE, sits down beside him.)

ANDREE: All hell's broken loose, Crooked Veit! The whole country's after us! We're not even safe outside the country!

VEIT: I know! Anybody who admits he knows Jackie has had it! You have to deny it! Then they can't hurt you!

ANDREE: Thanks for the tip, Veit! I already denied everything! It didn't do me any good! *(looks at VEIT for a while, in silence)* They've got lists of names!

(VEIT is silent.)

ANDREE: Somebody must've given them all those names!

VEIT: Yeah, probably! *(points around him)* There are lots of guys here! And real young ones, too! A couple of them must've squealed!

(Quick as a flash, ANDREE throws his chain over VEIT'S head, pulls it tightly around his neck. DIONYSUS grins with satisfaction.)

DOFFER: Help! Somebody's getting strangled! Somebody's getting strangled! Who's getting strangled here? *(crawls over)* Ah, it's Crooked Veit! You have my permission! Choke him some more!

ANDREE: You already turned us in once before! And now you've done it again! Right?

VEIT: Back then, yeah! Back then, yeah! I didn't steal those shoes! It was Raggedy Leni, your whore!

(*MAGDALENA punches VEIT in the face.*)

VEIT: Yeah, am I supposed to let them lock me up for something I didn't do? I still don't have any shoes!

MAGDALENA: You've betrayed us again! You told them our names! Admit it!

ANDREE (*tightening his stranglehold*): I'll kill you, you turd!

MAGDALENA: Admit it! Now!

DOFFER (*looking VEIT eye to eye*): Admit it, Veit, before you die!

VEIT: Okay! Okay! I admit it!

(*ANDREE stops choking him, hits VEIT in the face with the bell on his chains. VEIT falls over.*)

VEIT: You bitch! You dirty bitch! (*props himself up*) You'll name names, too! You will, too! Who do you think you are? Nobody can fool them! And you won't either!

(*Blackout*)

9. The office

(*The COMMISSIONER and the SCRIBE are sitting at their desks, the EXECUTIONER and his TWO HENCH-MEN on the bench to the rear. The chair is back against the wall. Standing before the COMMISSIONER is JOHNNY (age 6). He keeps sneaking a look at the EXECUTIONER, whose mask frightens him.*)

COMMISSIONER: So, you do not know your family name or where you come from?

JOHNNY: Yes!

COMMISSIONER: What do you mean, "yes"? You mean "no," do you not?

JOHNNY: Yes!

(*JOHNNY looks over at the EXECUTIONER who makes at face at him and sticks out his tongue. JOHNNY steps back, frightened. The EXECUTIONER and his HENCH-MEN grin.*)

COMMISSIONER: Stop that nonsense, Executioner!—Look at me, Johnny!

(*JOHNNY does.*)

COMMISSIONER: But you do know how old you are?

(*JOHNNY holds up both hands, shows him five fingers of the left hand and the index finger of his right hand.*)

SCRIBE: Six—is that it?

(*JOHNNY turns toward the SCRIBE, shows him the number of fingers too.*)

COMMISSIONER: Are you sure?

JOHNNY: That's what Michael told me!

COMMISSIONER: But Michael does not know where you come from?

JOHNNY: No. He's blind, don't you know.

COMMISSIONER: You are called the "Mow Catcher"? Where did you get that name?

JOHNNY: I catch mows for the farmers! I'm good at it! They don't get away from me too much!

COMMISSIONER (*to the SCRIBE*): "Mow"?

EXECUTIONER: Moles! A "mow" is a mole! Don't you know that?

COMMISSIONER: No, unfortunately. I am not terribly familiar with the way peasants speak, Sir! (*to JOHNNY*) Can you pray, Johnny?

JOHNNY: Yes!

COMMISSIONER: Do you know the Hail Mary?

JOHNNY: Yes!

COMMISSIONER: Then recite it for us.

(*JOHNNY kneels down, folds his hands and prays.*)

JOHNNY: Hail, Mary, full of grace, the Lord is with you, you are blessed among women and blessed is the fruit of thy womb, Jesus. Holy Mary, Mother of God, pee for us sinners now and in the hour of our death. Amen. (*gets up*)

(*With the words "pee for us sinners" the EXECUTIONER starts to laugh, his TWO HENCHMEN laugh too. The EX-ECUTIONER can barely control himself, slaps his thigh and roars with laughter. Even the SCRIBE cannot sup-press a grin.*)

EXECUTIONER (*laughing*): Pee for us sinners! Pee for us sinners! Pee for us sinners!

COMMISSIONER: That will be enough, Executioner.

(*The TWO HENCHMEN stop laughing, but the EXECU-TIONER simply cannot control himself.*)

COMMISSIONER (*enraged*): Stop it!

(*The EXECUTIONER stops laughing, though for several minutes he must make a concerted effort; he still lets out a couple of stifled guffaws.*)

COMMISSIONER: Pray for us sinners, Johnny, that is

the way it goes! Remember that! —Do you know
anything about the devil, Johnny?

JOHNNY: Yes!

COMMISSIONER: What is that?

JOHNNY: He's always trying something!

COMMISSIONER: What is he trying?

JOHNNY: Trying to make us do evil!

COMMISSIONER: What do you mean?

JOHNNY: Make us do evil, in words and in deeds!

COMMISSIONER: Very good, Johnny!—What does he
look like, the devil?

(*JOHNNY turns around and points to the EXECU-
TIONER.*)

JOHNNY: Like that man there!

(*The TWO HENCHMEN giggle, even the SCRIBE grins.
The EXECUTIONER is not amused.*)

COMMISSIONER: Do you go to church sometimes,
Johnny?

JOHNNY: A lot!

COMMISSIONER: With your brother Michael?

JOHNNY: Yes!

COMMISSIONER: Do you also take Holy Communion
sometimes?

JOHNNY: Yes! A lot!

COMMISSIONER: That is bread, is it not?

JOHNNY (*grinning*): Yes! (*seriously*) And the body of the
Lord!

COMMISSIONER: Where did you two meet Jackie?

JOHNNY: In Tittmoning! (*suddenly frightened*) No! No! I don't know Jackie! I don't know him!

COMMISSIONER: Michael told you to say that, did he not?

(*JOHNNY does not answer, his face contorts as he begins to cry. The COMMISSIONER looks at the EXECUTIONER who stands up, approaches, picks up JOHNNY under the armpits, lifts him up, looks him in the eye with a malicious expression. JOHNNY stares back at him, frozen in terror.*)

COMMISSIONER: Michael told you to say that, did he not?

JOHNNY: Yes!

(*The EXECUTIONER grins, puts JOHNNY back down, returns to his seat on the bench.*)

COMMISSIONER: So, you two met Jackie in Tittmoning?

JOHNNY: Yes! (*starts to cry*) Michael's gonna beat me! I promised him I wouldn't tell!

COMMISSIONER: Lying is a sin, Johnny! You know that!

JOHNNY: Yes!

COMMISSIONER: Well, then! Why did you two go along with Jackie?

JOHNNY: Because it's paradise!

COMMISSIONER: What do you mean?

JOHNNY: There's meat and money and a warm spot to bed down at night!

COMMISSIONER: How is that possible? How did you do that? By magic?

JOHNNY (*amazed*): No!

COMMISSIONER: Well, then, how?

JOHNNY: The farmers're afraid of him!

COMMISSIONER: Afraid of Jackie?

JOHNNY: Yes! (*smiles*) They give him whatever he wants!

COMMISSIONER: Why are they afraid of him, Johnny?

JOHNNY: Don't know.

COMMISSIONER: Think a moment!

JOHNNY: Don't know! He just says "I'm Jackie," and they give him whatever he wants!

COMMISSIONER (*losing his patience*): Why?

JOHNNY: Don't know!

COMMISSIONER: But Jackie does know how to cast spells! Did you know that?

JOHNNY: Yes!

COMMISSIONER: He also taught you and your brother how to cast spells, did he not?

JOHNNY: No! Wish he had! Only thing he gave us was a punch in the mouth!

COMMISSIONER: Why?

JOHNNY: Because we go to Mass!

COMMISSIONER: Because you receive Holy Communion?

JOHNNY: Yes!

COMMISSIONER: He made you two steal the Consecrated Host, did he not?

JOHNNY: No! Why?

(*Blackout*)

10. The office

*(The COMMISSIONER, the SCRIBE, and JOHNNY as in
the previous scene. Beside JOHNNY stands VEIT. At this
moment the FIRST HENCHMAN is leading MICHAEL
out of the torture chamber; MICHAEL has just been lashed.
Inside the chamber the EXECUTIONER puts the rod back
in the basin, then comes out into the office with the SEC-
OND HENCHMAN. They both sit down. The FIRST
HENCHMAN leads MICHAEL before the COMMIS-
SIONER, then returns to his own seat on the bench.)*

COMMISSIONER *(to VEIT)*: Tell him! Tell it to him, to
his face!

VEIT: "Phooey on you, you dirty Jew, you're not worth my
time!" you yelled! "You can kiss my ass!" you
yelled!

COMMISSIONER *(to MICHAEL)*: Is that the truth? Is
that the truth?

MICHAEL *(in desperation)*: Yes! Yes!

COMMISSIONER: What else? What else?

VEIT: "Just look, the whore . . . "

COMMISSIONER: Be quiet, he is supposed to say it himself!

MICHAEL *(enraged)*: Just look, the whore's there too,
that's what I yelled!

COMMISSIONER: Which whore?

VEIT: The Virgin Mary!

COMMISSIONER: Where?

MICHAEL: On the altar! In the field!

COMMISSIONER: How can you see anything? You are
blind, are you not?

MICHAEL (*yells*): I saw her, that goddamn whore!

COMMISSIONER: And then? What then?

MICHAEL: I spit on her! I wiped my shit on her mouth! I knocked her over! I broke her to bits!

COMMISSIONER (*to JOHNNY*): What about you? What did you do? Tell me! Now!

JOHNNY (*stammering*): Yeah, I . . . I . . . I pulled down—I pulled down my pants, and showed her my heinie!

MICHAEL (*yells*): I pulled Christ from the cross and broke him to bits! The thief on the gallows! The thief on the gallows!

JOHNNY (*eagerly*): And I . . . and I peed on the Virgin Mary, and . . . and . . . threw snowballs at her and . . . and . . . and smeared my snot on her! (*laughs*)

COMMISSIONER: The Consecrated Host! Let's talk about the Host, Michael! Tell me about the Host! You desecrated it, did you not! You took it out of the church, did you not! You did evil things to it, admit it!

MICHAEL: Yeah, I did evil things to it! I did evil things to the Host! I stabbed it with a knife, and blood gushed out, and all of a sudden it grew and changed itself into the Lord!

COMMISSIONER: How big was He? How big?

MICHAEL: As big as a crucifix, about nine inches long!—He raised His arms to me and looked at me! And I stabbed Him again! "Ohhh, my God, my God, don't stab me any more!" He cried! Then I threw Him on the floor and stomped on Him! He wiggled like a worm and cried and whined! Then I took Him and nailed Him to the side of the barn and stabbed Him some more! In the chest, in the face, in His private parts! "Ohhh, ohhh! Who's got such power over me?" He cried! And then He started moving, wiggling and arching His back like a cat! And then He was finished! Dead! Dead! Dead!

(*Blackout*)

11. The office

(*The COMMISSIONER, the SCRIBE, and the EXECU-TIONER as in the previous scene. The trapdoor is open, the TWO HENCHMEN lift DOFFER (age 13) out. DOFFER is curious, looks around, recoils at the sight of the EXECU-TIONER, then goes directly to the COMMISSIONER. The HENCHMEN close the trapdoor and sit down on the bench.*)

DOFFER (*leaning on the COMMISSIONER'S desk*): Sir, I've been sitting down there in that hole for twelve years, and now I forgot everything I wanted to tell you! Nobody can remember all that for twenty years! My head's buzzing! I've made statement after statement so somebody'll listen to me, but nobody wants to talk to me! And that's a big mistake, Sir, 'cause I, I know more than anybody else! There's no crime I haven't committed! There's no crime I'm not familiar with! There's no crime I haven't witnessed!

(*The EXECUTIONER and his TWO HENCHMEN have been grinning the whole time. The SCRIBE cannot afford to laugh, since he has to write down the entire testimony. The COMMISSIONER betrays no emotion.*)

COMMISSIONER (*calmly*): Be quiet, Doffer.

DOFFER (*surprised*): You know my name, Sir?

COMMISSIONER: Yes, I know your name. Take two steps back, please.

DOFFER (*steps back*): One, two, three! Three's better! Three is better! The Holy Trinity, that's also three! Three is always good! (*looks over to the EXECUTIONER, looks at the COMMISSIONER, looks back at the EXECUTIONER*)

COMMISSIONER: What is the matter?

DOFFER: Well, if he didn't have that mask on, I'd swear it's him!

COMMISSIONER: Who?

(*DOFFER takes a few steps over toward the EXECU-TIONER, peers at him, then walks back to the COM-MISSIONER'S desk and leans over it.*)

DOFFER (*whispers*): It's him!

SCRIBE: What?

COMMISSIONER: Who?

DOFFER (*whispers*): Who? Why, it's Jackie!

EXECUTIONER (*suspicious*): What'd he say?

COMMISSIONER: He said you are Jackie!

EXECUTIONER: What? But I'm not Jackie! I swear!

COMMISSIONER (*has to smile*): I believe you, Execu-tioner. I believe you. (*to DOFFER*) You must be mistaken, Doffer. That is the Executioner. He uses the rod and employs the instruments of torture. And he beheads people and burns them at the stake, when the time comes.

(*DOFFER looks at the EXECUTIONER suspiciously.*)

EXECUTIONER: I'll give you a sample right now! (*to the FIRST HENCHMAN*) He's crazy!

DOFFER (*to the COMMISSIONER*): I don't know, I don't know, Sir! If I were you, I wouldn't trust him as far as I could throw him!

COMMISSIONER (*smugly*): Well, perhaps there is a bit of a family resemblance. What do you think, Executioner?

(*The EXECUTIONER looks insulted.*)

COMMISSIONER: Well, Doffer. Please take two steps back. Or three, if you prefer.

DOFFER: Three is better! (*steps back*) One, two, three! (*looks over at the EXECUTIONER, shakes his head.*)

COMMISSIONER: How old are you, Doffer?

DOFFER: I'm two years old!

COMMISSIONER: Considering your age, you're big and strong and have the gift of gab!

DOFFER: After all, I come from a good family!

COMMISSIONER: Which family is that, Doffer?

DOFFER: I was born at the court in Vienna! The Royal Court Nigger was my father!

COMMISSIONER: Is that so? And your mother?

DOFFER: I didn't have a mother! The Royal Court Nigger baked me up in a dessert oven. Later on, I practiced my profession as the imperial bedpan emptier! They had my father stuffed!

(*The COMMISSIONER looks at the SCRIBE who taps his index finger against his temple.*)

COMMISSIONER: From his appearance, approximately thirteen years old. Possibly a shut-in.

(*The SCRIBE makes a note.*)

EXECUTIONER: Or else he's just trying to trick us! Maybe he's not as crazy as he acts!

COMMISSIONER: Please refrain from giving advice, Executioner!

EXECUTIONER: I'm sorry!

COMMISSIONER: You just warned him! You idiot!

EXECUTIONER: I'm sorry, Mr. Counselor! It won't happen again!

DOFFER (*to the EXECUTIONER*): Let's hope not! You carnival geek!—Mind your own business! We don't need you! We know how to have a lovely conversation without you barging in!

EXECUTIONER: Shut your mouth, or I'll shut it for you!

(*DOFFER is about to answer him.*)

COMMISSIONER (*impatient*): Look at me! At me! Look at me!

DOFFER: Be glad to! You have such a lovely robe! In fact, you're such a beautiful, dignified gentleman!

COMMISSIONER: Thank you, Doffer!—Do you feel healthy?

DOFFER: Sir, I'm healthy as a horse!

EXECUTIONER (*raising his hand*): Beg your pardon, Mr. Commissioner!

COMMISSIONER (*impatient*): What? What is it?

EXECUTIONER: When I searched him, I discovered that he's torn open in the rear!

COMMISSIONER: What?

EXECUTIONER: Well, he's torn open! And everything's inflamed! Do you want me to show you?

COMMISSIONER: No, thank you!

EXECUTIONER: I don't see how he can walk at all!

DOFFER: He doesn't see, he doesn't see! If I don't want to walk, I'll fly!—Let's get to the point, Judge! I admit everything!

COMMISSIONER: Why are you torn open, back there?

DOFFER: The devil! The devil!

COMMISSIONER: What?

DOFFER: You know, he does it to me. All the time! Everywhere! Even down below! (*points to the basement cell*) And you know for sure, he's got a gigantic organ!

COMMISSIONER: The devil is down below in the dungeon?

DOFFER: Of course! He's doing it to everybody! Let me tell you, there's a wild party going on down there!

COMMISSIONER: You made a pact with the devil?

DOFFER: The whole works! The whole shebang! Here's the sign! (*points to a scar on his forehead by tapping his index finger against it, indicating that he himself is crazy.*)

(*The COMMISSIONER looks at the SCRIBE who comes over and verifies the scar.*)

DOFFER: An unusual sign, wouldn't you say?

(*The SCRIBE goes back to his desk, sits down, makes a notation.*)

COMMISSIONER: What do you think about animals?

DOFFER: Animals? Our friends of the animal kingdom?

COMMISSIONER: Yes.

DOFFER: They taste good! Meat! Milk and honey!

COMMISSIONER: What else?

DOFFER: What else?

COMMISSIONER: Yes, what else can you do with them?

DOFFER (*to the EXECUTIONER*): Do you have any ideas?

COMMISSIONER: If you really feel the urge . . . if you cannot help yourself . . . if you have that certain feeling . . .

DOFFER: That certain feeling? (*looks at the COMMIS-SIONER, perplexed, then catches on*) Ah, I get it now! Yes, sure! I've done that, too! Do it with an animal, is that what you mean?

(*The COMMISSIONER nods.*)

DOFFER: Yes, sure! Now listen here: Jackie always used to cut off their tails first, so he could get a better grip! I never did that! Because animals are my one and only love!—Wait a minute, I'll try to remember so I can give you the exact figures!—Yup! I've got it! I've done it with 30 cows, three times each; with twenty different horses, each one five times; and with three-hundred goats, once apiece! I really prefer cows to goats! No comparison! They've got much prettier faces! One time—I've got to tell you this—there was this gray one! She had eyes on her, let me tell you—so beautiful, so beautiful! You'd have to have a heart of stone not to fall in love with her on the spot! (*thrusts his pelvis in and out, moans)* Ahhh! Ahhh! Ahhh!—*(stops in mid-thrust)* Oh, I almost forgot something! Cats and dogs! Well, I never could get interested in dogs, since the time one of them bit me real bad! But as far as cats are concerned, they're . . .

COMMISSIONER: That is enough, Doffer.

DOFFER: Is that enough? Fine! What else can I do for you?

COMMISSIONER: Can you name a few accomplices?

DOFFER: All of 'em! I'll tell you the names of all of 'em!

COMMISSIONER: Well? Go on!

DOFFER: Unfortunately they're all French and live in France! I don't know if that'll be of any help to you! Oh—there is one from around here!

COMMISSIONER: Who would that be?

DOFFER *(points to the EXECUTIONER)*: Him! If he's not Jackie, then he's got to be an accomplice!

(The SCRIBE grins, the EXECUTIONER leaps up.)

EXECUTIONER: Now I've had enough! I'll skin you alive, you little shit!

DOFFER: You want my skin? Why, you've already got one! *(to the COMMISSIONER)* Just take a look at his belt, Judge!

COMMISSIONER: What?

EXECUTIONER: Well, what can I say, Mr. Counselor! Your predecessor let me wear it!

COMMISSIONER *(confused)*: What?

EXECUTIONER: You know, the belt!

COMMISSIONER: What belt?

DOFFER: It's made out of human skin! Human skin!

COMMISSIONER: How do you know that?

DOFFER: When he was shaving my hair off, I touched it, touched his belt! And smelled it! I know human skin when I touch it! If you remember—my father was stuffed!

(*The COMMISSIONER looks at the EXECUTIONER.*)

EXECUTIONER: Your predecessor let me wear it!—I was suffering from gout! Since I've been wearing this belt, (*reaches down and clasps it*) it's gotten a lot better!

COMMISSIONER: And whose skin was it, if you please?

EXECUTIONER: A young woman who'd committed a murder!

COMMISSIONER: You are a strange fellow, Mr. Ehegartner! I do not know what to do with you! Perhaps this young man is not too far from the truth!

EXECUTIONER: Mr. Counselor, you have no right to talk to me like that! I'm an honorable man!

COMMISSIONER: All right. (*looks silently at DOFFER for a while*) Doffer, if you think you can make fun of me, then you are sadly mistaken! You will always come out on the short end, believe me!

DOFFER: Me, make fun of you? I've never made fun of a gentleman! I'm just a guy who likes to confess!

COMMISSIONER: Well, then let us continue with your confession! We will come back to your French accomplices. Let us try something else.—Did you practice malicious sorcery too?

DOFFER: Malicious sorcery? Weather and stuff like that?

COMMISSIONER: Yes!

DOFFER: That's difficult! Very difficult, Judge! If there weren't any bells to warn people about the weather—well, then it'd be a snap! But not now!— Let me give you an example! If I try to sneak through the Lueg Pass with the weather, then the watchdog in Werfen usually doesn't let me through; I've got to stay outside or travel over the meadow at Abt! But if the watchdog's asleep and I get by him without any trouble and go on through Fritz, then the big dog from Altenmarkt comes after me near Hell's bridge and won't let me over the Kreisten, in fact, most of the time I can't even get into the Upper Fritz! (*to the SCRIBE*) Did you get all that?—If I try to get away and go over the Gasthof Mountain to St. Martin, then that's when the real trouble starts! As soon as the dog at the inn starts barking, all the little inn puppies join in, and I have to take out my anger on the Höll Mountain, or I have to go back and then over the Brunnhäusl to get to St. Martin! But if I get lucky and sneak over Hell's bridge and go on to Filzmoos via the Upper Fritz, then the little pups in Filzmoos get after me and won't let me go on! What should I do? The Neuberg hounds won't let me into Neuberg, and I'm too tired to turn back, and the farmers' dogs in Fritz won't even let me sit down! Even though I'm dead tired, I've got to climb the mountains, cross over the Gsengplatte or the Rossbrand or, if I'm lucky, go over the Wurmegg and take out my anger on the innocent meadows and forests and take my revenge on the woods and animals, until I can finally sit down and rest on the Dachstein!—That's the way it is, Judge! It's not an easy job being a sorcerer! You can believe me!

(The COMMISSIONER gazes calmly at DOFFER for a while. The SCRIBE writes furiously until he has finished, drops his quill, stares at his writing hand.)

SCRIBE: My hand's falling off! Executioner, please sell me one of your salves!

EXECUTIONER: You sure you can afford it, Scribe?

COMMISSIONER: Silence! *(looks at DOFFER)* Well, Doffer, we are about to find out if your simplicity is real or feigned—in the torture chamber!

SCRIBE: The torture chamber? Then I'd better raise your estimate of his age to fourteen! Is that all right with you?

COMMISSIONER *(nods)*: That is all right with me! *(to DOFFER)* You are a rare bird, Doffer! Usually the miscreants are sent to the torture chamber because they talk too little! You are being sent because you talk too much!

DOFFER: Doctor, that's all my fault! I've never been average! That's always been the case! But you tell me: can a young man whose father was the famous Court Nigger—now stuffed, sadly—can a young man like that be mediocre? It's hard! It's hard! *(turns away)* Where is this chamber?

COMMISSIONER *(points to the door)*: Right next door!

DOFFER: Well, then, shall we? *(walks toward the door)* When you feel it, you've got it!

(DOFFER opens the door, looks into the torture chamber, recoils a bit when he sees the various instruments of torture. The EXECUTIONER and the TWO HENCHMEN watch him in amazement; they cannot believe that he could walk into the torture chamber so nonchalantly.)

DOFFER *(turns around)*: By the way, I'd like to thank you

for the lovely gown! It reminds me a little of my childhood at court! (*gathers up the shirt, courtsies*) Many thanks, your Excellency! (*turns back to the chamber*) Chamber, here I come! Sharpen your best steel and test it on me!

(*DOFFER walks into the torture chamber. Inside, he takes a close look at everything. The EXECUTIONER and the HENCHMEN get up.*)

EXECUTIONER: Just you wait! You won't think it's so much fun! (*walks over to the door*) Are you coming, Mr. Counselor?

COMMISSIONER: No, go ahead! Ask him his name and his hometown and his connection to Jackie! Do not stop until he gives us some reasonable answers!

EXECUTIONER: And which degree?

COMMISSIONER: Start with the rack, stretch him a bit!

EXECUTIONER: The riding horse with nails would be better! With a couple of weights on each foot!

COMMISSIONER: Why is that?

EXECUTIONER: Well, because he's torn open, in the rear!

COMMISSIONER: Fine! Do it!

(*The EXECUTIONER and the TWO HENCHMEN enter the torture chamber. Inside, DOFFER is leaning comfortably against the rack.*)

COMMISSIONER: Close the door! And remember to put a gag in his mouth! I have work to do!

(*The FIRST HENCHMAN closes the door.*)

SCRIBE: Should I write to the Supreme Court and belatedly ask permission to torture the subject?

COMMISSIONER: Yes, please.

(*The SCRIBE makes a note. The COMMISSIONER gets up, stretches, stomps his feet gently to get the circulation going. The SCRIBE does finger exercises.*)

COMMISSIONER: Exhausting, is it not?

SCRIBE: You can say that again!

COMMISSIONER: My back is sore! (*rubs the small of his back with his hands*) That comes from sitting all the time!—Nevertheless, we do not want to waste any time! The latest reports, please!

(*The SCRIBE searches through the mess of papers on his desk, looking for the reports, finds them.*)

SCRIBE (*glances at the first report*): The county judge in St. Johann has arrested Christian Fleis. During his first interrogation, Fleis said the following: (*reads*) When Jackie took him to a farm, the farmer fixed them a nice porridge and some fresh milk. While they were eating, the farmer went to the police, and in no time a hundred men had surrounded the farm. Jackie opened the door for them and said: "Come on in, you can't hurt me!" And then Jackie made himself invisible. The posse searched for him for more than an hour and finally took a stone along with them, thinking it might be Jackie. After the hundred men had left, Jackie made himself visible again and finished eating his porridge. When the farmer came back into the kitchen, Jackie said to him: "Take a look at your animals!" The farmer found all his farm animals dead. Then Jackie said, if that's not enough, then he'll also kill the farmer's two horses. The farmer started begging. Just then Jackie put a spell on him, so that the farmer ended up on all fours outside the front door. The farmer had to beg him some more until Jackie finally broke the spell; but he kept teasing the farmer, asking him where all the money was that he'd hoped to get as a reward. (*looks up*)

COMMISSIONER: Continue!

SCRIBE (*reads from the same report*): Maria Moser has accused a young beggar woman by the name of Susanna Kitzberger: If people didn't give her enough when she begged, Suzy would threaten them by saying she would conjure up Jackie. Then everybody'd be glad to give, once Jackie destroyed their crops with weather sorcery.—Fleis and Kitzberger are being transferred here. (*looks at the COMMISSIONER, picks up a new report*)—Report from Berchtesgaden: (*reads*) In spite of renewed search parties and inquiries, Jackie hasn't been caught. According to inquiries, he's holed up primarily around Hallein, Dürrnberg and in that area.

COMMISSIONER: Naturally! Their hands are clean!

SCRIBE (*glances at a new report*): Report from the Electoral Councilor in Munich. (*reads*) To prevent a major disaster, they have sent a general order to all officials in the country to keep a close watch out for the scoundrel, Jackie the Sorcerer, so that they can eventually bring him to justice. If he is brought in alive, there is a reward of 500 gold pieces, if dead, then only 100 ducats. They have made the neighborly proposal that an experienced man who is familiar with Jackie's description and personality be assigned from Salzburg to Munich, all expenses paid, and from there be sent out on a secret manhunt with two or three equally experienced officers. (*looks up*)

COMMISSIONER: We accept their offer! Send the huntsman from Liefering! He knows Jackie inside-out, does he not?

SCRIBE: Just a minute! Just a minute! (*searches frantically*) Where did I put that . . . ? (*finds a document, glances at it*) We can't do that! In the meantime the huntsman from Liefering has become a suspect himself!

COMMISSIONER: Then someone else!

SCRIBE: Wait a minute! (*searches, finds what he's looking for*) Simon Schönperger, previously fought in the army here! He has volunteered, since he knows Jackie and would like to take part in a manhunt—that is, if we'll pay his expenses and a modest salary! He was interrogated and found to be reliable!

COMMISSIONER: Good! Take him!—And raise the reward! Alive, 900 gold pieces; dead, 750!

SCRIBE (*making a note*) . . . dead, 750!

COMMISSIONER: Add the following: according to testimony from several miscreants, Jackie cannot make himself invisible between eleven and twelve o'clock and at those times when church bells are rung for the Angelus; therefore those are the best times to catch him.—In case the search drags on into winter: when the ground is frozen, Jackie cannot walk on it, and so this would also be a better time to catch him!

(*The SCRIBE writes furiously. The door to the torture chamber opens, the TWO HENCHMEN drag the unconscious DOFFER out. The EXECUTIONER, wearing a blood-stained apron, follows. DOFFER still has the gag in his mouth, blood is running down the inside of his legs. The HENCHMEN lay him down before the COMMISSIONER who retreats behind his desk, since it offers him protection.)*

COMMISSIONER: Unconscious?

EXECUTIONER: Or else the devil put him to sleep!

COMMISSIONER: Remove the gag! He could choke to death!

(The FIRST HENCHMAN removes the gag from DOFFER'S mouth, puts it in his pocket.)

COMMISSIONER: Holy water!

(The EXECUTIONER goes over to the basin with holy water, picks up the aspergillum, walks over to DOFFER, sprinkles water in his face. The TWO HENCHMEN sit back down. DOFFER wakes up, the EXECUTIONER returns the aspergillum to the basin, observes DOFFER. DOFFER props himself up, collapses, reaches down between his legs with a groan, looks at his hands; they are bloody, because his black shirt is saturated with blood. DOFFER licks the blood off his hands.)

COMMISSIONER *(to the EXECUTIONER)*: Well?

EXECUTIONER *(approaches the COMMISSIONER'S desk)*: He just talks gibberish!—I can't figure him out!—You're the judge!

COMMISSIONER: Even the judge has his limitations! *(to DOFFER)* How old are you, Doffer?

DOFFER *(moaning)*: A hundred! A hundred! Oh, Executioner, you really do good work!

EXECUTIONER: I hope so!

COMMISSIONER: Will you tell us the names of your accomplices, Doffer?

DOFFER: Oh, yes! Oh, yes! Glad to! Glad to!

COMMISSIONER: Not the French ones!

DOFFER: No, not the French ones!

COMMISSIONER: Well? What are their names?

DOFFER: I've forgotten their names, Sir, but I know their titles!

COMMISSIONER: Go ahead! What are their titles?

DOFFER: The Holy Roman Emperor in Vienna, the Holy Father in Rome! They, Sir, are the most God-awful accomplices!

(*The EXECUTIONER yanks DOFFER up by his shoulders.*)

EXECUTIONER: I'll hang him on the rack! I'll burn out his armpits!

COMMISSIONER: Let us not get carried away, Executioner! We have time!—Get him out of here!

(*Enraged, the EXECUTIONER drops DOFFER so that he plops on the floor. The TWO HENCHMEN approach, seize him, drag him over to the trapdoor. The FIRST HENCHMAN opens the trapdoor, the SECOND HENCHMAN shoves DOFFER down through it, the FIRST HENCHMAN closes the trapdoor.*)

(*Blackout*)

12. The office

(*The COMMISSIONER and the SCRIBE as in the previous scene. The EXECUTIONER, still wearing his bloody apron, is sitting on the bench with his TWO HENCHMEN.*)

The door to the torture chamber is open. In a black shirt but without chains, MAGDALENA PICHLER, alias "Raggedy Leni" (age 17) stands before the COMMISSIONER. She is looking with horror at her swollen and bloody forearms. She has endured the torture of lacing; her skin is red-blue and burst in several places where the laces were tightened.)

MAGDALENA *(to the COMMISSIONER)*: I told you all I know!

COMMISSIONER: Oh, no, Magdalena Pichler, you have not told me all you know, not by any means. We both know that, do we not? *(after a while)* You have two children?

MAGDALENA: No! I only have one!

COMMISSIONER: In Gastein they said you had two? At least you *had* two!

MAGDALENA: I only have one! I ought to know!

COMMISSIONER: And how old is your child?

MAGDALENA: Almost two!

COMMISSIONER: Is that so? That means that you had a child when you were only fifteen?

MAGDALENA: Yes, I was fifteen!

COMMISSIONER: And Andree Mayer, called the "City Reject," he is the father?

MAGDALENA: I guess!

COMMISSIONER: You are not sure?

MAGDALENA: Sir, it's easy to pick up a kid when you're on the road!

COMMISSIONER: Where is the child?

MAGDALENA: In Gastein. With relatives.—At first, the officer wanted to arrest the baby too! Can you imagine that? A two-year-old baby! (*screams*) What crime can a two-year-old baby commit?

COMMISSIONER (*calmly*): You do not need to yell at me, Pichler. We should not underestimate children. I have already heard a great deal from children.

MAGDALENA: From your children, Judge?

COMMISSIONER (*leaps to his feet, yells at her*): My children are innocent angels, you despicable slut! (*Embarrassed that he lost his temper, he sits back down, glances at his papers, regains his composure.*) They call you "Raggedy Leni"?

MAGDALENA: Yes.

COMMISSIONER: Why?

MAGDALENA: I buy colorful cloth from the gypsies! (*looks at him*) I like to look pretty!

COMMISSIONER: You think gypsy rags make you look pretty?

MAGDALENA: Oh, I'm pretty without them, Sir! Just the way God made me! Can't you see that for yourself?

COMMISSIONER: I am sorry. I suppose I am not able to appreciate your beauty.

MAGDALENA: Your wife probably does all her shopping at Kaltenhauser's, doesn't she? They have the prettiest red cloth in all of Salzburg! I'd like some of that myself! I just don't have enough guilders!

COMMISSIONER (*loudly*): My wife would never buy red cloth! We would not have the color red in our house!

MAGDALENA: What a shame! I guess you just have to get your red somewhere else?

COMMISSIONER (*stunned at first, he then screams*):

What do you think this is, some sort of private conversation? How dare you! A filthy whore like you does not have the right to a private conversation with me! Do you understand?!

(*MAGDALENA smiles.*)

COMMISSIONER (*calmly, coldly*): Where is your second child, Pichler?

(*MAGDALENA turns around, pulls up the back of her shirt, exposes her bare buttocks to the COMMISSIONER'S face.*)

(*Blackout*)

13. The office

(*The office is empty. A small coffee pot and a cup are sitting on the COMMISSIONER'S desk. The door to the torture chamber is open. The audience can see the lower part of the rack, the EXECUTIONER is turning the four hand levers on the pulleys that wind up the rope. We can hear MAGDA-LENA'S cries of pain: she is being stretched. Her feet are visible, hanging through a rope tied to a wooden pulley, so that the FIRST HENCHMAN who is standing below the rack has to push up MAGDALENA'S feet so that she can't stand and support herself on the rungs of the rack. The SECOND HENCHMAN, the COMMISSIONER, and the SCRIBE are out of view.*)

VOICE OF THE COMMISSIONER: Enough!

(*The EXECUTIONER stops tightening the ropes, but holds the levers tightly, so that the tension does not slacken. The COMMISSIONER is now visible, as he steps up to the rack.*)

COMMISSIONER: Your second child, Pichler!

MAGDALENA: Let me go! Please, let me go!

COMMISSIONER: You sacrificed it to the devil! Admit it!

MAGDALENA: No!

COMMISSIONER (*calls offstage*): Come over here!

(*VEIT appears, approaches the rack.*)

COMMISSIONER: Tell her!

VEIT (*to MAGDALENA*): You sacrificed it to the devil! At the witches' orgy!

MAGDALENA: No!

VEIT: Yes, you did! On the Untersberg Mountain! Last May!

MAGDALENA: No!

(*The COMMISSIONER gives a sign to the EXECU-TIONER who tightens the ropes. MAGDALENA'S feet are stretched further down.*)

MAGDALENA (*screaming*): No! No! (*Her shoulders are pulled from their joints, she screams in pain.*)

COMMISSIONER: Do you admit it?

MAGDALENA: Yes! Yes! Yes!

(*The COMMISSIONER gives a sign to the EXECU-TIONER who pauses.*)

COMMISSIONER: Everything? Will you admit everything?

MAGDALENA: Yes! Everything! Everything!

COMMISSIONER: Untie her. Take her out.

(*The COMMISSIONER emerges from the torture chamber, sits down at his desk. The SCRIBE appears with his writ-*

*ing utensils and paper, also comes out and sits down at his
desk; he is shattered by what he has just seen. VEIT looks
at MAGDALENA, then comes out too, stopping by the door.
Inside, MAGDALENA is being untied, she disappears from
view. The COMMISSIONER pours himself a cup of coffee,
takes a sip, looks at VEIT, points to a spot in front of his
desk. VEIT comes over, stops at a respectful distance. The
TWO HENCHMEN lead MAGDALENA out. She is wearing the black shirt once again, her arms are hanging down,
dislocated. The EXECUTIONER also comes out of the
chamber, closes the door behind him, sits down on the
bench. The HENCHMEN lead MAGDALENA before the
COMMISSIONER, then they too sit down on the bench.
MAGDALENA can barely stand up.)*

COMMISSIONER (*to the EXECUTIONER*): Put her
    arms back in their sockets! What is wrong with
    you?!

*(The EXECUTIONER stands up, looks at the FIRST
HENCHMAN who also gets up. They walk over to the girl.
The FIRST HENCHMAN holds MAGDALENA tightly, the
EXECUTIONER pulls on her arms until they are back in
joint. MAGDALENA cries out. The EXECUTIONER and
the FIRST HENCHMAN sit back down.)*

COMMISSIONER (*to MAGDALENA*): How do you get to
    a witches' orgy?

*(MAGDALENA does not answer immediately, so VEIT an-
swers for her.)*

VEIT: She flies! On a roofing shingle! Or on a straw!

COMMISSIONER: I was asking you, Pichler!

MAGDALENA: Yes, I fly! But not on a straw! Sir, the devil
    comes to get me personally—That's how badly he
    wants me!

VEIT: Yeah, that's right! He came to get her!

COMMISSIONER: In what form?

MAGDALENA: As a goat, a black goat! What else?

COMMISSIONER: And your boyfriend? The City Reject?

MAGDALENA: Why would I need the City Reject, when I can have the devil?!

(The COMMISSIONER looks at VEIT.)

VEIT: Of course the City Reject was there!

MAGDALENA: Shut your mouth, kid! I don't need you to tell me the answers!

VEIT *(to the COMMISSIONER)*: He was there! He was at the orgy! I saw him!

COMMISSIONER *(to MAGDALENA)*: So, you flew up to the Untersberg Mountain . . . and everyone was there?

MAGDALENA: Yes! All of them! Even the superintendent of the Salzburg cathedral!

VEIT: No! That's not true!

COMMISSIONER *(to the SCRIBE)*: Do not enter that in the transcript! *(calmly, to MAGDALENA)* I am warning you, Pichler. If you continue to give false statements, then you will be back on the rack in no time.—So, they were all there, the beggars and the beggar women! The country's entire un-Christian scum! Tell me their names!

MAGDALENA: You know, Sir, I wasn't too interested in who else was there! *(smiling)* I was the devil's favorite mistress that night!

VEIT: They were all there! All the ones who are down there in the cell! And a whole lot more, too!

COMMISSIONER *(to MAGDALENA)*: Jackie too, eh?

MAGDALENA: Of course, Jackie too! He's also the devil's favorite lover! As you know, the devil doesn't put up with wallflowers!

COMMISSIONER: Tell us more, Magdalena. What happened?

MAGDALENA: Oh, we greeted the devil the way he likes it . . .

COMMISSIONER: You kissed his behind!

MAGDALENA: Oh, yes, and that's not all! And we licked him there too, with our tongues!

VEIT: Not me!

MAGDALENA (*looks at VEIT, grinning*): You even ate his shit, Crooked Veit!

VEIT: Not true at all!

COMMISSIONER: Go on. Go on, Pichler.

MAGDALENA: I licked his ass, and the rest of him too! You should try that sometime, Sir! Try it on your wife! Or—if she's too prudish—then go to a whorehouse!

(*The COMMISSIONER is shocked. Then he slowly stands up, looks at MAGDALENA, goes over to the basin with holy water, picks up the aspergillum, goes back over to MAGDALENA, looks at her. He suddenly starts beating her with the aspergillum. MAGDALENA cowers, covers her head with her arms to protect herself; she does not take it seriously, grins.*)

EXECUTIONER (*smugly*): Why, Dr. Zillner! Do you want to trade places? Do you want me to sit behind the desk in your chair?

(*The COMMISSIONER stops beating MAGDALENA, looks at the EXECUTIONER, puts back the aspergillum.*

*The EXECUTIONER and his TWO HENCHMEN grin at
each other. The COMMISSIONER straightens his wig and
his robe, sits back down.*)

COMMISSIONER (*softly*): May God help you, Pichler!

MAGDALENA: God? God never helped me! I can do without your God!

COMMISSIONER: Go on! Tell us more!

MAGDALENA: Can you really stand to hear any more? It seems to me, it gets you too upset!

COMMISSIONER (*softly*): Talk, or I will have you tortured beyond all legal and humane limits!

MAGDALENA: Whatever you say, Sir!—Well, everything worked out the way it was supposed to! Now we come to the partner swapping!

VEIT: The meal! You forgot the meal!

MAGDALENA (*smiling*): You've always got just one thing on your mind, Crooked Veit, and that's eating . . .

VEIT (*to the COMMISSIONER*): Well, sure! A huge banquet! Meat, sausage and grapes and . . . and . . . (*he can't think of anything else*) . . . donuts and pastries and everything, just everything! Only no bread and no salt! The devil doesn't like 'em!—And then everybody dances! A wild dance, with everybody dancing with each other!

MAGDALENA: Yes, that's right, everybody dances! Everybody dances! It's wonderful! (*begins to dance*) Wonderful! You get so dizzy! So dizzy! But nobody falls down! Everybody floats on air!

VEIT: Fiddlers and bagpipers and zither pluckers and trumpeters and drummers—all of 'em are little devils with horns! They go wild! Just wild!

MAGDALENA: Yes!—And suddenly the lights go out—
and everybody, everybody falls on the ground and
indulges in carnal lust! (*stops dancing in front of
the COMMISSIONER*) A mad passion, Sir! You
probably can't imagine how mad! Or can you?

COMMISSIONER (*gets up*): I do not want to imagine
your orgy, but I know all about it! Dionysus with
his sister, his sister with their father, the father
with Dionysus, Jackie with the father, Blind Bat
Michael with his brother, Veit here with a witch,
the devil with him, from the front and the rear,
doggy-style—I know everything, it is all here in
the records! (*sits down*) An abyss! The worst abyss
imaginable! Hell on earth!

MAGDALENA: But you don't know the whole story, Sir!

COMMISSIONER: What could be worse?

MAGDALENA: The host! I brought along a Holy Communion wafer!

COMMISSIONER: What?

MAGDALENA: In my rearend!

COMMISSIONER (*in a stunned monotone*): What?

MAGDALENA: In my rearend! I brought along a Holy
Communion wafer in my rearend!

COMMISSIONER: And what did you do with it?

MAGDALENA: Well, what else? It stayed where it was! It
was just pushed around a bit! By the devil!

(*The COMMISSIONER is speechless, horrified.*)

MAGDALENA: But that's not all, Sir! You were asking
about what happened to my second child. Well, I'll
tell you! My baby was there, at the witches' orgy!
And when the devil was enjoying me, at the peak

of our carnal pleasure, I shoved the baby under my body! And it suffocated!—Now you know all there is to know, Judge!

(*Suddenly the COMMISSIONER lets out a roar.*)

(*Blackout*)

14. The cell

(*Filled to the brim with prisoners. MAGDALENA (17), back in chains, is sleeping beside ANDREE (18) who is sitting and playing a shell game. VEIT (14), DIONYSUS (12), LISL (8), and JOHNNY (6) are watching. BLINDBAT MICHAEL (10) is sitting, leaning back-to-back with JOHNNY, with his head cocked, listening. DOFFER (13) is lying off to one side, very sick, staring into space with a glassy look. ANDREE has woven three cups out of straw and rolled a little pea-shaped ball out of straw and mud. He pushes the straw aside, lays the "pea" on the ground, places one cup over it, places the other two cups on either side, and then moves all three cups back and forth a few times.*)

ANDREE: Where is it?

DIONYSUS (*points*): There!

(*ANDREE lifts the cup, the pea is lying under it.*)

ANDREE: You've got it!—What'll we bet that next time you won't be able to find the pea?

DIONYSUS: Bet you our evening soup that I can find it!

(*ANDREE moves the cups back and forth several times.*)

ANDREE: Where is it?

DIONYSUS (*pointing to a cup*): There!

(*ANDREE lifts the cup, the pea isn't there.*)

ANDREE: You lose! (*picks up another cup*) There it is!

DIONYSUS: Nah! I could've sworn it was under the other one! (*points to the first cup*)

ANDREE (*looks at VEIT*): Want to try your luck, Veit?

VEIT (*knows ANDREE'S trick*): Find some other sucker!

(*ANDREE takes VEIT'S hand and slaps VEIT's face with it, presses VEIT'S cheeks together.*)

ANDREE: What did you say?

JOHNNY (*tugs at the hem of his shirt, trying to pull it down*): Leave me alone! Leave me alone!

MICHAEL: Johnny! What's wrong?

(*ANDREE lets VEIT go, JOHNNY gets up, so that MI-CHAEL falls over, since he had been leaning against JOHNNY'S back. JOHNNY grasps the hem of his shirt and pulls it down.*)

JOHNNY: They make fun of me when you do that! Cut it out!—Michael, help me!

MICHAEL (*sits up, desparately cranes his neck to find out what's going on*): What are you doin' to Johnny? Let him alone! Who did that?

(*ANDREE crawls over to JOHNNY, knocks him to the ground.*)

ANDREE: Shut your goddamn mouth!

MICHAEL: Johnny! Is it the City Reject?

ANDREE: Shut your trap, you blind jerk!

(*ANDREE crawls back over to MAGDALENA, sits down beside her. MICHAEL crawls around, looking for*

JOHNNY, finds him, feels his face, pulls JOHNNY under his wing.)

MICHAEL: Johnny! Johnny!

(JOHNNY regains consciousness, hugs MICHAEL.)

MICHAEL: Johnny! What's wrong?

JOHNNY *(sobbing)*: He's always pulling up my shirt!

MICHAEL: Who? The City Reject?

ANDREE: You ass, I've got somebody else here to play that game with! *(lays his hand on MAGDALENA'S buttocks.)*

MICHAEL: Then who was it, Johnny?

JOHNNY: Beelzebub!

LISL: Pray a lot, Johnny! Pray a lot!

JOHNNY *(kneels down, folds his hands)*: Hail, Mary, full of grace, the Lord is with you . . .

(The small door upstage opens, the EXECUTIONER crawls in; he is not wearing his white apron.)

EXECUTIONER: Dionysus Feldner and his sister! Get over here!

(DIONYSUS and LISL crawl toward the EXECUTIONER who notices the sick DOFFER in the meantime.)

EXECUTIONER: Well, Doffer? Guess I shut your big mouth!

DOFFER: It's just resting! It's just resting! I'll open it again on Judgment Day!

(LISL and DIONYSUS have reached the EXECU-TIONER.)

EXECUTIONER: Today I'm going to burn your father at

the stake! Lisl is supposed to watch! On orders from the Counselor!

(*DIONYSYS and LISL are stunned.*)

DIONYSUS: What are you going to do?

EXECUTIONER: Your father! He confessed to every-thing, the verdict is in. I'm going to burn him!

LISL (*sobbing*): No, don't burn him! Don't burn him!

DIONYSUS: I take back everything I said! I take it all back!

EXECUTIONER: You take back what?

DIONYSUS: Everything I said! All those things he was supposed to have done!

EXECUTIONER: You're not taking anything back! Got it? That's all I need! It's all down on paper! You under-stand? It's all on paper, everything you said about him! For all eternity! It's permanent! Written in stone!

ANDREE: Hey, you, Joe Hangman!

(*The EXECUTIONER looks in astonishment at AN-DREE.*)

ANDREE: Do we really look that stupid, hey?

EXECUTIONER: Who in hell are you?

ANDREE: Andree Mayer, the City Reject! You cut off all my hair, don't you remember?

EXECUTIONER: What did you just say?

ANDREE: I said, did you really think we looked that stu-pid!

EXECUTIONER: I'll hang you right up on the hoist with 110-pound weights, if you get smart with me!

ANDREE: I know our rights, Executioner! Of course, anybody can take back an accusation!

DIONYSUS: Yes, please! Please, Mr. Executioner!

EXECUTIONER: He confessed, he's made his peace with God, and so he's going to burn! (*to LISL*) And you're going to watch! So that you can see what happens when you get involved with the devil!

(*The EXECUTIONER grabs LISL, drags her along with him toward the little door.*)

LISL: Dionys! Dionys!

(*DIONYSUS crawls after LISL, reaches out for her, but the EXECUTIONER shoves him away and disappears with LISL through the door. DIONYSUS tries to follow, but the FIRST HENCHMAN appears, shoves him back into the cell, closes and bolts the door.*)

DIONYSUS: Lisl!—Daddy! Daddy! (*beats his fists against the door*) I want to see my daddy! Please! Please! (*collapses at the door, reaches into his mouth and tries to yank out his tongue.*)

(*Blackout*)

15. The office

(*The COMMISSIONER and the SCRIBE are sitting at their desks, the TWO HENCHMEN on the bench. ANDREE MAYER, alias "City Reject" (age 18) stands in chains before the COMMISSIONER, his shirt pulled down over his shoulders. The EXECUTIONER is standing behind him, wearing a freshly washed apron and holding the needle in his hand. Beside ANDREE, in chains, stands*

MAGDALENA. The COMMISSIONER looks at ANDREE, looks down at papers on his desk.)

COMMISSIONER: Andree Mayer, called the City Reject, eighteen years old, from Klausen in Tyrol? (*looks up at ANDREE*)

ANDREE: Yes!

(*The COMMISSIONER looks at the EXECUTIONER who, quick as a flash, sticks the needle into a mole on ANDREE'S back. ANDREE scarcely reacts. The COMMISSIONER looks at the SCRIBE who makes a note. The EXECUTIONER wipes off the needle on his apron and sits down. ANDREE pulls his shirt back up.*)

COMMISSIONER: I would say that you have had a stormy life, Andree.

ANDREE: Yes, I've been around a bit, seen a few things!

COMMISSIONER: What all have you done?

ANDREE: Traveled a lot!

COMMISSIONER: Have you ever had a job?

ANDREE: Lots of them!

COMMISSIONER: Really! Tell us. Start at the beginning.

ANDREE: When I was around eleven, I went with my mother over the Brenner Pass to Innsbruck. Then my mother died in the infirmary in Haller, and I was all alone.

COMMISSIONER: Your father?

ANDREE: Hanged himself. Way before my mother died.

COMMISSIONER: Brothers or sisters?

ANDREE: Six or seven. No idea where they are. One brother was shot dead in Friaul. He was a mercenary.

COMMISSIONER: And then?

ANDREE: In Innsbruck I got to know the son of a noble family! He got me a job as a beater, at the royal hunting parties!—Later on I traveled with soldiers. Went with the Rist expedition to Germany. Spent a year in Kaiserslautern. Went to Salzburg. Then I drove cattle—thousands of 'em—to Germany for Mr. Lindl, the royal district supervisor in Sondermoning. Then I got stuck in Munich. And had to . . .

COMMISSIONER: You stole cattle! That is why you got fired.

ANDREE (*taken aback for a second, then collects himself*): None of that's true! It's all lies!

COMMISSIONER: That is not at issue here. Continue. Munich . . .

ANDREE: I was a gold-diver!

COMMISSIONER: A what?

ANDREE: Gold-diver! (*grins*) King of the night!

COMMISSIONER: What is that supposed to mean?

ANDREE: I was a cleaning man in the public lavatories!

COMMISSIONER: You still smell like it! (*to the EXECU-TIONER*) Why does he smell so badly? I thought I told you to . . .

EXECUTIONER: He was washed! (*looks at his TWO HENCHMEN*) You did wash him, didn't you?

(*The FIRST HENCHMAN nods.*)

COMMISSIONER: Apparently the cells have fallen into a deplorable state again!

(The EXECUTIONER gets up, goes over to ANDREE, smells him.)

EXECUTIONER: He smells like piss! *(to ANDREE)* Why do you smell so much like piss?

ANDREE: 'Cause I washed with it!

COMMISSIONER: What? Why would you do that?

ANDREE: It's the scabies, Sir! It burns so bad!

COMMISSIONER: We will find out if you did it because of the scabies or not.

EXECUTIONER: There's got to be some satanic reason behind it!

COMMISSIONER: After the hearing, wash him with holy water. His whole body.

EXECUTIONER: Yes, Sir! *(sits back down)*

COMMISSIONER *(to ANDREE)*: Then you left Munich and returned to Salzburg . . . When was that?

ANDREE: Three years ago.

COMMISSIONER: They call you the City Reject? Why?

ANDREE: Because the watchmen threw me out of the city lots of times!

COMMISSIONER: And what do you do when they throw you out of a city?

ANDREE: What am I supposed to do?

COMMISSIONER: They toss you out, and you sneak right back in. Am I right?

(ANDREE grins. The COMMISSIONER looks at the SCRIBE who frantically riffles through his papers, finds the one he has been searching for, glances at it.)

SCRIBE: Incarcerated in Salzburg six times already!

Taunting the watchmen at the city gates! Harrassing and molesting passersby! Two decent citizens were attacked because they refused to give him alms; various fights. And the theft of four guilders!

COMMISSIONER (*to ANDREE*): What do you have to say to that?

(*ANDREE shrugs his shoulders.*)

COMMISSIONER: You and your companions hang around the goat stalls? East of the New Gate?

ANDREE: Among other places. It's warm there in the winter.

COMMISSIONER: That is where you met Jackie, too, is it not?

(*ANDREE doesn't answer.*)

COMMISSIONER: Is it not?

ANDREE: No! I don't know the guy! Who is he?

COMMISSIONER: Do not play dumb with me, Andree! Your whore here, Magdalena Pichler, she has admitted it! You two had a good long talk with Jackie at the goat stalls!

(*ANDREE does not get angry at MAGDALENA. He knows how she has suffered.*)

ANDREE: That can't be right, Sir! She must be mistaken! I wasn't there!

(*The COMMISSIONER looks at MAGDALENA.*)

MAGDALENA: At least it seemed like he was there!

COMMISSIONER: Admit it, Andree! Even Veit Lindner saw you there with Jackie!

ANDREE: He lies like a rug!—(*loudly*) How can I admit

something if it's not true? You want the truth, don't you?

(*The COMMISSIONER gazes at ANDREE for a while in silence.*)

COMMISSIONER: We have ways to get at the truth, Andree.

ANDREE: I believe it!

COMMISSIONER: So, you will not admit that, with Jackie's help, you made a pact with the devil?

ANDREE: 'Course not!

COMMISSIONER: But Magdalena has already told us everything!

ANDREE: But I'm not Magdalena!

COMMISSIONER: She has implicated you in serious crimes!

ANDREE: I don't understand that word, Sir!

COMMISSIONER: She has accused you!

ANDREE: That's her business!

COMMISSIONER: So, you deny it?

ANDREE: No, just the opposite! I'm telling the truth!

COMMISSIONER (*to the EXECUTIONER*): Take him into the torture chamber! First, put him on the hoist. For the amount of time it takes to say the Lord's Prayer three times! Then hang weights on him! First, 42 pounds, and if that still doesn't work, 110 pounds!

(*The EXECUTIONER and the TWO HENCHMEN rise. The HENCHMEN approach, grab ANDREE and drag him into the torture chamber. The EXECUTIONER follows.*

The SCRIBE rises and picks up his writing utensils and paper.)

COMMISSIONER (*calls to the EXECUTIONER*): Make sure Pichler watches!

(*The EXECUTIONER turns around, motions to MAGDA-LENA, she hesitates.*)

COMMISSIONER (*to the SCRIBE*): Stay here, Mr. Deputy.

SCRIBE: But I've got to . . .

COMMISSIONER: The executioner will give us a full report. The main thing is that the boy's resistence is broken.—Rest yourself.

SCRIBE: Thank you, Mr. Counselor! I need it!

(*During this last exchange, the EXECUTIONER impatiently gestures a second time to MAGDALENA, she approaches him. The EXECUTIONER shoves her into the torture chamber, follows her inside, closes the door. The SCRIBE massages his writing hand, does finger exercises, looks over to the door of the torture chamber.*)

SCRIBE: A tough nut!

COMMISSIONER: We will soften him up.—Anything on Jackie?

SCRIBE: Not a thing! Lots of reports, but it's all so vague! He's been seen everywhere! In Bavaria, in Tyrol, in Carinthia, in Styria, here in Salzburg! Nobody can catch him!

(*Silence for a while. From inside the torture chamber we can hear the sound of the hoist creaking, but not a sound out of ANDREE the entire time.*)

SCRIBE (*after a while*): Mr. Counselor!

COMMISSIONER: Yes?

SCRIBE: I'm sorry, I don't mean to be impudent, but I have a request!

COMMISSIONER: What is it?

SCRIBE: Please don't misunderstand me! I enjoy my work, and I don't consider myself underpaid! But—I just can't take it anymore! I'm finished, Mr. Counselor! Look how my hands shake! (*shows the COMMISSIONER*) I've never had to write so much in my entire life! We've already conducted eighty-five interrogations! Day after day after day! And there's no end in sight! Everything has to be written twice! After all, I've got to make a clean copy of everything! And when do I do it? At night! Every night I sit here and copy the records! I barely get two hours sleep! In there (*nods toward the torture chamber*) I lie down on the rack. I just can't take it anymore, Mr. Counselor! I can't take it anymore! We need additional stenographic help!

COMMISSIONER: Unfortunately, we will not get any, Mr. Finsterwalder. I put in a request for assistance a long time ago. The Court Treasury has already complained about the cost of these procedings. It was not anticipated in the budget. Well, of course not! Who sets aside money in the budget to combat the devil?!

The VOICE of MAGDALENA (*screams from within the torture chamber*) No!

SCRIBE (*hearing her voice, in desperation*) I just can't take anymore!

COMMISSIONER: We must see it through, Mr. Finsterwalder! Do you think I enjoy this? I need you, Mr. Finsterwalder! What would I do without you?—Listen! I will request a special subsidy for you from the Prince himself! 150 guilders! How does that sound?

SCRIBE: I don't care about the money, Dr. Zillner!

COMMISSIONER: I know, Mr. Finsterwalder! It was only meant as a temporary remedy.—When all this is over, we will take a nice long vacation! I promise!

(*Silence. The SCRIBE stares off into space. His incidentally notices a piece of paper, picks it up.*)

SCRIBE: The Executioner has handed in his bill for old man Feldner! Seems a bit too high to me!

COMMISSIONER: How much?

SCRIBE (*reads*): One bonfire with accessories: two guilders, thirty farthings. Fee for reducing one person to ashes: one guilder. Ash removal: fifty farthings. Honorarium for the skinner's wagon: three guilders. For a total of seven guilders and ten farthings.

COMMISSIONER: We must speak to him about that!— (*listens*) It's so quiet!

(*After a while the door to the torture chamber opens, the EXECUTIONER comes out, a few small bloodstains on his white apron. ANDREE is not visible, but we can see MAGDALENA sitting on the floor with her hands over her face.*)

COMMISSIONER: Did you gag him?

EXECUTIONER: He didn't need a gag! Didn't make a peep! I've never seen anything like it in my entire career!

COMMISSIONER: Did you wash him down with holy water?

EXECUTIONER: Yes, of course!

COMMISSIONER: Did you hang on 110 pounds?

EXECUTIONER: 110 pounds! His arms were yanked out of their sockets a long time ago!

COMMISSIONER: And he admits nothing?

EXECUTIONER: He won't say anything! He won't say one damn word!

COMMISSIONER: Well, all right, we will just have to escalate the punishment! Put on thumbscrews, and Spanish boots on both legs!

(*The EXECUTIONER nods, starts to return to the torture chamber.*)

COMMISSIONER: You have blood on your apron! Since when does a man bleed on the hoist?

EXECUTIONER: He had a nose bleed!—What do you care? Why don't you just leave the torture to me?!

COMMISSIONER: Do not get excited, Executioner! Calm down!—By the way, the Scribe just read me your bill! Could you please explain how you manage to spend more than two guilders for a bonfire?

EXECUTIONER (*momentarily stunned, than angrily*): Ninety carts of firewood, two carts of shavings, three carts of straw! And the pole in the middle!

COMMISSIONER: Ninety carts of firewood? It did not appear to be that many! Would you be putting a few carts aside? For the cold winter months?

EXECUTIONER (*beside himself*): Why, that's just . . . ! Are you accusing me . . . ?

COMMISSIONER: All right! All right! In my opinion, sixty carts would have been sufficient!

EXECUTIONER: Well, I don't work on a low burner! I

might as well try to set the people on fire with a piece of kindling!

COMMISSIONER: Just try to be less extravagant, for Heaven's sake! The same with the gunpowder! You hung a sack of gunpowder around Feldner's neck, so that parts of his head were blown into the audience! You almost hit me, too!

EXECUTIONER: Then you'll have to sit farther back, if you're afraid of getting your good suit dirty!— (*stretches*) The punishment must have force, Sir! Or else people don't get the point! I can still remember how the Executioner in Munich fixed Witch Gamperle. He cut off her breasts and tied them around her children's ears! Now that makes a point! That's got deep meaning, Sir!

COMMISSIONER: Now, would you please—

EXECUTIONER (*interrupts him*): And while we're talking about money: the cells have been crammed to overflowing for some time now, but the maintenance money still hasn't been increased! I've already spent four hundred guilders out of my own pocket to take care of the prisoners! If the Court Treasury doesn't reimburse my four hundred guilders in the next two days and grant me additional funds, then I'll let the prisoners starve to death! You understand?

COMMISSIONER: I beg your pardon, you will have to settle that with the Court Treasury yourself!

EXECUTIONER (*bellows*): They don't even answer!

COMMISSIONER: Sad to say, they are having financial problems, Executioner!

EXECUTIONER: That'd be easy to solve, in fact child's

play, Mr. Counselor! As Commissioner of Charity, you administer over seven thousand guilders a year! Why don't you just put the money in this trial? Then all your financial problems'd be over!

COMMISSIONER: Impossible, Executioner! These seven thousand guilders are donations from the citizens of Salzburg! Donations intended for distribution to the poor!

EXECUTIONER: Sure! To the beggars and riff-raff! To bums like the one in there! (*nods toward the torture chamber*)

COMMISSIONER: No, Executioner! Bums like that do not receive one red cent! Only our own beggars, only the sick, the crippled, and those who cannot work receive something!

EXECUTIONER: Oh, come on! Nobody ever checks on that!—Just toss 'em all in the same hole, pour pitch on 'em, and set 'em on fire! Then we're all finished!—That's the way you solve the beggar problem! That's the only way! You sure don't do it with an expensive trial like this!

COMMISSIONER: Mr. Executioner! Are you implying that the purpose of this trial is the extermination of beggars?

EXECUTIONER: What else could it be?

COMMISSIONER: Our job here is to combat a diabolical conspiracy! Do you not understand that?

EXECUTIONER: I understand more than you think, Mr. Commissioner!

SCRIBE: Now, that's enough, Executioner! If the Counselor is so polite that he won't tell you to shut up, then I will!

(The EXECUTIONER looks at the SCRIBE in astonishment.)

SCRIBE: Get back to your work, Executioner! Go! Go!

EXECUTIONER: Why, you . . . I'll squeeze your head so hard, your brains'll come out your ears!

COMMISSIONER *(stands up)*: Enough!

(The EXECUTIONER goes over to the door to the torture chamber, turns back.)

EXECUTIONER *(to the SCRIBE)*: From now on, you'll kindly address me as Master! I have a right to that title! Make a note of that, Scribe!

SCRIBE: Fine! Fine! And in the future you'll kindly address me as the High Court Deputy Tax Appraiser!

(The EXECUTIONER enters the torture chamber, slams the door shut. The SCRIBE looks at the COMMISSIONER, looks down at the bill on his desk.)

SCRIBE: I'm going to investigate this bill! Something's wrong here! Three guilders for the wagon! The skinner demands three guilders for driving the miscreants in his wagon to the execution site! What nerve!

COMMISSIONER: In the future, only approve one guilder!

SCRIBE: Obviously, the Executioner's in on this with him! One skinner scratches another skinner's back! As always!

(Silence for a while. From inside the torture chamber ANDREE'S scream can be heard. The door is ripped open, MAGDALENA tries to get out, but is pulled back inside by the SECOND HENCHMAN. The door is slammed shut. We can hear ANDREE moaning.)

SCRIBE: Doctor, I must admit that it's not just the stenography alone that gets me!—All these horrible confessions . . . ! Sometimes I'm afraid, Mr. Counselor! I'm afraid! At night when I sit here by candlelight and write, I see the devil lurking in every corner! (*momentary silence*) And I also have to admit that sometimes I feel sorry for the children. Not for him . . . (*nods toward the torture chamber*), but for the children!

COMMISSIONER: If you have compassion for these children, then you have compassion for God's enemy!

SCRIBE: I know it's wrong, but I just can't help it!

(*Extended silence*)

COMMISSIONER: Sometimes, when I come home late in the evening and look at my children while they are sleeping so peacefully, I think to myself: Has the devil already gotten inside them, too?

The VOICE of MAGDALENA (*screams*): Admit it! Please, just admit it!

(*The COMMISSIONER and the SCRIBE look over at the door. After a while the door opens, the EXECUTIONER comes out, sweating, with bloody hands and bloody apron. He wipes his hands off on his apron, looks at the COMMISSIONER helplessly. The FIRST HENCHMAN appears behind him in the doorway.*)

COMMISSIONER: Nothing?

EXECUTIONER: Nothing!

COMMISSIONER: I say, what is the matter with you, Master? Your skill usually never fails!

EXECUTIONER: That bitch! She must have some kind of protective powers!

COMMISSIONER: Then get her out of there!

(*The FIRST HENCHMAN goes back inside, drags out MAGDALENA.*)

MAGDALENA (*calling back inside*): Tell them! Please tell them! I die when you suffer like that!

(*The FIRST HENCHMAN opens the trapdoor, shoves MAGDALENA down, closes the trapdoor.*)

COMMISSIONER: Then there is only one option left: torture by fire! Burn under his armpits! And insert burning splints under his fingernails and toenails!

(*The EXECUTIONER nods, goes back into the torture chamber with the FIRST HENCHMAN, closes the door.*)

COMMISSIONER (*after a while*): Maleficium taciturnitatis—the evil power of silence!

(*After a while, ANDREE begins to scream in pain from within the torture chamber.*)

VOICE OF THE EXECUTIONER (*yells*): Talk! Talk! Talk! Open your mouth! Talk! You bastard! You bastard!

(*ANDREE'S screaming suddenly stops. For a while there is silence. Then the door opens, the EXECUTIONER emerges with a burning torch in his hand. In the background, the audience can see the lower half of ANDREE'S legs on the rack, can see his bloody, squashed calves and the burned toes. On his toenails we can still see the smoldering wooden splints.*)

EXECUTIONER: I'm at the end of my rope! I burned his fingers and toes and roasted the skin under his arms down to the ribs! Now he's unconscious!

COMMISSIONER (*smiling*): That has never happened to you before, eh, Executioner?

EXECUTIONER: No, that's never happened to me before!

(*The SCRIBE grins.*)

EXECUTIONER (*yells*): The Pope himself would confess to being a sorcerer, if I ever got him in my torture chamber! (*to the SCRIBE*) You, too! (*to the COM-MISSIONER*) And you, too, Dr. Zillner!—How am I supposed to fight the power of the devil?

COMMISSIONER (*after a while*): Perhaps he is innocent, Executioner?

EXECUTIONER: Him? Innocent? If he's innocent, then I'll burn myself at the stake!

COMMISSIONER (*looks at the SCRIBE*): This inquiry is concluded! It took place extra and in loco torturae, the miscreant denied everything, although he was subjected to the horrible screams of several other accomplices and although several degrees of torture were employed. I thank you, gentlemen! (*gets up, takes off his wig*)

(*Blackout*)

16. The office

(*The COMMISSIONER and the SCRIBE at their desks, the EXECUTIONER—without his apron—and the TWO HENCHMEN are sitting on the bench. Standing in front of the COMMISSIONER, in black shirts and chains, are DIONYSUS (12) and his sister LISL (8).*)

COMMISSIONER (*to DIONYSUS*): The advocate for the poor assigned to you has handed in a defense plea to the Archbishop and to the Prince on your behalf.

When you have attained the age of twelve years, he will plead for mercy. I support his plea! And the Archbishop, in fact, has shown mercy! Therefore, you will not be burned at the stake alive, but rather you will be beheaded first, and then your corpse will be consigned to the flames! That is your judgment, Dionysus Feldner!

(*DIONYSUS is dumb-struck and shows no reaction, he just stares at the COMMISSIONER. The SCRIBE feels sorry for DIONYSUS.*)

COMMISSIONER (*to LISL*): You, Lisl, are also guilty of a conspiracy with the devil, but since you are only eight years old (*He smiles.*), we feel that you are too young to die! Therefore I have suggested to the High Court that you be provided with spiritual guidance, and after a sufficient time, when your soul has been purged, that you be employed in the home of a good Christian couple! This office will bear all related expenses!—Say goodbye to your brother! You will not see him again in this world!

(*LISL looks at her brother. She has not understood the sentence yet either. DIONYSUS suddenly suffers an epileptic fit and crashes to the floor.*)

(*Blackout*)

17. The cell

(*Filled to the rafters with prisoners. VEIT, DOFFER—who still cannot sit—, blind MICHAEL, his brother JOHNNY, MAGDALENA, and ANDREE. ANDREE'S fingertips and toes are burned, both thumbs and his calves are crushed,*) *his head is resting in MAGDALENA'S lap; he has a fever and stares blankly off into space. The door opens. The EX-ECUTIONER—without his apron—crawls in; he is furious. In the doorway we see the FIRST HENCHMAN; grinning at the EXECUTIONER'S plight, he closes the door behind him. The EXECUTIONER looks around, sits down. ALL but MICHAEL and ANDREE turns their heads to watch him.)*

MICHAEL: Another one?

MAGDALENA: Yeah! Another one! But this time it's somebody special!

MICHAEL: Well, who?

MAGDALENA: It's the butcher! The famous man who skins human beings!

MICHAEL: Who?

VEIT: Now the world's upside down!

MICHAEL *(reaches out for JOHNNY)*: Johnny, tell me who it is!

JOHNNY: It's the Executioner!

MICHAEL: The Executioner! Is he here to get us?

MAGDALENA: I don't think so! It doesn't look like he's here on his own free will!— To what do we owe this honor, Master!

(The EXECUTIONER does not answer.)

MAGDALENA: Did they accuse you of sorcery too? I wouldn't be surprised!—I guess you don't want to talk to us, huh?

(The EXECUTIONER does not answer. Suddenly MAG-DALENA jumps him, scratches his face, punches him, pulls his hair, kicks him in the groin with her knee, throws her chain around his neck and strangles him. The EXECU-

TIONER is so surprised by her attack that he cannot properly defend himself for some time. But then he grabs MAGDALENA, hits her with his fists, pulls the chain free from around his neck, strikes MAGDALENA again and again. After she falls to the ground unconscious, he kicks her limp body several more times.)

EXECUTIONER: Dirty whore! You miserable witch!

(He kicks MAGDALENA one last time, crawls away from her, and then props himself up against the wall, exhausted. During the fight, ANDREE did not move a muscle, DOFFER sat upright and watched with excitement, MICHAEL listened closely. DOFFER crawls over to MAGDALENA and shakes her.)

MICHAEL: Johnny! What happened?

JOHNNY: They were fighting!

MICHAEL: Who?

JOHNNY: Raggedy Leni and the Executioner!

MICHAEL: Who won?

JOHNNY: The Executioner won!

MICHAEL: If she'd'a won, it'd been a miracle!

VEIT *(politely)*: If you don't mind my asking, Executioner!—Are you here on a visit?

(The EXECUTIONER does not answer.)

DOFFER: They've sentenced the Executioner to ninety-nine years in prison! Because he tortures so gently! Am I right, Executioner?

EXECUTIONER: Just you wait, Doffer! I'll settle your hash!

DOFFER: Ah, if all you're going to do is put me up on that

riding horse . . . ! I thought I was sitting on the Emperor's throne!

EXECUTIONER: I've got other ways!

DOFFER: What other ways are there? The kind you used on the City Reject?—Sure, sure, you've got a tough job! One fellow says too much, the next fellow won't say anything! By the way—would you be so kind as to inform Mr. Commissioner-Counselor the next time you see him that I would very much like to make a dozen more confessions? I'm not only a great sorcerer, but also a great robber and murderer! Let me tell you a couple of stories about my past crimes! Just listen!

EXECUTIONER: If you don't shut your trap this minute, I'll kill you right here and now!

(*MAGDALENA regains consciousness, sits up, looks around, looks at the EXECUTIONER, crawls over to AN-DREE.*)

DOFFER (*during the above*): Oh, please! Do whatever you like! It would've been a pleasure to help you kill some time! How long will we be enjoying the pleasure of your company?

(*The EXECUTIONER leans forward, grabs DOFFER, takes him by the throat, chokes and shakes him, then flings him aside.*)

DOFFER (*gasping for breath*): Well, I guess you'd better find somebody else to entertain you!

(*Silence for a while.*)

MICHAEL: Come on, tell us what you're doin' here!

EXECUTIONER: Zillner, that asshole! He put me in here with you little shits! For the whole weekend! The only two days when I've got time to visit my mother! She'd made her wonderful sour tripe just for me! She's waiting for me! She'll start to worry!

VEIT: But why? Why did he do that to you?

EXECUTIONER: Because Feldner got away! Is it my fault that dumb kid got away?

VEIT: The Shitspotter? How? (*crawls closer*) Come on, tell us!

EXECUTIONER (*stands up, bumps his head on the low ceiling*): He's kneeling down in front of me, I raise my sword for the horizontal chop, it whistles through the air—and what does he do? He pulls away, to the side, and I just cut off the top half of his head! People are screaming, the Counselor jumps up and cusses me out in front of the whole crowd! Of course I'm upset, so I hack away at Feldner who's lying on the ground with half his head! It took me three times till his head was properly chopped off!—And for that Zillner's got me locked up in here! For the whole weekend! What do you think of that?

VEIT: That's unbelievable! Completely unfair!

EXECUTIONER (*sits back down*): I'll lodge a complaint with the Bishop! That Zillner can't just lock me up down here with you disgusting animals!

(*Blackout*)

18. The office

*(The COMMISSIONER and the SCRIBE at their desks,
the EXECUTIONER—without his apron—and his TWO
HENCHMEN are sitting on the bench. Standing before the
COMMISSIONER are VEIT, MICHAEL, and JOHNNY.
On the floor to one side, sitting up on one knee, is DOFFER.
Beside him is ANDREE, sick, lying on his back.)*

COMMISSIONER *(to DOFFER)*: Would you like a chair?

DOFFER: No, thank you, Mr. Commissioner! My hind-
quarters are still a bit warm, thanks to the
Executioner's treatment!

COMMISSIONER *(looks at MICHAEL)*: Well, Michael,
what should we do with you? Since you do not
know where you come from, we also have not been
able to ascertain how old you are.

MICHAEL: I'm ten! I'm not fourteen!

COMMISSIONER: I believe you when you say you are not
fourteen. But it is difficult to say whether you are
nine, ten, or eleven.

MICHAEL: Ten, I think!

COMMISSIONER: You have already turned ten?

MICHAEL: Just barely, yes!

COMMISSIONER: Well, Michael, you should know that
it is not unimportant for you, whether you have
completed your tenth year or not. If you are still
nine, then you will live; but if you are ten, then you
will have to die.

*(MICHAEL "stares" in the direction of the COMMIS-
SIONER, confused.)*

COMMISSIONER: In our country, persons under ten are

not executed. Even in the case of a diabolical conspiracy.

(*MICHAEL now understands, becomes afraid, is silent for a while.*)

DOFFER: Michael can't be ten! Why, he used to pee on my arm when I'd carry him around, oh, just three . . . four years ago!

(*Silence for a while.*)

MICHAEL: I don't think I'm really ten yet!

COMMISSIONER: At the beginning you said otherwise.

(*MICHAEL falls silent in despair.*)

COMMISSIONER: Never before has anyone committed such a despicable act of desecrating the host, as you have. Except for Magdalena Pichler. I believe that, considering the seriousness of your crime, the doubts about your age will have to be set aside. Nevertheless I will suggest to the High Court that you not be burned alive, but that you first be strangled to death at the stake. (*to the EXECU-TIONER*) Is that all right with you, Master? We will just forget about beheading people for awhile! Until you have had a little more practice!

EXECUTIONER: Beheading people is always risky business, Mr. Counselor! And it'll always be that way, believe me! But I've got a better idea, Mr. Counselor!

COMMISSIONER: What would that be?

EXECUTIONER: I put my weekend in prison to good use! I've come up with an idea for a contraption! A guillotine! An automatic guillotine! That way, nothing could ever go wrong again!

COMMISSIONER: Fine. Build a model and you can demonstrate it for me.

EXECUTIONER: Be glad to, Mr. Counselor! Next weekend!

(*The COMMISSIONER looks at MICHAEL who is standing motionless, his head held high.*)

COMMISSIONER (*to MICHAEL*): Do you understand what I have said, Michael?

MICHAEL: Yes!

(*JOHNNY does not understand what they are talking about, looks at MICHAEL desparately.*)

MICHAEL: You there, Johnny?

JOHNNY: Yes! (*takes MICHAEL'S hand*)

(*The COMMISSIONER looks at MICHAEL, feels sorry for him.*)

COMMISSIONER: Do you regret what you have done, Michael?

MICHAEL: Yes! Yes! I really do!

COMMISSIONER: Then nothing evil can happen to you. You will confess your sins, you will receive Holy Communion, the body of our Lord Jesus Christ which you desecrated and Who forgives you nonetheless; and you will be free from the devil! He will no longer have power over you. You will be free! Completely free! And you will rise up from the darkness, and the light of God will no longer be inaccessible to you. You will go up unto it and radiate in chaste innocence and purity. Do you understand what I have just said?

MICHAEL: Hope so!—And Johnny? Will he get to live?

COMMISSIONER (*smiling, to JOHNNY*): The little Mow Catcher will live!

MICHAEL: That's good!

COMMISSIONER: And as for you, Doffer, I have arrived at the conclusion that your simplicity is only a pretense. On account of this special deception, before you are strangled to death, glowing pincers will reach in and clasp your heart.

EXECUTIONER: There you go, Doffer! What did I tell you?

DOFFER: And I told you, too—we'll meet again on Judgment Day!

COMMISSIONER: However, the Archbishop has decreed that you be spared the glowing pincers if you repent your misdeeds and your deception beforehand.

DOFFER: All the things I did weren't misdeeds, they were wonderful, and I don't repent anything! It's even better this way! Besides, I've always liked to be pinched! One time, when I was with Jackie and his woman at the Mondsee—it was a warm summer night—well, I was lying there when Rosina, that was the wench's name—

COMMISSIONER: Enough! I do not care to hear any more! You have already said enough!

EXECUTIONER: You can say that again!

DOFFER: I'll tell you all about it at the bonfire, Executioner! You'll laugh yourself to death!

EXECUTIONER: I'm gonna make an extra special effort to burn his mouth out!

COMMISSIONER (*to VEIT*): Veit Lindner.

VEIT (*hopeful*): Here, Mr. Counselor!

COMMISSIONER: Veit, you have been extremely helpful to us these many months! We owe the capture of numerous accomplices of Jackie the Sorcerer all to you!

DOFFER: Our gratitude will be eternal, Veit!

COMMISSIONER: During the cross-examinations you bravely told them their crimes face-to-face!

DOFFER: Flung—that would be a better word!

COMMISSIONER: If you are not quiet, Doffer, I will hand you over to the Executioner right here and now!

EXECUTIONER: Just give him to me!

DOFFER: No, thanks! Our meeting at the bonfire is enough for me!

COMMISSIONER (*to VEIT*): Taking the above into consideration, you will therefore not be burned alive, despite your horrible crimes—you will be strangled to death beforehand.

(*VEIT is stunned.*)

VEIT: But . . . but . . . Mr. Counselor! You told me . . . you told me you'd consider my cooperation at sentencing!

COMMISSIONER: That is correct, Veit. That is correct, as you see.

VEIT: No! No! I take it back! I take it all back! I lied! I made everything up! (*raises his right hand, his index and middle fingers*) I swear it!

(*A long, embarrassed silence ensues.*)

SCRIBE: Why, that's madness, Mr. Counselor! Then we'd have to start the entire trial all over again! Not only against him, but also against all the people he accused!

COMMISSIONER: Do you realize what you are saying, Veit? If you recant, then we would have to start over again, from the very beginning! You are already fourteen, therefore you are eligible for torture! You have been spared all that thus far!

EXECUTIONER: Don't be so stupid, Veit! Or I'll make mincemeat out of you!

COMMISSIONER: Do you want to end up like him? (*points to ANDREE*) Please, spare yourself all that! And spare us, too!

(*VEIT looks at ANDREE, looks around in desperation.*)

VEIT: No! I can't take anymore! I want out of here! I want to get out of here!

(*VEIT runs over to the door. The EXECUTIONER and the TWO HENCHMEN leap up and grab him. VEIT resists out of desparation.*)

VEIT (*to the COMMISSIONER*): You tricked me! You tricked me! You tricked me!

COMMISSIONER: Take him away! Put him in the special cell!

(*The TWO HENCHMEN drag VEIT out the door, the EXECUTIONER sits back down on the bench.*)

DOFFER (*giggling*): Now I feel a lot better! Crooked Veit'll be going with us! Now that's justice, Judge! Never thought you could do it!

COMMISSIONER (*rises, looks at ANDREE*): And as for you, Andree Mayer . . . (*walks around the desk, steps up to ANDREE*) Can you hear me, Andree?

ANDREE (*softly*): Yes! Make it short!

COMMISSIONER: Today your whore, Magdalena Pichler, has recanted her testimony against you. Therefore you are no longer under indictment by a major witness. Moreover, in spite of severe torture, you never confessed. Whether you had the help of the devil or were really innocent, that I cannot judge. But without a confession there is no proof of your guilt. Thus you will be set free as soon as you are able to walk again. (*to the EXECUTIONER*) You will take care of his wounds, Executioner.

(*The EXECUTIONER considers the acquittal to be an error in judgment.*)

EXECUTIONER: As your Excellency requests!

COMMISSIONER (*to ANDREE*): When you have regained your health, you will take the oath of amnesty, that means that you will promise to exact no revenge for the imprisonment you have suffered. Subsequently, you will be taken to the Tyrolean border and banished forever from the Archdiocese of Salzburg. Have you understood me, Andree?

ANDREE: Yes! I just can't believe it!

(*DOFFER leans down to ANDREE, pats him on the shoulder.*)

DOFFER: Congratulations, City Reject! All my best to the world outside! I've seen some wonderful things in my day!

MICHAEL: Me, too!

(*Blackout*)

19. Cell

(Jammed full of prisioners. MAGDALENA and ANDREE embrace under the blanket.)

MAGDALENA: Don't leave! Please, don't leave!

ANDREE: I'm right here!

MAGDALENA: He's saving me for last! He's saving me for last!—I don't want to die!

ANDREE: Don't make it any harder on me!

MAGDALENA: Why is it so hard on you?! You get to leave! I'm going to burn! I'm going to burn!

ANDREE: Nobody said that yet! They haven't pronounced sentence yet!

MAGDALENA: My sentence was pronounced before I was born! *(sits upright)* Go get Jackie! Join forces with him! Set their houses on fire and murder their children!

ANDREE: I can't go get Jackie! —Jackie's dead!

MAGDALENA: What? What'd you say?

ANDREE *(sits upright)*: Jackie's dead!

MAGDALENA: No!

ANDREE: Yes, he is! Believe me!

MAGDALENA: So that wasn't him, in St. Wolfgang!

ANDREE: No, that wasn't him! But he's dead, anyway! I saw him! Near Werfen! Beside a creek, ants running in and out of his mouth!

MAGDALENA: That can't be true! That can't be true!

He's alive! He's got to be alive! He just has to be alive!

(*Blackout*)

20. The office

(*The COMMISSIONER and the SCRIBE at their desks, sitting on the bench to the rear are the EXECUTIONER— without his apron—and his TWO HENCHMEN. MAGDA- LENA stands before the COMMISSIONER in black shirt and chains.*)

COMMISSIONER: Magdalena Pichler, I have requested the following for you: (*glances down at a piece of paper*) To be dragged to the place of your execu- tion, to have strips cut from your flesh, and to be burned alive with a sack of gunpowder hung from your neck. His Serene Highness, the Archbishop and Prince, in his usual spirit of generosity, has dispensed with the dragging and the stripping, and has ordained that you only receive three clasps with the glowing pincers, those being: one on the upper arm, one on the breast, and one on the cheek. Do you have anything else to say?

MAGDALENA: You wade through our blood like it was dew on the grass!

COMMISSIONER (*to the EXECUTIONER*): Take her away. Put her in a special cell until the execution.

(*The TWO HENCHMEN rise, approach MAGDALENA,*

lead her to the door where she turns to face the COMMIS-
SIONER.)

MAGDALENA: Even if you burned the whole country at
the stake, there's one person you'll never catch—
Never!—, and that's Jackie the Sorcerer!

(MAGDALENA exits. The TWO HENCHMEN follow her
out, the door is closed after them.)

COMMISSIONER *(to the EXECUTIONER)*: Executioner,
you are dismissed for today.

EXECUTIONER *(stands up)*: Tomorrow I'll set up the
guillotine, Mr. Counselor!

COMMISSIONER: Fine.

EXECUTIONER: That makes me feel a lot better! All this
strangling, day after day . . . ! I'm basically a sensitive man, Mr. Counselor!

(The SCRIBE grins with contempt.)

COMMISSIONER: I do not doubt it for a moment, Master. Good night.

EXECUTIONER: Good night, Mr. Counselor!

(The EXECUTIONER exits. The COMMISSIONER and
the SCRIBE exchange glances.)

COMMISSIONER: Tired?

SCRIBE: Yes!

COMMISSIONER: I am, too! *(takes off his wig)*

SCRIBE: Did you know, Mr. Counselor, that we've conducted one of the largest trials that this century
has ever seen?

COMMISSIONER: Is that so?

SCRIBE *(proudly)*: Yes, that's so! 198 prisoners! On the

average that I've calculated from similar procedings, 140 of them will die! We'll go down in history, Dr. Zillner!

COMMISSIONER: Oh, no, not us! The children! The children will go down in history! Do not delude yourself! Criminals are the heroes of the future, Mr.
Finsterwalder! Criminals, not the representatives
of law and order!

SCRIBE: But the criminals die, Mr. Counselor! At least
that's an advantage!

COMMISSIONER: We shall die, too, Mr. Finsterwalder!

SCRIBE: No! I don't think anybody'll ever remember
these beggar children! Who wants to remember
them? The citizens and the farmers they tormented? Their families? Most of these kids don't
have families!—No, Mr. Counselor! As soon as
their ashes are cast to the wind, people'll forget all
about them!

COMMISSIONER: There is one person we certainly will
not forget: Jackie the Sorcerer! The Arch Magi-
cian! Who leads our children astray! (*after a while*)
We live at the apex of all times. We now know that
the things we believe to be real are mere appearance, and appearances are reality. We have found
an order in geometry, in the flesh, and in the heart.
Symmetry determines our lives. Everything is
mirrored in this symmetry, and everything is a
mirror of God, and therefore a mirror omnium in
omnibus! We have absolute politics, absolute sci-
ence, absolute theology! The task of administration is the highest principle of order! We seemed to
be saved from chaos!—And now this! Plague, in-
surrection, devil worship, Islam at our doorstep!

The Prince of Darkness is breathing down our necks!

SCRIBE: We should trust in God! He'll save us!

COMMISSIONER: Yes! Yes! (*crosses himself*) May the glory of the Lord last for ever and ever!

SCRIBE: Amen!

(*Blackout*)

21. MAGDALENA PICHLER BURNS AT THE STAKE.

THE END

One Everyman

Translated by
Todd C. Hanlin

CHARACTERS

GOD THE FATHER

GOD THE SON

GOD THE HOLY GHOST

DEVIL (in traditional costume, and as TROUBLE-SHOOTER)

DEATH (in traditional costume, and as OFFICE BOY)

EVERYMAN (CHAIRMAN OF THE BOARD)

EVERYMAN'S MOTHER

EVERYMAN'S WIFE

EVERYMAN'S GOOD COMPANION (FEDERAL CHANCELLOR)

POOR NEIGHBOR (INDUSTRIALIST)

DEBTOR (INDUSTRIALIST)

MISTRESS (EVERYMAN'S SECRETARY)

FAT COUSIN (CARDINAL)

THIN COUSIN (DOCTOR)

MAMMON (INVESTMENT BANKER)

WORKS (UNION PRESIDENT)

STARVING CHILD (AFRICAN)

AMPUTATED CHILD (ORIENTAL)

COUGHING CHILD (EUROPEAN)

FIRST BODYGUARD

SECOND BODYGUARD

THE VOICE OF MAMMON'S SECRETARY

WORKERS, MEMBERS OF THE BOARD OF DIRECTORS AND THEIR WIVES, COLLEAGUES, FRIENDS, SECURITY GUARDS, WAITERS AND WAITRESSES

STAGE SETTING:

Executive office suite in a skyscraper (*desk, sitting area, conference table, bar, TV monitors, elevator doors, door to the outer office*)

PART ONE

(**Morning.** *The blinds covering the glass front are half closed. From far below, rising from the asphalt caverns, we can hear sirens from police, fire, and rescue vehicles during the course of the play. Above EVERYMAN's private elevator are luminous buttons: Basement-10 to Basement-1, Ground, Floors 1 to 50—the very last floor, 51, is designated as CEO. Beginning from the extreme right, a white triangle lights up, races down toward the floor marked CEO, as if the elevator is coming from somewhere high above. Finally the CEO lights up, a bell chimes, the elevator doors open. A radiant white light streams from the elevator, GOD THE FATHER, GOD THE SON, and GOD THE HOLY GHOST step out of the light and into the room. The elevator doors close behind them. GOD THE FATHER is a somewhat grumpy, yet understanding old gentleman, smooth shaven, wearing an expensive conservative suit with hat and tie. GOD THE SON is unshaven, wearing a thorn crown, t-shirt, old and faded jeans, gym shoes, with wounds on his palms. GOD THE HOLY GHOST is a jittery, fluttering, transparent being: ageless, sexless, shapeless. The THREE look around. GOD THE SON goes over to the bar, pours himself a double whiskey on the rocks, takes a big gulp, exhales appreciatively, goes over to the sitting area, lounges around on the leather sofa, puts his feet up on the table, pulls out tobacco and cigarette paper, rolls a cig-*

*arette, then smokes it. GOD THE HOLY GHOST walks
over to EVERYMAN's desk, observes with curiosity the various
objects on it, the telephones, the computer, the various
buttons. HE presses one of the buttons, activating the TV
monitors which hang from the ceiling on steel frames. On
one monitor we can read the stock reports, on the others we
see catastrophes—earthquakes, conflagrations, starvation, demonstrations, crime, wars. He has also activated
the sound, and now there is an indescribable noise. GOD
THE HOLY GHOST becomes terribly frightened, looks at
the monitors, retreats in horror. GOD THE SON casts a
fleeting glance at the monitors. GOD THE FATHER looks
with irritation at GOD THE HOLY GHOST, goes over to
the desk, immediately presses the right button, the monitors and noise grow silent. The spell is broken.)*

GOD THE FATHER: Judgment Day.

*(GOD THE SON makes a weary gesture, groans out loud.
GOD THE FATHER gives him a reproachful look.)*

GOD THE HOLY GHOST (*pointing to the monitors*): What
kind of a spirit is that? Certainly not my kind! How
can a spirit be like that? How can a spirit create
something like that?

GOD THE FATHER: Humans are free!

GOD THE HOLY GHOST: But why? I don't understand
that! I will never understand that! They hurt each
other. They murder each other. Everyone is someone else's enemy.

GOD THE SON (*taking his feet off the table*): Don't talk
such hogwash! You don't understand it at all!

GOD THE HOLY GHOST (*to GOD THE FATHER*): Do I
have to put up with that, Father?

GOD THE FATHER (*annoyed*): Why do the two of you always have to argue?

GOD THE HOLY GHOST (*to GOD THE SON*): You human!

GOD THE SON: Thank you!

GOD THE HOLY GHOST: You brutal human!

GOD THE SON (*stands up*): You'd better watch what you say!

GOD THE FATHER: Children!

GOD THE SON: Let me tell you something, Holy Ghost! I wish you had five minutes! Just five minutes as a human being! Then you'd know how great it is. (*beating his chest*) That's life! That's strength! That's flesh! God, you're a real jerk!

GOD THE HOLY GHOST (*fluttering around*): Stop it! Stop it! Leave me alone! That doesn't interest me in the least!

GOD THE SON: The agony! The ecstasy! The pleasure!— Senses! Senses, you idiot! Feelings! You haven't the foggiest idea how wonderful that is, you boring scarecrow.

GOD THE FATHER (*in a loud voice*): That's enough!

GOD THE HOLY GHOST: Brutal! Brutal! You're just such a brute!

GOD THE SON: That's fine with me. Brutal, sure. That's all part of being human! All of it! Oh, God! The chance to be human again! I'd give anything!—And even if they butchered me all over again! And even if the blood just squirted out of me! (*cries out*) Life!

GOD THE HOLY GHOST: Shame! Shame! Shame!

GOD THE FATHER (*screams*): Stop! No more! What do you think you are doing? This is outrageous! What a way to behave! You are God!

GOD THE SON: Excuse me, Dad! I'm sorry! (*goes over to*

the bar, refills his glass) You shouldn't have brought me along. *(takes a drink)* It grabs me. It grabs me, Dad. I can't help it. You just don't know what it's like. You don't know what it's like!

GOD THE FATHER: Tell me, have you gone completely mad or something? *(yells)* I know everything!

(The door to the outer office opens, MISTRESS (EVERY-MAN'S SECRETARY) enters, carrying a tray. She cannot see the HIGHER BEINGS, goes over to EVERYMAN's desk, puts down the tray with a bouquet of flowers in a vase, a thermos of coffee, a cup, and a glass of orange juice. She places the objects on the desk, picks up the empty tray, looks at the blinds, presses a button on the desk, the blinds rise into the ceiling, the morning light streams in; we can see a view of the city below. GOD THE FATHER and GOD THE HOLY GHOST watch MISTRESS without showing any special interest. GOD THE SON is entranced by MIS-TRESS, he approaches her, looks at her longingly. She walks over to the glass window, looks out over the city. GOD THE SON puts down his glass, follows her, looks her up and down, lifts his hand, carefully touches her shoulder; MISTRESS feels something, looks in amazement at her shoulder, lightly brushes her shoulder, goes back to the door to the outer office and exits. GOD THE SON watches her go, longingly.)

GOD THE SON *(softly, after the door has closed behind her)*: Oh, Mary Magdalen . . .

GOD THE HOLY GHOST *(to GOD THE FATHER)*: Did you hear what he just said?

GOD THE FATHER *(this is getting on his nerves)*: Yes . . !

GOD THE HOLY GHOST: He said: 'Mary Magdalen!'

GOD THE FATHER: Yes, yes, I heard it.

GOD THE HOLY GHOST: He's incorrigible. In-corrigible!

I told you it was a mistake to send him down here.
Like this. As a human being! A human being can't
redeem anyone.

GOD THE SON (*furious*): Only a human being can redeem
another human being! Who else, you idiot?

GOD THE FATHER (*tired*): Please stop it, son! Calm
down! Behave yourself!

GOD THE SON (*softly*): I can't calm down.

GOD THE FATHER: I command you! You must obey me!
You understand?

GOD THE SON: I always obeyed you, in all those 33 years.
Always. (*raising his voice*) Do you know how difficult that was? (*pointing to GOD THE HOLY
GHOST*) He's right! You never should have sent me
down here!

GOD THE FATHER: The same old accusations!

GOD THE SON: Do you know how I felt, up there on the
cross? Do you know?

GOD THE FATHER: Of course I know how you felt.

GOD THE SON: You can't know. Otherwise you'd never
have let it happen.

GOD THE FATHER (*lovingly*): I know how you felt, my
son.

(*GOD THE SON spreads out his arms, as if he were being
crucified. The wounds on his palms are now visible for the
first time.*)

GOD THE SON (*cries out in despair*): My God, my God,
why hast Thou forsaken me?

(*GOD THE FATHER goes over to him, puts his hand on his
shoulder. GOD THE SON drops his arms, stares straight
ahead in despair.*)

GOD THE FATHER: I did not forsake you. I really didn't.

GOD THE HOLY GHOST: Certainly not. (*to GOD THE SON*) Why do you make such a big fuss about all this? Why are you always setting yourself apart from us? You're no better than we are!

GOD THE FATHER: I was always with you, my son. Always.

(*GOD THE SON begins to cry, he sobs. GOD THE FATHER puts his arms around him, hugs him.*)

GOD THE HOLY GHOST: Now he's going to cry, on top of everything else!

GOD THE FATHER (*to GOD THE HOLY GHOST*): Be quiet!

GOD THE HOLY GHOST: Water is running down his face. (*flutters around*) I'll never understand that. Water is running down his face. Water! (*flutters over to the TWO, looks at the face of GOD THE SON*) Just like out of a spring. The head is a mountain. Eh? Maybe it's groundwater. It rises up from down below. Up from the inside. Is that the way it works . . . ? Man is a landscape that cries! Is that the way it is? I'll never understand!

GOD THE SON (*stepping out of GOD THE FATHER's embrace*): Come on, Dad, let's put it all behind us!

GOD THE FATHER: Good.—Judgment Day. (*looks over at EVERYMAN's executive swivel chair*) Here is a man who bears responsibility for many and for much.

GOD THE SON: A human being!

GOD THE FATHER: Yes, a human being!—Let me finally get a word in edgewise!

GOD THE HOLY GHOST (*to GOD THE SON*): In the beginning was the word! But not yours!

GOD THE FATHER (*to GOD THE SON*): A human being. I know that. You don't have to tell me! But one with power! With responsibility! He doesn't care. About anybody. Not even about himself. Kills others and himself. There must be consequences. We must set an example.

GOD THE HOLY GHOST (*to GOD THE SON*): That's right! An example!

GOD THE FATHER: I will grant him some time. From now until midnight. He can prove his worth, if he chooses to.

(*GOD THE SON accepts the decision with reluctance. GOD THE FATHER takes his pocketwatch from his vest pocket, looks at the time, looks at the elevator. Above the elevator a glowing red inverted triangle lights up, beginning from the extreme left of the standard numbers. The light races forward, toward the Basement-10 light, as if the elevator were coming from far below the building.*)

GOD THE HOLY GHOST: He is on his way!

(*The numbers for the individual floors light up—in red—at amazing speed, finally the CEO light goes on, the doors open. In the elevator stands the DEVIL in his traditional costume, enveloped in a sufur-yellow light. He steps out into the room, the elevator doors close behind him.*)

DEVIL: Gentlemen! What can I do for you?

GOD THE SON (*bursts out laughing*): What a ridiculous outfit!

DEVIL (*grinning*): I know you don't approve of my being here.

GOD THE SON (*sits down on the sofa, takes out his tobacco*): You're part of the play, so what? (*rolls him-*

self a cigarette) You just overestimate your own importance.

DEVIL (*grinning*): Jesus Christ, I am important! You must have noticed that on your earthly travels. Didn't you?

GOD THE FATHER (*to the DEVIL*): A bit more respect, if you don't mind!

DEVIL: I beg your pardon! Beg your pardon, God, sir! He was a human being. I have a hard time forgetting that. (*enraged*) He insulted me!

GOD THE SON (*lighting his cigarette*): How can I insult someone who doesn't even exist?

DEVIL: Well! That's about the . . . (*looks over at GOD THE FATHER*).

GOD THE FATHER (*to GOD THE SON*): Why do you always have to upset me?

GOD THE SON: He doesn't exist!

DEVIL (*laughs out loud*): I guess the boy would have been excommunicated long ago, if he were still here on earth.

GOD THE SON: Well, you're right about that.

GOD THE HOLY GHOST: Well, I'm not about to get involved in this discussion.

GOD THE SON: Sure, sure, just keep hovering over the waters! It's better that way!

GOD THE FATHER: Now I've had just about enough! Are you going to be quiet, or not?

(*GOD THE SON raises his hands in a sign of surrender.*)

GOD THE FATHER (*to the DEVIL*): Here we are! (*indicating the entire room*) This is his bailiwick. Go to work!

DEVIL: No problem! He already belongs to me. For a long time now. From the womb to the tomb. He's destroyed himself, all by himself. He always has to be on top.—Even then, he can't enjoy himself. Those are the real sad sacks!

GOD THE SON: How would *you* ever know who the real sad sacks are?

DEVIL (*ignoring GOD THE SON; to GOD THE FATHER*): Shall we just raise the stakes a bit . . . ?

GOD THE FATHER: Good. I'll give him a few more tests, as a last chance.

(*The elevator—which had returned to the ground floor shortly before—approaches at a normal speed. GOD THE HOLY GHOST notices.*)

GOD THE HOLY GHOST: He is on his way!

(*ALL look over to the elevator. It arrives, the doors open. It is black inside, DEATH is standing there in traditional costume, a scythe over his shoulder. He steps out, the doors close behind him, pinching the blade of the scythe between the doors. DEATH is jerked backwards. The doors open automatically, having sensed an impediment. DEATH, who was just about to yank the scythe free, stumbles forward and falls to the floor. The elevator doors close. Because of this pratfall, GOD THE SON is almost convulsed with laughter. DEATH looks up in consternation, grasps his scythe, stands up while leaning on the scythe, looks at the THREE GODS and the DEVIL, looks up at GOD THE SON who simply cannot stop laughing.*)

GOD THE FATHER (*loudly*): Stop it!

(*GOD THE SON stops laughing, but cannot help grinning.*)

GOD THE FATHER (*to DEATH*): At midnight his time is up. Inform him. One chance to come to his senses.

DEATH: As you command, Lord and Creator. Is there any special way you want him to die? An accident, murder, suicide?

GOD THE FATHER: It doesn't matter to me. Whatever works out.

DEATH (*shouldering his scythe*): Then I'll be on my way. (*bows*) Praise be to the Holy Trinity!

(*DEATH purposely ignores the DEVIL, goes over to the elevator, the doors open. Inside it is still pitch black.*)

GOD THE SON: Hey, skeleton man!

(*DEATH turns around.*)

GOD THE SON: One more thing I wanted to tell you: You don't exist either, you Mardi Gras clown!

(*DEATH stares at him.*)

GOD THE FATHER: Tell me, son, why are you getting all worked up about this? What's the point?

GOD THE HOLY GHOST: Well, I think he's right, for once! I agree, I agree!

DEATH: I'll be there!

GOD THE SON (*to GOD THE FATHER*): He doesn't exist! (*points at the DEVIL*) Neither one of them! I can't believe it!

GOD THE FATHER (*in a conciliatory tone*): It's an arrangement. An image.

GOD THE SON: I don't like it! (*looks at DEATH*) The man with the scythe! What's that supposed to mean? In earlier times, people just passed over. Not down. Not into some dark hole. Not down and not up. Over. It was universal. I liked that.

DEATH (*stepping forward*): What do you think I am, God the Son? Don't you think I know? Don't you think I know all that? Your Father just said it: an image. People need images. It helps them.

GOD THE SON: Oh, for Heaven's sake! It's a threat. I hate threats.

DEATH: I didn't create that image. It could be a different image. There are others. I am many things to many people. Also a consoler. Also a friend. Though less and less these days. I never really had any special ambitions. I just wanted to do my job, in peace, when the time came. But because of him (*points to the DEVIL*) they force me to come, they force me. Prematurely! Sometimes I get really tired.

(*DEATH steps into the elevator, the doors close, the elevator travels down to the GROUND FLOOR, then comes right back up.*)

DEVIL: What a sentimental fool!

GOD THE FATHER: An image. Like you. Like all of us.

GOD THE HOLY GHOST (*noticing the lighted numbers over the elevator* : He is on his way!

(*ALL glance over at the elevator. GOD THE FATHER reaches back and massages the base of his spine.*)

GOD THE FATHER: Oh, my aching back!

(*The elevator arrives, the bell chimes, the doors open. Standing at the back of the elevator, leaning against the railing, is EVERYMAN (in overcoat, suit, and carrying an attaché case), holding his hand over his heart, feeling pressure, pain, because DEATH has given him the prearranged "sign." EVERYMAN pulls himself together, steps out of the elevator, the doors close behind him. With his hand on his heart, EVERYMAN walks over to his desk, sets down his attaché case, takes off his overcoat and hangs it up, sits down in his executive swivel chair, listens to his heart, takes a pillbox out of his coat pocket, takes out one pill, inserts it in his mouth, takes a drink of the orange juice, swallows the pill, leans back, puts his hand back over his heart, waits, the pain passes. EVERYMAN notices the bouquet of flowers, looks at it, looks over at the door to the outer office, places the bouquet off to one side, looks up at the monitors, presses a button: the stock market results, financial news, and catastrophes re-appear with hellacious noise. GOD THE HOLY GHOST jumps with fright, EVERYMAN presses another button which mutes the sound while the pictures continue. EVERYMAN opens his attaché case, takes out files and lays them on the desk in front of him, pours a cup of coffee, adds sweetener, lights a cigarette, takes a drink of coffee, studies the files while making notes, boots up his personal computer, types on the keyboard, looks at the screen, is concerned, worried, then gets angry. The THREE have been watching him. GOD THE SON now empties his glass, goes over to the elevator, the doors open (though EVERYMAN doesn't notice). GOD THE FATHER follows. GOD THE HOLY GHOST, prancing, hovers behind them, the DEVIL grins over at EVERYMAN. The THREE are already waiting in the elevator, the DEVIL sees them, quickly steps into the elevator, and with a grin waives goodbye to EVERYMAN; the elevator doors close. The white triangle above the elevator races upwards to the right, simultaneously the elevator travels down to Basement-10 and then the red inverted arrow races on down below that. EVERYMAN presses a button; after a while MISTRESS enters from the outer office with a legal pad, pencil, and a pack of congratulatory telegrams in her hand. She has a guilty conscience concerning EVERYMAN, but still thinks she acted correctly.)*

MISTRESS: Good morning, sir!

EVERYMAN (*doesn't look up*): Morning! (*looks up, lost in thought*) Morning . . .

(*MISTRESS is slightly irritated, walks over to him, kisses him on the cheek.*)

MISTRESS: Happy Birthday! (*places the pack of telegrams down on his desk*) Birthday telegrams . . .

EVERYMAN: Thanks. Emergency board meeting! Eleven o'clock!

MISTRESS: Two board members are out of the country.

EVERYMAN: What? I told them to be on call! Things are heating up!

MISTRESS: They are trying to firm up two potential deals! We can certainly use the business!

(*With a frigid glance, EVERYMAN puts her in her place. She leaves his desk, sits down in an armchair, strikes a conscious pose of the typical secretary with pencil at the ready, waiting for further instructions.*)

EVERYMAN: Notify them to hop the next flight back!

(*MISTRESS makes a notation.*)

EVERYMAN: Cancel my flight and cancel appointments with my business partners. Also cancel all other appointments. Have the finance department prepare a current balance.

(*MISTRESS makes a notation.*)

MISTRESS: The heads of those two bankrupt firms are waiting outside. Should I send them away?

EVERYMAN: No. I'm going to buy out their companies.

MISTRESS: Your mother is also waiting outside.

EVERYMAN: My mother? What's she doing here?

MISTRESS: I have no idea.

EVERYMAN: Get rid of her!

MISTRESS: She'll wait until midnight, if she has to. That's what she said.

EVERYMAN (*loudly*): I don't have time!

MISTRESS (*loudly*): She won't leave! She just keeps yacking and yacking! Shoots poison darts at me! I can't take it any more! She's crazy!

(*EVERYMAN looks at her coldly. His glance hits her like a slap in the face, but she doesn't flinch.*)

EVERYMAN: All right, fine . . . But first send in those two failures!

MISTRESS: That fellow who runs the union is also on his way over. Should I let him in?

EVERYMAN (*irritated*): Of course I want you to let him in! Right now everything depends on him! What's the matter with you? Have you forgotten what we're here for?

MISTRESS: I'm doing my best. (*looks down at her legal pad*) By the way: half the government has already called: the Chancellor, the Minister of Finance, the Minister of Welfare. Your good friend, the Chancellor, wasn't very friendly, this morning!

EVERYMAN: Just have them wait, if you don't mind! Now they're on the phone. Usually they just have their spokesmen deny everything.

MISTRESS (*looks down at her notepad*): Oh, yes. A call from Caracas. They confiscated your son's passport.

EVERYMAN: What?

MISTRESS: Suspicion of drug running.

EVERYMAN: What? (*stands up*) That can't be true! Caracas?

(*MISTRESS nods.*)

EVERYMAN: What the hell is he doing in Caracas?

(*MISTRESS shrugs her shoulders.*)

EVERYMAN: Well, let him see what it's like!

MISTRESS: He doesn't have any money. The consulate says that without bail he'll have to sit in jail until the trial.

EVERYMAN: That bum! On top of everything else, now he's turning into a criminal! I've got a criminal for a son! Well, isn't that just great!—Call up that guy at the State Department; you know which one! He owes me a favor.—I want to see my son here first thing tomorrow. Here! On the spot!—The diplomatic courier should take a check along with him! And the plane ticket! Business Class.

MISTRESS (*taking notes*): Is that all?

EVERYMAN: That's all!

(*EVERYMAN sits back down, types on the computer, MISTRESS stands up, goes over to the door, reaches for the doorknob, stops, turns around.*)

MISTRESS: Your wife also called twice.

EVERYMAN (*doesn't look up*): I'm not in.

MISTRESS (*hesitating*): I . . . I talked to her.

EVERYMAN (*doesn't look up*): Yes—so what?

MISTRESS: I told her.

EVERYMAN (*looks at the computer screen*): What?

MISTRESS: About us.

(*EVERYMAN stops, stares straight ahead, dumbstruck.*)

EVERYMAN (*tired, tormented*): Why did you do that?

(*MISTRESS doesn't answer.*)

EVERYMAN (*looks at her*): Why did you do that? What good will that do?

(*MISTRESS doesn't answer.*)

EVERYMAN (*stands up, furious*): Right now we're in the middle of one of the most difficult hours in the history of capitalism! I've got enough on my mind already! And you pull something like this! At a time like this!

MISTRESS (*approaches him*): We've been together for five years now. To the very day. It was at your birthday party, you seduced me.

EVERYMAN: Beg your pardon? Seduced? I seduced you?

MISTRESS: I don't want to be a whore any longer!

EVERYMAN: Come on! Don't get pathetic on me, okay?! (*goes over to the bar, makes himself a scotch on the rocks*) God, that's all I need right now! Now I'm really going to catch hell!

MISTRESS: She was completely calm. She said she'd let you go. She won't miss you. Because she's been living without you for years anyway.

EVERYMAN: She'll never let me go! Never!

(*He drinks his scotch, sits down, lights a cigarette.*)

MISTRESS (*in a conciliatory tone*): Thomas!

EVERYMAN (*doesn't look at MISTRESS*): Now get out! Don't forget, you've still got work to do around here!

(*MISTRESS goes to the door.*)

EVERYMAN (*sorry for his brusqueness*): When this is all over, we'll talk about it again.

(*MISTRESS doesn't turn around again, exits, closes the door behind her. A moment later the door opens again, the POOR NEIGHBOR starts to enter, MISTRESS waves him back outside, so he closes the door behind him. One of the gadgets on the desk hums. EVERYMAN presses a button.*)

VOICE OF MISTRESS (*coming from the intercom on the desk*): Your wife, sir!

(*A momentary musical interlude over the intercom.*)

VOICE OF EVERYMAN'S WIFE (*from the intercom, drunkenly*): Hello! Hello! Put me through, please, you whore!

EVERYMAN: What's wrong? What do you want?

VOICE OF EVERYMAN'S WIFE: What do you think I want? I want to wish you a happy birthday!

EVERYMAN: Thanks.

VOICE OF EVERYMAN'S WIFE: You didn't come home last night?

EVERYMAN: No! Please, let me get back to my work!

VOICE OF EVERYMAN'S WIFE: Guess what I'm doing right at this very moment?

EVERYMAN: Haven't the faintest idea. Quit playing games! We'll talk about it later.

VOICE OF EVERYMAN'S WIFE: I'm sitting in the bathtub.

EVERYMAN: That's wonderful. You called just to tell me that?

VOICE OF EVERYMAN'S WIFE: I've just slashed my wrists!

(*From the depths—the glowing red inverted triangle lights up—the elevator races upward. EVERYMAN angrily takes a deep breath. MISTRESS, agitated, enters and closes the door behind her, looks at EVERYMAN.*)

VOICE OF EVERYMAN'S WIFE: I said I'm sitting here in

the bathtub with slashed wrists! Would you do me
the honor of a response!

(*The elevator has arrived, the bell chimes, the doors open,
out steps the DEVIL, a young, elegantly dressed Wall Street
broker, in one hand a laptop computer. He goes over to the
conference table, puts down the computer, opens it, sits
down.*)

VOICE OF EVERYMAN'S WIFE (*during the above*): Do
you hear me?

EVERYMAN: Yes, I hear you.

VOICE OF EVERYMAN'S WIFE: Would you please speak
louder!

(*EVERYMAN sees the DEVIL who takes a diskette out of
his briefcase, puts it in the computer, types on one key, looks
at the monitor.*)

EVERYMAN: Who are you?

DEVIL (*grinning*): I'm the troubleshooter.

(*MISTRESS just now notices the DEVIL.*)

VOICE OF EVERYMAN'S WIFE: This will cause a scan-
dal, I promise you! I've sent a farewell letter to the
newspapers!

EVERYMAN (*to the DEVIL*): Dammit, get the hell out of
here! I don't need you!

(*The DEVIL grins, keeps typing.*)

VOICE OF EVERYMAN'S WIFE: Do you hear me?

EVERYMAN: That's ridiculous, Brigitte. You've had your
share of affairs, too! (*to the DEVIL*) Now beat it!—
Brigitte! Are you drunk?

VOICE OF EVERYMAN'S WIFE: Oh, no! For once I'm not!
Just some tranquilizers! Do you think it's easy to
commit suicide?

EVERYMAN: But why, for Heaven's sake? I haven't done anything to you!

VOICE OF EVERYMAN'S WIFE: That's just it! You don't do anything to me. I can't even feel you. It's like living with a corpse. With a ghost. I can't take it anymore.

MISTRESS: I'll call the doctor.

DEVIL (*lightly, in passing, without looking up from his computer*): No.

(*MISTRESS doesn't look at the DEVIL, hesitates briefly, picks up one of the telephones on the desk, calls the THIN COUSIN. The DEVIL, surprised, grins and wags his head in admiration. We cannot understand what MISTRESS is saying, since she is whispering into the phone.*)

VOICE OF EVERYMAN'S WIFE (*during the above*): Who was that? Is she there, the whore?

EVERYMAN: Of course! Stupid jealousy! That's all it is!

VOICE OF EVERYMAN'S WIFE (*sobbing*): Tell her to go! Tell her to go! This is something between us! She's always there! She's always with you!

MISTRESS (*hangs up, whispers to EVERYMAN*): He'll drive on over.

EVERYMAN: Brigitte! I won't leave you!

(*MISTRESS casts a glance at EVERYMAN, as if to ask: "Do you really mean that?"*)

VOICE OF EVERYMAN'S WIFE: Tell her to go! I want to speak with you alone!

MISTRESS (*loudly, in the direction of the intercom*): I'm going now! (*goes over to the door*)

DEVIL: No.

(*MISTRESS stops in her tracks, turns around.*)

MISTRESS: That's just like me. I always give up without a fight. After all, I'm only his mistress. His mistress has got to clear out. But why?

EVERYMAN: Go! Please!

MISTRESS: Can't you see how beautiful I am?

EVERYMAN (*in desperation*): She's just slashed her wrists!

DEVIL: Theatrics.

MISTRESS: Nonsense! Theatrics!

VOICE OF EVERYMAN'S WIFE: Throw her out! Throw her out, for God's sake!

(*EVERYMAN is torn both ways.*)

DEVIL: She is ugly—

MISTRESS: She is ugly, old, dried up. A millstone around your neck!

VOICE OF EVERYMAN'S WIFE: Fire her, on the spot! I demand that you fire her on the spot!

DEVIL: No.

EVERYMAN: No! She knows everything! Everything! She can ruin our company!

MISTRESS: And how, Mrs. Chairman of the Board! I'd have a few things to tell the newspapers, too!

VOICE OF EVERYMAN'S WIFE: I beg you, Rita! You can get other men. Who is he, anyway? He's nothing special.

MISTRESS: No, he's not. But I'll keep him, just the same.

DEVIL: Buzz off.

MISTRESS: And, as for you, you old hag, buzz off!

EVERYMAN (*to MISTRESS*): Are you out of your mind? Shut up, for God's sake!

VOICE OF EVERYMAN'S WIFE (*howling*): Where is my son? Where is my son?

DEVIL: He ran away.

EVERYMAN (*simultaneously*): He ran away, away from you! Like everybody else!

VOICE OF EVERYMAN'S WIFE: Oh, God! Oh, God! (*slips under water, gurgles*) Oh, my God!

EVERYMAN: Brigitte! Brigitte! (*to MISTRESS*) Get out!

(*MISTRESS goes out the door.*)

EVERYMAN: Brigitte! Brigitte! Do you hear me?

VOICE OF EVERYMAN'S WIFE (*spitting water, coughing*): I can't go on! You'll pay for this! You'll pay for this! I've left my stock portfolio to your worst enemy (*gets water in her mouth again*) . . . just so you know! (*gurgling, coughing*).

DEVIL: Drown.

EVERYMAN: Drown! Drown! Then I'll be rid of you for good!

(*Sounds of struggling, of splashing bathwater.*)

VOICE OF THE THIN COUSIN: Thomas!

EVERYMAN: Yes?

VOICE OF THE THIN COUSIN: I've got her!

EVERYMAN: Is that you, Doctor?

VOICE OF THE THIN COUSIN: Who else?

EVERYMAN: Did she really slash her wrists?

VOICE OF THE THIN COUSIN: Yes! But it looks worse than it is. She'll make it.

DEVIL: Lock her up.

EVERYMAN: Take her to your clinic! Lock her up! Don't tell a soul!

VOICE OF THE THIN COUSIN: Yes, yes! Got it! 'Bye!

(*Static. Silence. EVERYMAN goes over to the bar, refills the whiskey glass, lights another cigarette, sits down exhausted on the leather sofa. The door to the outer office opens, MISTRESS enters, behind her we can see the nervous POOR NEIGHBOR. MISTRESS closes the door, approaches.*)

MISTRESS: Well, what did I tell you? Theatrics! And you swallowed the whole thing, hook, line, and sinker!

EVERYMAN (*sees the DEVIL*): Are you still here? Beat it, I didn't ask for you!

DEVIL: I'm the troubleshooter, I told you before.

EVERYMAN: Out, or I'll call the security guards!

DEVIL (*glances at his monitor*): The stock market is not particularly bullish.

EVERYMAN: What? (*goes over to the DEVIL, looks at his monitor*) What's going on here?—That's just not possible!

(*EVERYMAN glances up at one of the monitors suspended from the ceiling, immediately learns that there is not the slightest hint of a falling market. He looks back at the DEVIL's monitor, back up at the others above him.*)

EVERYMAN: That's not right! Just look up there!

DEVIL (*doesn't look up*): These are the real figures, sir! Believe you me! My information is the best. Always a step ahead of the competition.

(*For the first time, EVERYMAN takes a close look at the DEVIL who meets his glance, smiles. EVERYMAN looks back down at the DEVIL's monitor.*)

DEVIL: Don't you believe me?

EVERYMAN: Yes. It had to happen, sooner or later. If

we're shaky at home, we'll fall throughout the world.

DEVIL: That's the way it goes.

(*EVERYMAN looks depressed.*)

DEVIL: But we'll get on top of it. Don't worry! (*aside to MISTRESS*) Wimp.

MISTRESS: You, wimp! Now you've got her around your neck again!

DEVIL: Apartment.

EVERYMAN: I'm going to give you your own apartment. For our anniversary.

MISTRESS: Thanks alot. I've already got one. Nothing luxurious, as you're well aware, but it's good enough for me.

EVERYMAN: An apartment for the two of us!

MISTRESS (*hesitates*): You'll move in with me?

DEVIL: Yes.

EVERYMAN (*in anguish*): Not entirely. Not yet!

(*The DEVIL looks surprised.*)

MISTRESS (*laughs out loud*): A sleazy love nest! Thanks heaps! (*goes to the door*).

(*The DEVIL types on his computer.*)

DEVIL (*looks at the monitor*): In the heart of the city. A wonderful old building, renovated. Penthouse apartment. 2,000 square feet. Roof garden. Elevator. View of the cathedral. Accept.

(*MISTRESS turns around, doesn't want to give in.*)

DEVIL: Accept!

MISTRESS: Well, all right . . .

DEVIL (*grinning*): A kiss!

(*MISTRESS goes over to EVERYMAN, kisses him on the cheek, he smiles with relief. She looks at him, sees how exhausted he is, suddenly feels sorry for him, hugs him. The DEVIL looks disgusted. MISTRESS goes to the door.*)

MISTRESS: I'll send the first one in.

(*MISTRESS goes out, leaves the door open. EVERYMAN sits down at his desk.*)

DEVIL (*typing*): We'll write it off as a business expense.

EVERYMAN: What?—Okay, fine.

(*POOR NEIGHBOR—wearing suit and tie, with briefcase in hand—enters through the open door, closes the door behind him.*)

POOR NEIGHBOR: Thank you, sir, for taking time to see me.

EVERYMAN: I don't have any time. But, please . . .

(*EVERYMAN points to the armchair in front of his desk. POOR NEIGHBOR sits down, places his briefcase between his feet.*)

POOR NEIGHBOR: Hard to get through this morning. All the bridges blocked. The whole city packed. Workers, thousands of workers. They're gathering around the Central Square. In their filthy blue overalls. With the yellow hardhats. They didn't even bother to wash up. So they look real working-class. Those assholes, those primitive assholes! It's like it was 100 years ago! 100 years ago! My great grandfather used to tell me about it, when I was a kid, dressed in my sailor's suit with a spit part in my hair. But back then the police came, on horseback. With their sabres! And when they couldn't control the crowds, they called out the soldiers. Kaboom!—And today? Today the TV crews come. The politicians come. And bow down in front of the workers. Grant the most absurd demands. Put a knife to the throats of us industrialists. So that they'll get the workers' vote in the next election. The vote of that mob! Why does every vote count the same? Can you tell me why? The vote of the dumbest asshole in my company counts exactly the same as mine! Is that right? There are three things I hate more than anything else in the world: workers, politicians, and democracy!

EVERYMAN: Don't lecture me, get to the point!

POOR NEIGHBOR: That is the point, my friend. Yesterday they ruined me, tomorrow you're next! Or maybe even today! Those are your workers out there, marching in the streets.

EVERYMAN: They aren't my workers. They aren't mine! They're free. I'm not your great grandfather.

POOR NEIGHBOR (*laughs*): Well, of course they're free! Free to find a new job, right?

EVERYMAN: That'll depend on negotiations. Did you come here just because you were worried about my company?

POOR NEIGHBOR: You know why I'm here. So you can help me! But when I saw the proletarian masses, I thought to myself: My good neighbor, my dear friend—maybe he can't help me anymore either, maybe he's going under himself.

EVERYMAN: I'm a little too big for that, my friend! If we go under, then the whole country goes under.

POOR NEIGHBOR: Yes, I know, you're big all right.

EVERYMAN: And you're at the end of your rope, right?

POOR NEIGHBOR: Not at the end . . .

EVERYMAN: You've overextended yourself. You didn't know your own limits.

POOR NEIGHBOR: I ran my business the way a business should be run!

(*The DEVIL types away on his computer.*)

EVERYMAN: Who cares? As long as the balance sheets tally and you pay dividends.

POOR NEIGHBOR: I could have prevented the bankruptcy. With new capital investments. But the banks won't lend me any more money.

DEVIL (*looks at his monitor*): No wonder!

(*POOR NEIGHBOR looks in astonishment at the DEVIL, just now notices him for the first time.*)

DEVIL (*points to his monitor*): Just take a look at that!

(*POOR NEIGHBOR gets up, goes over to the DEVIL, looks at his monitor. EVERYMAN does the same.*)

POOR NEIGHBOR: Where did you get my balance sheets?

EVERYMAN: You're not just at the end of your rope, you're dead and buried.

POOR NEIGHBOR: We were a dynasty. For five generations. The workers loved us, before the Reds came. We were the first ones to build them houses, decent apartments, fit for human beings. They used to kiss my grandfather's hand. A gentleman! A patriarch! And me—they're tearing me to pieces. I'm fair game for every gypsy newspaper hack. The union boss props his filthy boots up on my desk.—The workers, why they've got everything! Everything! Just like us. There's no difference between us any more. Except for one thing—I'm responsible for everything. I have to carry everything on my own two shoulders. As far as they're concerned, why, they sit there in their bars and drink away their unemployment checks. The government stuffs them full, left and right.

EVERYMAN: Please, do me a favor and quit whining at me. You've only got yourself to blame!

POOR NEIGHBOR: What?

EVERYMAN: You're too soft. You've always been too soft. Even as a child. A big mouth, and nothing to back it up. You were always playing the martyr. Do you remember?

POOR NEIGHBOR: Thomas! 3 million! Then I'll be back on my feet again! Just 3 million.

(*EVERYMAN doesn't answer.*)

POOR NEIGHBOR: The stockholders are stoning me to death! I don't dare set foot in the office any more!—Thomas! We've been friends for so long!

(*The DEVIL types on his computer. POOR NEIGHBOR hears the clack of the keyboard, looks at the monitor, steps closer, stares uncomprehendingly at the monitor, looks at EVERYMAN. EVERYMAN steps up, also looks at the monitor, is not surprised.*)

POOR NEIGHBOR (*drained*): That's not possible! That's just not possible! (*looks at EVERYMAN*).

DEVIL: What's the matter? You've got every reason . . .

EVERYMAN (*simultaneously*): What's the matter? You've got every reason to be happy. Your company is saved. (*points to the monitor*) I didn't invest 3 million, I put 30 million in your company!

POOR NEIGHBOR (*stunned*): How did you do that? Why didn't I know anything about this?

DEVIL: Overnight.

EVERYMAN: Oh, it happened practically overnight. A few
  banks bought up stock on my behalf.

DEVIL (*grinning*): Nice and quiet!

(*POOR NEIGHBOR sits down, crushed.*)

POOR NEIGHBOR: You swallowed up my company. You
  bastard!

EVERYMAN: I saved jobs, my friend. Everybody will give
  me the credit for that.

(*POOR NEIGHBOR gets up, goes over to the monitor, looks
at it.*)

POOR NEIGHBOR (*triumphantly*): I still hold 30 percent
  of the stock!

DEVIL: Brother. Vice President.

EVERYMAN: That's right, together with your brother.
  He's the new Vice President. He's on my side.

(*POOR NEIGHBOR almost collapses.*)

POOR NEIGHBOR: But I promise you one thing! You'll
  feel my 15 percent! I won't let you dump me just like
  that!

DEVIL: Manila. A girl.

EVERYMAN: In Manila a girl died. A little girl. Just a
  baby.

(*POOR NEIGHBOR just stares at EVERYMAN, suddenly
collapses unconscious on the floor. EVERYMAN is frightened, kneels down, props up POOR NEIGHBOR. The
DEVIL types something into his computer, the printer immediately prints out a contract in triplicate.*)

EVERYMAN: Anthony!

DEVIL: Don't worry, he'll come out of it in a minute.

EVERYMAN (*suddenly, with horror*): What are we doing? (*looks at the DEVIL*) What are we really doing?

DEVIL: The same as always, sir. Just with a little more intensity. And with more honesty.

(*In anguish, EVERYMAN laughs out loud.*)

DEVIL: Get ahold of yourself, if you don't mind my saying! Stick to your guns! You are who you are!

(*EVERYMAN nods slowly, looks at the POOR NEIGHBOR who starts to regain consciousness. EVERYMAN helps him up. POOR NEIGHBOR looks around, disoriented, remembers, is overcome with horror.*)

POOR NEIGHBOR: It was an accident, Thomas! An accident! I didn't want it to happen! (*as if to excuse himself*) She was a prostitute!

(*The printer has finished printing out the contract, the DEVIL gets up, tears the pages from the printer, lays them on the table, pulls out a fountain pen, holds it in front of POOR NEIGHBOR who looks at EVERYMAN.*)

DEVIL: Sign.

EVERYMAN (*resisting from his heart*): You know, Anthony . . .

DEVIL (*more emphatically*): Sign!

EVERYMAN (*suddenly completely cold*): You'll sign over your 15 percent to me. As a symbolic gesture.

(*POOR NEIGHBOR stares at him.*)

EVERYMAN (*threatening*): Understand?

(*POOR NEIGHBOR staggers to the table, the DEVIL puts the pen in his hand, POOR NEIGHBOR signs the three copies. The DEVIL places the third copy in POOR NEIGHBOR's left hand, takes the pen out of his right hand. POOR NEIGHBOR supports himself with one hand on the*

table, is on the verge of passing out again, pulls himself to-
gether, drags himself over to the door.)

EVERYMAN: Your briefcase!

(POOR NEIGHBOR doesn't react. EVERYMAN picks up
POOR NEIGHBOR's briefcase from the floor, brings it over
to him, presses it in his hand.)

DEVIL: Fired.

EVERYMAN (*tormented*): No!

DEVIL (*more emphatically*): Fired!

EVERYMAN (*to POOR NEIGHBOR*): You're fired!

(POOR NEIGHBOR stands there, stunned. The door
opens, DEATH enters as an old OFFICE BOY, documents
requiring EVERYMAN's signature under his arm. POOR
NEIGHBOR looks up, sees DEATH, goes over to the open
door and thus straight toward DEATH. It looks as if POOR
NEIGHBOR wants to turn to DEATH for help, but DEATH
steps aside.)

DEATH (*points out the door, to POOR NEIGHBOR*): After
    you . . . !

(POOR NEIGHBOR looks at DEATH, goes out, DEATH
closes the door after him.)

DEATH (*to EVERYMAN*): These require your signature,
    sir!

EVERYMAN: Yes, that's fine . . .

(EVERYMAN goes over to the bar, pours himself another
glass of whisky, DEATH looks at the DEVIL.)

DEVIL (*grinning*): Hi there!

(DEATH doesn't answer, goes over to the desk, waits there
for EVERYMAN.)

EVERYMAN (*to the DEVIL*): How about you?

DEVIL: No, thanks. I don't drink.

(*DEATH looks at the DEVIL with some disdain. EVERY-MAN, drink in hand, returns to his desk, lights another cigarette.*)

EVERYMAN (*pointing to the DEVIL*): Henry, this is my new consultant! (*sits down*).

DEATH (*already knows it*): Yes.

DEVIL: Well, old boy? How's business?

(*DEATH doesn't answer, lays out, in order, various documents requiring EVERYMAN's signature. EVERYMAN quickly skims through each document, signs.*)

DEVIL: I guess he doesn't talk to just anybody.

EVERYMAN: Henry is a leftover. From my father's time. (*smiles*) I inherited him from my father.—Right, Henry?

(*DEATH nods.*)

EVERYMAN: Shortly before my father's death, he made me promise to take on old Henry. Henry belongs to the firm, just like our company logo.—How are you doing? How's your health?

DEATH: I'm healthy, sir.

EVERYMAN: Glad to hear it. May I offer you something to drink?

DEATH: But, sir! You know I don't drink!

EVERYMAN: Oh, yes, of course! I'm sorry!—My new colleague is apparently a teetotaler, too. You two belong together.

(*DEATH looks at the DEVIL who grins back.*)

DEATH: I don't think he's a teetotaler, if you don't mind my saying.

EVERYMAN (*smiling*): No? What makes you think so?

(*DEATH doesn't answer.*)

DEVIL: The old man's right, of course! I'm a hedonist. Absolutely! My work is my pleasure. There can be no greater pleasure than one's work. To do whatever you want. Anything. Everything. Recklessly.

(*DEATH takes the folder with the signed documents and closes it, takes it under his arm.*)

DEATH (*suddenly, to the DEVIL*): Schemer! Agitator! You snake!

EVERYMAN (*surprised*): Why, Henry! What's wrong?

(*The DEVIL grins.*)

DEATH: Beg your pardon, sir! I beg your pardon!

(*EVERYMAN shakes his head, signs the last document, DEATH picks up the folder and sticks it under his arm with the rest, slowly walks to the door. EVERYMAN watches him go.*)

EVERYMAN: He's getting old. And strange. I won't be able to keep him on much longer.

DEVIL (*grinning*): I'm afraid he'll be with you to the very end.

EVERYMAN (*smiling*): You're probably right.

(*DEATH reaches for the door knob, the door is shoved open, DEBTOR—in suit and tie, carrying a briefcase—enters, obese and sweating, collides with DEATH so that the latter almost falls down. DEBTOR walks right up to EVERYMAN, collapses into the armchair in front of the desk, holds his briefcase on his knees. DEATH looks over briefly at him, exits, closes the door behind him.*)

DEBTOR: I've got a kidney stone, a huge one! And diabetes. That's the only reason I'm not in prison right now. Been declared unfit for incarceration.

(*EVERYMAN doesn't answer.*)

DEBTOR: I would've paid them! They didn't have to confiscate all my property right off the bat!

EVERYMAN: Now, listen, I'm not some savings and loan office.

(*The DEVIL types on his computer, looks at the monitor.*)

DEVIL: 1.3 million in outstanding debts. For more than a year. Your checks bounced! (*grinning*) That's fraud!

DEBTOR: But you've got a huge company here. A conglomerate! What are 13 million to you? My house is gone. My very own house! This morning I got the eviction notice. Where am I supposed to live?

(*The DEVIL types on the computer, looks at the monitor.*)

DEVIL: Don't you still have a little home in the mountains?

(*DEBTOR is stunned for a moment, because he thought no one knew about it.*)

DEBTOR: What am I going to do in the mountains? I have to be here. To bring my company back to life.

DEVIL (*looking at the monitor*): And a little home at the shore. Even though it's listed in your wife's name.

DEBTOR (*ignoring the DEVIL*): I've got a fabulous deal in the works. With an Arab country. Absolutely blue-chip. The deal of a lifetime!

DEVIL (*looking at the monitor*): We know all about it.

DEBTOR: And now you're going to tie my hands? You do that, and it'll be impossible for me to repay you!

EVERYMAN: You don't have enough capital to bring off the deal. You're just dreaming.

DEBTOR (*gasping for air*): I need my insulin!

(*He stands up, unbuttons his pants, pulls them down, sits back down, frantically opens his briefcase which is chock full of papers and private items, digs around until he finds a vial, breaks off the top, quickly looks for a disposable syringe, finds one, draws the insulin into the needle, presses out the air, injects the insulin into his thigh, then pulls his pants back on.*)

DEBTOR (*talking non-stop, during the above*): Yesterday, I collapsed right in the middle of the street! A 16-wheeler almost ran over me. My cholesterol count is way too high. Here, here in my groin, I'm all swollen up. Have to have an enema first thing in the morning and late at night, just so I can take a shit. Here! My stomach is hard as stone! I think I'm dying!

DEVIL: Old bitch. (*begins to type*)

DEBTOR: My wife, the old bitch, is down there on the beach, with all her fur coats and jewels and won't let go of a penny. Where does she think she got all that junk? From me! She gives it all to her Italian gigolo. Left and right! If I still had a car, I'd drive right down there and bump her off.

(*The contract that the DEVIL had typed into his computer is now printed in triplicate.*)

DEVIL: Jump in.

EVERYMAN (*getting up*): I'll jump in on your deal. Give you the 1.3 million as your share. I'll withdraw the restraining order.

DEBTOR: What? Really?

(*EVERYMAN nods. DEBTOR gets up, his briefcase slides off his knees, dumping the entire contents on the floor.*

DEBTOR *rushes over to EVERYMAN, takes his hand and shakes it vigorously with both hands.*)

DEBTOR: I'll never forget you for this. Never! Now my wife'll get hers! Now I'm going to get a divorce. I'll send a bunch of goons after her muscle-bound boyfriend.

(*The DEVIL tears the contract from the printer, the noise distracts DEBTOR. The DEVIL pulls out his fountain pen, offers it to DEBTOR who walks over. The DEVIL lays the contract on the table.*)

DEBTOR (*to EVERYMAN*): The contract?

EVERYMAN: The contract. We're partners!

(*DEBTOR picks up the contract, glances through it.*)

DEBTOR: I ought to have my lawyer . . .

EVERYMAN: I don't have time!

(*The DEVIL puts the fountain pen in DEBTOR's hand; the latter is furiously trying to skim through the contract.*)

EVERYMAN: Well, something wrong?

DEBTOR: I've got a lump in my throat, I don't feel well!

EVERYMAN: Either you sign right now, on the spot, or the deal is off.

(*DEBTOR resigns himself, signs the three copies, the DEVIL gives him the third copy for his records. DEBTOR rushes over to his briefcase, stuffs the contents back inside, shuts the case, totters to the door, all the while glancing down at the contract.*)

DEBTOR (*reading the contract*): Oh, shit! Oh, shit! I think I'm going to throw up.

EVERYMAN: Not in my building, please!

(*DEBTOR opens the door. EVERYMAN's MOTHER has*

been standing just outside, a lap dog in her arm. DEBTOR bumps into her, disappears. Indignant, EVERYMAN's MOTHER watches DEBTOR go, then enters, leaving the door wide open. MISTRESS appears in the doorway, gives EVERYMAN's MOTHER a dirty look, closes the door.)

MOTHER: You've kept me waiting a long time!

EVERYMAN: If I were father, you'd never have gotten in the door. No one in the family would. Except me, as his heir apparent. On my 14th birthday, for the very first time, he allowed me to enter his sanctuary.

MOTHER: What am I supposed to do? You never come to see me anymore.

EVERYMAN *(lighting a cigarette)*: But you know how that is, mother! It was the same way with father. The company eats us up. It's always been that way. No time for a private life. Do you think I enjoy it?

MOTHER: I'm alone! I'm depressed! I can't sleep!

EVERYMAN: Who can, these days . . . Take something!

MOTHER: I have been. All the time. Too much. Most people would never wake up again. But nothing helps. I can't sleep because I'm afraid. Afraid!

EVERYMAN: Of what?

MOTHER: Of my dreams! I have dreams! Horrible dreams.

EVERYMAN: Here, have a drink!

(EVERYMAN makes her a drink.)

MOTHER: And when I wake up, the dreams continue. They just keep going. Do you know what I'm saying? They never stop!

(EVERYMAN gives her the drink, she sips from the glass, only now becoming aware of the DEVIL's presence, glances

over at him. Grinning, the DEVIL raises his hand in greeting. MOTHER looks at him, becomes frightened, looks at EVERYMAN.)

EVERYMAN: My new consultant! This man has an unbelievable power, simply unbelievable. *(to the DEVIL)* We'll discuss your salary later. And, of course, you'll get a healthy commission.

DEVIL: Why, that's just fine! Makes me very happy.

MOTHER *(anxiously)*: Would you please send him away?

EVERYMAN: What?

MOTHER: I would like to speak with you, in private.

EVERYMAN: Mother! We've got work to do!

MOTHER: Send him out! Please!

DEVIL: No.

EVERYMAN *(to MOTHER)*: Five minutes!

(EVERYMAN gives a sign to the DEVIL who gets up, slightly miffed, goes over to the elevator, presses the button, the elevator doors open, the DEVIL steps in, the doors close, but the elevator doesn't move—the light remains at CEO.)

MOTHER *(softly)*: I dream of the devil. Do you hear me? I dream of the devil.

EVERYMAN: Aren't you in therapy any more?

MOTHER: Son, therapists aren't worth a damn!

EVERYMAN: Well, if you're dreaming about the devil, why don't you go see Uncle George!

MOTHER: I went to see Uncle George. The Cardinal advised me to find a good therapist.—Oh, my son, I dream things . . . ! *(approaches him, in a hushed voice)* You're in danger!

EVERYMAN: What?

MOTHER: You're in danger, my son!

EVERYMAN (*fed up*): What danger is that?

MOTHER: It's not my fault. Believe me! It overwhelms me all the time. My head is about to explode. It's not my fault. I used to be so normal. Rational. You remember. I was always a good wife to your father. Never hysterical.

EVERYMAN: What danger, mother?

MOTHER (*not listening to him*): On the ride over, a young man was standing by the roadside, a hitchhiker. Out by the interstate exit. I picked him up. My chauffeur was furious. The old codger, you know him, of course. He's got more class-consciousness than I do.

EVERYMAN: What are you talking about?—Listen, mother, I . . .

MOTHER: I found him touching.

EVERYMAN: What?

MOTHER: The young man. He had some chocolate. And a piece of bread. He shared them with me.

EVERYMAN (*impatient*): Mother, please!

(*MOTHER begins to cry. Helpless, EVERYMAN heaves a loud sigh. MOTHER sits down on one of the leather armchairs, places her glass on the table, pulls out a handkerchief, wipes away her tears.*)

MOTHER: We had to stop. There was a group of demonstrating workers. They gave me some dirty looks. A big car with a chauffeur—that was all they needed to know. Somebody picked up a rock and was about to throw it. But then he saw the young man beside me, and put down the rock. (*looks at EVERYMAN*)

You can't fire these people! Father never would have wanted it! You have a responsibility!

EVERYMAN (*sits down in the leather armchair across from his MOTHER*): Of course I have a responsibility. To the company.

(*MOTHER doesn't answer.*)

EVERYMAN: Please, mother, you really don't understand any of this!

MOTHER: Just then a black Porsche raced past. Right through the middle of the workers. They leaped back out of the way.—He was inside (*points over to the DEVIL's computer*) And he laughed. (*insistently*) He's not the proper consultant for you, my son!

EVERYMAN (*getting up*): Mother, today is really a rough day. Everything is going wrong. Everything. The company's in trouble, and Brigitte—

MOTHER: Something's happened to her, hasn't it?

EVERYMAN: Yes. Attempted suicide. Uncle Sebastian was able to get there in time. How do you know about it?

MOTHER: That woman out there, she listens in on all your calls. I could read it in her eyes . . . —Send her away, Thomas! She's not for you. She's just a little floozy who wants to sleep her way to the top. A pretty face, but inside a gaping void. Uncultured.

EVERYMAN (*growing angry*): Mother!

MOTHER (*rises*): She doesn't love you! She's just using you!

EVERYMAN: Please don't butt in on my affairs, okay? I'm not a child anymore.

MOTHER: It's your birthday. Excuse me! Of course, that

was the other reason why I'm here. (*hugs him, kisses him*) Many happy returns, my son!

(*From her handbag MOTHER pulls out a small jewelry box, opens it and takes out a small gold chain with a cross, hangs it around EVERYMAN's neck. He permits it, reluctantly.*)

MOTHER: It's to protect you!

EVERYMAN: Thank you, mother!— And now, you'll have to excuse me—

MOTHER: Certainly! I'm on my way out!—This young man, Thomas, he got out of the car downstairs, right in front of your building. And he said: "He doesn't have much time left. You are his mother. Maybe you can help him. It won't take much. Just some insight. Some understanding. That would be enough." We drove down into the parking garage in the basement, and he waved goodbye. I was very happy. The nightmare, my non-stop nightmare was over. And no sooner do I walk in here, than he (*points to the DEVIL's computer*) . . . he's sitting here. And my nightmare starts all over again! Thomas! I beg you . . .

VOICE OF MISTRESS (*from the intercom*): Tell her to stop chattering, you've got work to do! The phones won't stop ringing!

(*EVERYMAN goes over to his desk, presses a button.*)

EVERYMAN (*furious*): Who do you think you are? If you don't shut up, right now, I'll throw you out!

VOICE OF MISTRESS: Go ahead, throw me out! Do you think I need you? Do you really think this uncultured floozy needs you? I don't need you in bed, and I don't need you for a boss. There are ten more where you came from.

EVERYMAN: You're fired! As of now!

VOICE OF MISTRESS: Okay, Mr. CEO! I'm on my way out the door. But before I go, I've got some news for you. First, your good friend, the Chancellor, says that if you insist on firing 15,000 workers, he'll destroy you. Second, our garbage scow, the one that's been wandering around the globe for over three years now, just sank off the Canadian coast. Supposedly on your orders. The crew is in good health, but, unfortunately, in jail; Canada's going to sue you. Third, the Africans won't pay! Instead, they're offering 300,000 tons of soybeans over the next 10 years. Hope they taste good!—Fourth, Southeast Asia reports losses of over 20 billion. The manager put a bullet through his head.—Fifth, take a quick look at the stock report! You're out of business! You can pack it in! Bye-bye, sweetie!

(The sharp crack of static over the intercom. Silence. EVERYMAN looks at the monitor that gives the market report, is shocked, comes closer to the monitor, stares at it, stunned.)

MOTHER: I'll be going now. Use your time wisely, my son!
    (goes to the door)

EVERYMAN *(bellowing)*: Where's that goddamn trouble-shooter?!

(EVERYMAN clutches his heart, feels pain, quickly takes out a pill and swallows it. MOTHER is about to reach for the door to the outer office when it opens and in comes the DEVIL. Right behind him is WORKS as UNION PRESIDENT, who also wants to get in. The DEVIL pushes him back out, steps aside with a grin so that MOTHER can exit, closes the door behind her.)

DEVIL *(happily)*: Here I am!

EVERYMAN: Disaster! One right after the other! (*points to the monitor*) Look! Our stock is falling through the floor!

DEVIL: We'll get on top of it. Cut your losses short, let your profits run! (*sits down at his computer, starts typing*).

EVERYMAN (*frantically*): What profits? What profits are you talking about? (*crushed*) I'm ruined.

DEVIL (*grinning*): Not yet!

EVERYMAN: What can I do?

DEVIL: First of all, you ought to keep your marvelous secretary.

EVERYMAN: She can't talk to my mother like that!

DEVIL: Don't be silly, that was a completely normal reaction. Get going! Talk to her!

(*EVERYMAN ponders, overcomes his reluctance, goes over to his desk and presses a button.*)

EVERYMAN: Rita!—Rita!

VOICE OF MISTRESS: What do you want now? I'm just cleaning out my desk. Leave me alone!

DEVIL (*looking at his monitor*): I need you.

EVERYMAN: I need you, Rita!

VOICE OF MISTRESS: You need a mommy, not a woman!

EVERYMAN: I need you, I really do!

DEVIL (*typing continuously*): You're beautiful.

EVERYMAN: You're beautiful. So beautiful! I can't live without you!

VOICE OF MISTRESS: There are lots of other pretty faces out there!

DEVIL: I love you.

(*EVERYMAN hesitates.*)

DEVIL: I love you.

EVERYMAN: I love you, Rita!

(*A long silence.*)

VOICE OF MISTRESS: No more talk. Prove it!

EVERYMAN: Prove it—how?

VOICE OF MISTRESS: No more floozy! No more bimbo. I want to be "the woman at your side!"

EVERYMAN: But, Rita! My wife just . . .

DEVIL: Agreed.

EVERYMAN (*angrily*): Okay, fine, agreed! You've got me. I'll marry you!

VOICE OF MISTRESS: I want it all in writing!

EVERYMAN: Okay, dammit, fine with me! Can it wait for a couple of minutes? I really ought to take some time and save our company! Is that possible?

VOICE OF MISTRESS: Of course, you've got to save our company. I'll send the head of the Union in right away. He's about to explode anyway.

(*EVERYMAN sits down in his executive swivel chair, the door to the outer office opens, WORKS as UNION PRESI-DENT enters, leaning on a cane, limping on one leg.*)

WORKS: I guess you've gone completely off your rocker, huh? Outside, the mob is gathering, and you, you let me wait. Who the hell do you think you are, anyway? I'm not some beggar, goddammit! If you think you can screw around like this with the President of the Union, then you've got another think coming! Not even your father would've tried something like this. If I want to, I can break you. Break you, you got that? I just snap my fingers—and you're history. I've got 100,000 workers behind me, and don't you forget it!

EVERYMAN: So sorry, Mr. President. I'm under a bit of pressure. Please, (*points to the armchair opposite his desk*) . . . sit down!

WORKS (*doesn't sit down*): You can't do that to us, Mr. Chairman! The barn's already on fire, let me tell you! My workers are already blockading the entire city. Everywhere you look, wanted posters with your name: "Dead or alive!" They're burning effigies, hanging effigies. With your likeness. In just a couple of minutes the mob'll be here. 100,000 workers! 100,000! They'll storm your office, Mr. Chairman. Nobody can stop them. (*sits down in the armchair*) Nobody but me!

DEVIL (*gets up*): A drink?

WORKS: What?—Yeah, sure! Something strong!

(*The DEVIL goes over to the bar, pours a whisky.*)

WORKS: I shouldn't even be sitting here. I should be outside. At the head of the demonstration. Lots of 'em already think I'm a traitor. Because I'm sitting here, talking with you. It's a dangerous game for me. A very dangerous game! But you know how it is—I'm no lunatic, I'm a nice guy, deep down in my heart; a man of moderation, of peace. Of peace for the workers. I'm a guy you can talk to. Anytime. If you've got good intentions.

(*The DEVIL approaches with the drink in one hand and an open box of cigars in the other. WORKS takes the glass and drinks, reaches into the box, squeezes a few cigars, takes one out, bites off the tip, spits it out. The DEVIL gives him a light, sits back down at his computer, types something. WORKS drinks and puffs away, looks at EVERYMAN encouragingly.*)

EVERYMAN (*resigned*): What can I tell you?

DEVIL: The age of blacksmiths is past.

EVERYMAN: The age of blacksmiths is past, Mr. President! This branch of industry has no future. Who needs steel and weapons anymore? In the age of synthetics and disarmament.

WORKS: Oh, get off it! There's still plenty of wars! Sure, mostly localized wars, but it all adds up in the long run, wouldn't you say?

EVERYMAN: None of them have any money! They want to pay with soybeans!

WORKS (*grinning*): But some of 'em will pay with oil, won't they?

DEVIL: The government.

EVERYMAN: The government's constantly on my back! It interferes with business! (*types on his computer, looks at the monitor*) Here! Here's a list of the countries where I'm not allowed to sell weapons!

(*WORKS guffaws.*)

DEVIL: Great numbers of workers.

EVERYMAN: I don't need great numbers of workers anymore! I've got to down-size. Retool to robots. I need skilled workers. Specialists!

DEVIL: Working stiffs.

EVERYMAN: No more burly, beer-drinking, soot-covered working stiffs! Their brains burned out by the heat from the foundry!

WORKS (*puts his glass down, gets up*): Hey, don't insult my workers! I even worked in the foundry myself! Burly working stiffs! Damn, now the barn's really on fire! Outrageous! A lot of those guys are highly intelligent! They just need to be retrained!

EVERYMAN: Retrained, my foot!

DEVIL: The government.

EVERYMAN: Fine with me. Retrain them. But that's the government's job. Not mine.

WORKS (*looks at his watch*): Won't be long now, and they'll be here.

DEVIL: We've known each other . . .

EVERYMAN (*simultaneously*): We've known each other for a long time now, Mr. President!

DEVIL: Benefits package.

EVERYMAN: I've really gone as far as I can go. I've always met you half-way. Our benefits package is exemplary! Company-financed apartments, company-financed vacations, home-heating allowance, additional retirement benefits, subsidies, overtime pay, bonuses. You're eating me alive! You're just eating me alive!

DEVIL: 5,000.

WORKS (*simultaneously*): 5,000!

EVERYMAN: What?

WORKS: 5,000! 5,000 lay-offs!

DEVIL: 15,000.

EVERYMAN (*simultaneously*): 15,000! That's the best I can do!

WORKS: Then there'll be a riot! Then heads'll roll!

DEVIL: And my head—

WORKS (*simultaneously*): And my head'll roll, too! And then other people'll take charge. Completely different kinds of people! They're hard. A lot harder than I am! Then there'll be another struggle. A class struggle!

EVERYMAN: 15,000! I really should let 25,000 go, if I were only looking out for the company's interests!

(*WORKS goes up to the desk, stubs his cigar out in the ashtray.*)

WORKS: I'm going to leave you alone now. When my workers get here, I'll be leading the charge. That's my job.

(*WORKS goes to the door, EVERYMAN frantically looks over at the DEVIL who is calmly typing on his computer, looking at the monitor.*)

DEVIL: Company sports club.

EVERYMAN: I've spent 23 million for the company sports club.

WORKS (*turning around*): I really appreciate it. Believe me, Mr. Chairman, I'd rather march my workers on down to the stadium than come up here. I'd rather be yelling "Score!" than "Strike!" (*reaches for the doorknob*)

DEVIL: Halfback.

EVERYMAN: I'll buy you the best halfback in the world!

(*WORKS pauses, slowly turns to face EVERYMAN, freezes, with his mouth wide open.*)

WORKS: What?

EVERYMAN: The best halfback in the world. The best defenseman. The best goalie.

DEVIL: President.

EVERYMAN: And you'll be the club president! Highly paid! With your hand free to do as you please. Complete control. You can buy whoever you want. Price is no object. We'll win the European Cup!

(WORKS just stands there, flabbergasted, on the verge of surrender.)

DEVIL: Another drink?

(WORKS nods, slowly returns to the desk, sits back down in the armchair. The DEVIL makes him a drink. On the street down below, we can hear the increasing noise of 100,000 demonstrating workers as they approach the building—the sound is like roaring surf. We can't quite make out the slogans shouted through bullhorns. The DEVIL brings another drink to WORKS who takes a big swallow. The DEVIL sits back down at his computer.)

WORKS: Actually, I've always been a soccer player. But I had to go to work in the foundry. Like my father did. And my grandfather. The foundry ruined me. Destroyed me. *(unbuttons his vest, opens his shirt collar)* Here, my whole stomach was burned! *(stands up, pulls up his left pantleg)* And my left leg. Muscle deterioration. Just skin and bones. *(sits down, buttons up his shirt and vest)* All my hopes destroyed. So I became a steward. The union . . .

DEVIL: I hate it—

WORKS *(simultaneously, as he rises)*: The union . . . to tell the truth, I hate it! Solidarity . . . ugh! I'm a loner. If I'm around more than ten people, I start to sweat. Even in the soccer stadium I've got my own box seat.—Envy! Everything's based on envy. I could afford God-knows-what: a villa, a yacht, expensive cars, women! I'm forced to enjoy everything on the sly. How's that going to look? A union president who enjoys life. That's not right. A union president isn't allowed to enjoy life! Or else his colleagues and the union membership'd make mincemeat out of him. 100,000 union members are watching me. Are watching my lifestyle. It's unbearable. Even as a child I enjoyed life. Even as a child I hated poverty. Really hated it! That's why I wanted to be a soccer player! To get rich! Rich! To enjoy luxury! Once I saw his picture in my mother's magazines (*looking at EVERYMAN*) A picture of your father. At a New Year's Eve party. In the background, the buffet. What a spread, and piled so high! That night I snuck down to the pantry! Gorged myself on sausage. Gorged myself on our entire stock of sausage until I was ready to explode. And, of course, I got a whipping for it. From my soot-covered father. He beat me black and blue. I threw up from fear and pain. Threw up all that good sausage, right there on my mother's clean kitchen floor! Then and there I swore to myself: Wealth and power! No matter what it costs!—Now I'm sixty. Never had anything.

EVERYMAN: It's not too late.

WORKS: Right! I want to enjoy these last couple of years before I kick the bucket!

(*The noise from the workers swells, ALL THREE listen.*)

WORKS: The unchained masses! Frightening!

DEVIL (*grinning*): Who unchained them?

WORKS: Me. I stirred 'em up. (*frightened, to EVERYMAN*) They'll kill us!

DEVIL: The government.

WORKS: The government! That's our only chance! (*goes over to EVERYMAN*) You'll keep your word?

EVERYMAN: 15,000?

WORKS: 15,000.

EVERYMAN: Part-time work for another 10,000?

(*WORKS stares off into space, regains his composure.*)

WORKS: Okay. Done.

EVERYMAN: Elimination of the additional retirement benefits.

WORKS: What?

EVERYMAN: I've got to eliminate the additional retirement benefits.

WORKS: No! No! Now you've gone too far. No! (*turns away from EVERYMAN*) Then the whole deal's off. Sorry.

DEVIL: One-time severance pay bonus.

EVERYMAN: A compromise. I'll offer the retiring workers a one-time severance pay bonus: 150 million dollars.

(*WORKS paces around the room, struggles with himself, deliberates.*)

WORKS (*screams out*): Yes! Okay! Shit! You goddamm pirate!—But don't announce it now. I don't want them to tie that to my tail! Three months from now. But not before!

EVERYMAN: Fine! (*reaches out his hand to WORKS*): Well, have we got a deal?

(*WORKS approaches, shakes hands with EVERYMAN.*)

EVERYMAN: You'll have your contract later today. As president of the soccer club. Back-dated, of course. So that there's no connection to today's events.

WORKS: That's the way I want it.

(*Sudden noise outside in the outer office, the door flies open, WORKS quickly pulls his outstretched hand back. WORKERS in blue overalls and yellow hardhats storm in. A few SECURITY GUARDS try in vain to stem the tide. Even MISTRESS is fighting like a lioness to force the WORKERS back outside.*)

MISTRESS: Out! Out! Out! Out!

(*ONE WORKER pushes her out of the way, MISTRESS flies across the room.*)

WORKS (*raising one hand*): Hold it! Hold it!

(*The WORKERS pause, MISTRESS gets up, primps her hair back into place.*)

WORKS: I've had a look at the books. He's got to lay off somebody, or the whole company'll go belly up. Then you'll all be out of work!

(*Nevertheless, A FEW WORKERS try to get at EVERY-MAN. WORKS holds them back.*)

WORKS: It's the government's fault! The government! Come on, let's go! Let's go kick some asses! (*heads for the door*) Down with the government!

(*THE WORKERS follow WORKS.*)

THE WORKERS: Down with the government!

(*WORKS exits, THE WORKERS follow him. A SECURITY GUARD looks at EVERYMAN apologetically, closes the door from the outside. The nightmare is over, it's quiet, though we can still hear the WORKERS shouting down on the street below. A little later we hear WORKS down on the street, shouting through a bullhorn. He wins over the WORKERS, incites the crowd, the mob roars approval, the procession of 100,000 WORKERS slowly moves off into the distance, the noise subsides.*)

MISTRESS (*astonished, to EVERYMAN*): How in the world did you do that?

EVERYMAN (*grinning with scorn*): Huh, no problem . . . !

(*EVERYMAN goes over to the bar, makes himself a drink. The DEVIL types something into his computer, gestures to MISTRESS to come over, points at the monitor; she looks at the monitor.*)

MISTRESS: What? A date for the wedding? Next week? (*to

EVERYMAN) Is that true? But ... what about your wife ... ?

EVERYMAN: Do you think a computer would lie?

(*MISTRESS throws herself around EVERYMAN's neck. One of the telephones starts ringing. EVERYMAN reaches over with one free arm to press a button on his desk, since MISTRESS won't let go of him.*)

EVERYMAN: Yes?

VOICE OF THE THIN COUSIN: Thomas?

EVERYMAN: Yes?

VOICE OF THE THIN COUSIN: Some bad news. Your wife just died.

(*MISTRESS lets go of EVERYMAN, stares at the intercom.*)

EVERYMAN (*taken aback*): What? Why ... what do you mean?

VOICE OF THE THIN COUSIN: Well ... It's awfully hard for me to tell you ... She jumped out the window. Can't imagine where she got the strength to do it. I gave her enough injections to knock her out.

(*EVERYMAN sits down.*)

VOICE OF THE THIN COUSIN: She left a message for you. Do you want to hear it?

DEVIL: No.

EVERYMAN (*softly*): Yes.

(*The DEVIL raises his eyebrows.*)

VOICE OF THE THIN COUSIN (*reads*): I am an unbearable burden on you. On everybody. On myself as well. I can't go on. I want to die. There won't be any note for the newspapers. That was just a threat. As always. My stock portfolio is willed to you, naturally. Good bye. I love you.

EVERYMAN: Really dead?

VOICE OF THE THIN COUSIN: Yes, I'm afraid so.

EVERYMAN (*gets up*): Goddammit, you've got all those machines! Hook her up! That can't be true! What kind of a doctor are you, anyway?

VOICE OF THE THIN COUSIN: When someone's brain is splattered all over the street, there's not much even I can do. I'm dreadfully sorr . . .

(*EVERYMAN angrily presses a button, the VOICE OF THE THIN COUSIN is interrupted. EVERYMAN sits down in his chair, depressed.*)

MISTRESS: I'm very sorry. (*goes to the door, turns around*): We'll set a later date, naturally.

EVERYMAN: Date for what?

MISTRESS: For the wedding.

EVERYMAN (*screaming*): I wouldn't marry you—

DEVIL (*in a loud, cutting voice*): Yes, you will!

EVERYMAN (*in despair*): I can't go on! I can't go on!

(*MISTRESS comes back over to EVERYMAN, puts her hand on his shoulder.*)

DEVIL: I want you.

(*EVERYMAN doesn't speak.*)

DEVIL (*louder*): I want you!

EVERYMAN (*softly*): I want you. I really do want you.

MISTRESS: I know.

(*MISTRESS exits. The DEVIL looks over at EVERYMAN.*)

DEVIL: Don't quit on me now! We've got to bring the company back to life. Today. Now!

EVERYMAN: I can't go on.

(*The DEVIL looks at him, decides to take matters into his own hands.*)

DEVIL: Will you grant me complete authority?

EVERYMAN: Do whatever you want!

(*The DEVIL types on his computer, looks at the monitor.*)

DEVIL: 1,000 tanks in stock . . . (*types some more, looks up*) 50,000 anti-tank missles . . .

(*The DEVIL stands up, takes off his jacket, drapes it around the back of the chair, rolls up his sleeves, goes over to EVERYMAN, motions to him to stand up. EVERYMAN stands up, goes over to the sitting area, lies down on the sofa. The DEVIL sits down in the executive swivel chair behind the desk, picks up the telephone, punches in a number, waits.*)

DEVIL: Troubleshooter here! His Excellency is expecting my call—Thank you! Hello, old buddy!—Yes, it's me. Long time no see.—Fine! Fine! Tremendous! Business is great. Yours too?—It's not? What's wrong?—You don't say? Well, then I can help. When the masses are restless, they need an external enemy.—Of course there's one. Your neighbor's buying arms, and covets your country's charms! (*laughing*) He's after a small chunk of your real estate!—Well, as you know, I've got my sources.—I know, your weapons systems are out-of-date. That's precisely why I'm calling. I can get you the most modern tanks in the world. The best of the best! 1,000 units!—At a great price! These tanks are practically indestructible.—No problem, I can arrange for credit.—Sure, naturally!—Of course you can have a commission. 10 per cent, okay?— Deposited to the same old account, right?—Don't worry, my phone line is absolutely safe.—Naturally, it'll all be taken care of very discretely. We don't want to make anyone nervous, now do we?—As scrap metal. We'll just declare everything as scrap metal!—Great!—Don't thank me, your Excellency! I'm always happy to be of service, as you well know. So, my best wishes to your family, we'll talk again!—*(hangs up, punches in a new number)* Troubleshooter here! Put me through!—Hello, Mr. President, it's me!—*(laughs)* Yes, you're right! The devil's on the loose again! Listen, your neighbor has just purchased 5,000 tanks. The latest model.—Yes! Yes! Of course! They've got something up their sleeve!—Well, in that case your intelligence agency's been asleep on the job again.—That's right. 5,000! They're hard to knock out, they're tough mothers.—Calm down, calm down, just get ahold of yourself! No need to panic! I can get you anti-tank missles.—Yes, of course! The only ones that are capable of knocking out these new tanks. Fully automated guidance system. Just hold them up and shoot. Any fool can operate one.—Naturally! Immediate delivery!—50,000 units! Immediate delivery!—Fine.—Fine. I'll get the ball rolling. Of course you'll receive the normal commission.—You don't need to thank me! Talk to you later!—*(hangs up, punches in a new number)* Reconnect me to his Excellency!—Hello? It's me again!—Right, unfortunately! I just learned that your neighbor's covering his flank with the latest anti-tank missles.—No need to worry, your Excellency! We've got a counter-weapon.—Of course! The latest anti-tank missile protection system.—Okay, I'll send 'em right along.—Boy, have they got a surprise in store for them! They'll run into a firestorm. We'll blow 'em all to hell! *(shouts out loud)* Yippie!

(hangs up) Okay, not bad for starters! *(to EVERY-MAN)* 16 billion!

(During the DEVIL's conversations above, EVERYMAN sits up and listens with growing interest to the details.)

EVERYMAN: 16 billion?

DEVIL: For starters!

EVERYMAN *(gets up)*: Incredible! You really know your business!

DEVIL: That's my job.

(EVERYMAN looks up at the monitor above with the stock prices.)

EVERYMAN: Prices are still falling.

DEVIL: So what? What do they know?

(EVERYMAN looks uncertain.)

DEVIL *(gets up, impatiently)*: Do I have to explain everything to you?—Buy low, sell high! Right?

EVERYMAN: How can I buy anything? I don't have any money!

DEVIL *(upset)*: Are you listening to me, or not? I just made you 16 billion! Those are airtight contracts.

EVERYMAN: I don't feel very well. I really don't feel very well at all!

DEVIL: Would you just forget your private troubles for a moment! The only thing that counts now is business! The only thing!

(EVERYMAN contemplates, goes over to the desk, DEVIL makes room for him. EVERYMAN sits down in his executive swivel chair, punches some buttons on his desk console, waits.)

VOICE OF MAMMON'S SECRETARY *(over the inter-*

com): Bank, main office, secretary to the President
. . . ?

EVERYMAN: Everyman!

VOICE OF MAMMON'S SECRETARY: Oh, good morning,
Mr. Chairman! Good that you called. We've tried to
reach you several times. Just a moment, please!

(*The brief sound of background music over the intercom.*)

VOICE OF MAMMON (*excited*): Thomas?

EVERYMAN: Yes!

VOICE OF MAMMON: Finally! Listen up! My shareholders are waiting outside. They're demanding that
you pay back your loans, immediately.

EVERYMAN: Really? That's nice!

VOICE OF MAMMON: Just scrape up as much as you can.
They're crucifying me. They're accusing me of giving you money without the proper guarantees. And
they're right. You're pulling me down with you.
You're pulling me down into the abyss with you!—
To hell with friendship! A man should never do
business with his friends!

EVERYMAN: Come on, now, why are you getting so hysterical?

VOICE OF MAMMON: Your workers are blockading the
city! The price of your stock can't go any lower!
You're finished!

EVERYMAN: Oh, not at all, my friend. I've just closed several deals. Worth 16 billion!

VOICE OF MAMMON: What?

EVERYMAN: And now I need 20 billion from you. Right
now!

VOICE OF MAMMON: What? Have you gone crazy?

EVERYMAN: No, not at all. I want to buy up my stock. I'll
never get a better price, never again. Come on, old
friend, give it to me as a birthday present! You can't
win if you don't play the game!

VOICE OF MAMMON: You and your deals! Tell me something—

VOICE OF MISTRESS: Excuse me, Mr. Chairman! It's the
Chancellor! urgent!

EVERYMAN: Put him through! Just a moment, Gunther,
the Chancellor's on the line. Please hold!

VOICE OF MAMMON: Okay, I'll wait.

EVERYMAN (*pressing another button on the desk*): Mr.
Chancellor?

(*The noise of 100,000 workers is audible over the phone, in
addition to WORKS' incomprehensible rantings over a
bullhorn.*)

VOICE OF GOOD COMPANION: Do you hear that? Do
you hear the riot?

EVERYMAN: Yes, I can hear it.

VOICE OF GOOD COMPANION: They've surrounded the
Chancellry! 100,000 of them!

EVERYMAN: That's life! They surrounded my office first.

VOICE OF GOOD COMPANION: Hey, what did I do to deserve this? You're the one who wants to lay off
15,000! Not me!

EVERYMAN: Sorry, old friend, it's your problem now. You
represent the government's social programs. I only
have to represent my company. And my company is
not some welfare office.

VOICE OF GOOD COMPANION: I'll crush you! Either
you cancel those lay-offs, or—

DEVIL: All of them.

EVERYMAN: I'll lay off all of them, Mr. Chancellor!

VOICE OF GOOD COMPANION: What? What did you just say?

EVERYMAN: I'll lay off all of them. If you don't help me. All 100,000! And if you count those companies we sub-contract, that's a total of half-a-million people who'll be out of work.

VOICE OF GOOD COMPANION: I'll have you arrested!

VOICE OF MAMMON: I think I'll call back later.

EVERYMAN: You stay on the line, you hear?

DEVIL: Election.

EVERYMAN: In the next election your party's going to take a bath, my dear Mr. Chancellor! Due to incompetence! The workers already know why they're knocking on your door. You're responsible.

VOICE OF GOOD COMPANION: I've pumped millions into your company!

EVERYMAN: You certainly didn't do it for me, you did it for the workers. Didn't you?

(*No answer. The DEVIL is satisfied, sits back down at his computer, begins to type.*)

EVERYMAN: Are you going to help me, or not?

VOICE OF GOOD COMPANION: How am I supposed to help you?

DEVIL: Contracts.

EVERYMAN: Well, for instance, by negotiating some contracts for me!

VOICE OF GOOD COMPANION: What contracts are you talking about?

DEVIL (*looking at his monitor*): Hospital.

EVERYMAN: There's going to be a new hospital built right here in the city.

DEVIL: 5 billion.

EVERYMAN: For 5 billion we'll serve as general contractor.

(*Silence.*)

EVERYMAN: Well, what's it going to be? I don't have much time.

VOICE OF GOOD COMPANION: All right! I'll see what I can do.

DEVIL (*looking at his monitor*): State visit.

EVERYMAN: Second of all, next week you're scheduled to make a state visit.

VOICE OF GOOD COMPANION: Yeah—so what?

DEVIL: Three nuclear power plants. 70 billion.

EVERYMAN: In case anybody asks you if our country could provide three fully operational nuclear power plants, then just say yes, and suggest my company. 70 billion.

VOICE OF GOOD COMPANION: Tell me something! How in the hell do you know about that, that's—

EVERYMAN: A good businessman has to keep up with the latest developments. Will you do it, or won't you?

VOICE OF GOOD COMPANION: All right, goddammit! I'll try. Is that it for now?

EVERYMAN: And tell them we've got a huge quantity of soybeans! *grins over at the DEVIL who grins back*).

VOICE OF GOOD COMPANION: Anything else?

DEVIL (*looking at his monitor*): Howitzers. Friendly relations.

EVERYMAN: Just one little thing. Then we can go back to playing tennis together, in peace and friendship.

VOICE OF GOOD COMPANION: What? What is it? Just tell me! (*audible sound of breaking glass, the VOICE OF GOOD COMPANION fades off into the distance*). Why, that's unbelievable! You get me the Secretary of State immediately! (*comes back on the line*) Tell me what you want! But make it fast!

EVERYMAN: I've heard that you have what we might call friendly relations with a gentleman who wants to outfit his army with new howitzers.

(*Silence. Through the intercom we can hear the raging mob of workers, and WORKS who is egging them on.*)

EVERYMAN: Are you still the Chancellor, Fritz?

VOICE OF GOOD COMPANION: That's the last straw! You hear? I've had it!

EVERYMAN: What are you talking about? We all have to exploit our friendly relations! For the good of the local economy.

VOICE OF GOOD COMPANION: There's an embargo against that country! You know that as well as I do! The world press would make mincemeat out of me! They'd call me before the United Nations!

EVERYMAN: But my dear Mr. Chancellor! I can provide you with a bill of sale listing whatever final destination you want. You can choose one yourself. Wouldn't be the first time, now would it?

VOICE OF GOOD COMPANION: That's outrageous! Outrageous! And even worse, you tell me all this over the telephone! What are you trying to do? Ruin me?

EVERYMAN: Not at all! You wanted to ruin me!

DEVIL: Party.

EVERYMAN: I suggest, Mr. Chancellor, that we discuss these matters this evening, at my birthday party. You are coming, aren't you?

VOICE OF GOOD COMPANION: I'm not coming to your goddammed party! That'd be political suicide! (*tumult over the intercom, it sounds as if the WORKERS are trying to storm the Chancellor's office.*)

EVERYMAN: It seems to me that the entire work force is descending on your office, my dear Mr. Chancellor!

VOICE OF GOOD COMPANION (*fades into the distance*): Reinforcements! Where are the reinforcements? For God's sake, where's the Chief of Police? (*The door to the Chancellor's office is apparently smashed, WORKERS storm in.*)

VOICE OF WORKS (*at some distance, through a bullhorn*): You can't do that to us, Mr. Chancellor! Let me tell you, now the barn's on fire!

VOICE OF GOOD COMPANION (*at some distance*): Calm down! Please, Mr. President! (*now back on the line*) Thomas! Mr. Chairman!

EVERYMAN: I'm right here!

VOICE OF GOOD COMPANION: Cancel the lay-offs! Please! Help me!

EVERYMAN: Scratch my back, I'll scratch yours. What do you say about the howitzers?

VOICE OF GOOD COMPANION: All right, goddammit! You'll get the deal!

EVERYMAN: Thank you very much. Tell the President that there won't be any lay-offs!

VOICE OF GOOD COMPANION (*speaking off in the distance*): No lay-offs! There will be no lay-offs! Not one single one! (*cheering from the WORKERS*).

EVERYMAN: For the time being. Contingent upon the success of our deals. Do you hear me?

VOICE OF GOOD COMPANION: Yes! Yes! I hear you. I'll see you at your party after all. Bye!

(*Silence on the line.*)

EVERYMAN: Gunther, are you still there?

VOICE OF MAMMON: Yes, I'm still here! Congratulations, Thomas! That was a stroke of genius.

EVERYMAN: So, you heard everything. That's another 15 billion to my account.

VOICE OF MAMMON: God, am I relieved! My shareholders will be amazed. I'm really proud of you, Thomas.

EVERYMAN: Thanks, Gunther! Does that mean I get the money?

VOICE OF MAMMON: Certainly! Will 20 billion be enough? I'll be glad to give you more.

EVERYMAN: That's enough for starters. I'll see you tonight, won't I?

VOICE OF MAMMON: Now you will! A couple of minutes ago wild horses couldn't have dragged me to your party. But you understand—money can only be seen where there's already money.

EVERYMAN: I know, my friend. See you later!

(*Presses a button, starts to sigh with relief and lean back in his chair.*)

DEVIL: Now—let's get buying! Quick!

(*EVERYMAN picks up the phone, punches in numbers.*)

EVERYMAN: Main office! The boss.—Yes, I saw it! And what do you do when prices are falling?—Well?— Where did you go to school, buddy?—Buy low, sell high! That's the ticket!—That means, buy up everything that the stockholders have dumped! Everything!—Money? The bank is behind us with 20 billion. We've got a surplus of over 30 billion.—Yes! Yes!—By the way, there'll be no lay-offs! The company's back on solid ground!—Spread the word! Leak it to the media! But first of all: buy! Buy everything! We had too many stockholders interfering with company business, anyway! Got it?— Good!

(EVERYMAN hangs up, leans back and exhales, casts a triumphant glance at the DEVIL, lights a cigarette. MISTRESS enters, radiant.)

MISTRESS: You're incredible! You're unbeatable! *(rushes to him, hugs him)* Fantastic! Let's see somebody try and top that!—We've got to drink to your success!

(MISTRESS starts toward the bar, the DEVIL waves her off, gets up, goes to the bar himself.)

MISTRESS: Champagne!

(The DEVIL nods, takes a magnum of champagne out of the refrigerator.)

EVERYMAN *(to the DEVIL)*: But this time you've got to join us!

(The DEVIL smiles, nods, pulls out three glasses, opens the bottle. Just as the cork pops, the door opens and DEATH enters, waits at the door. The DEVIL looks at him, grinning, pours champagne in the three glasses.)

EVERYMAN: What is it, Henry?

(DEATH doesn't answer.)

EVERYMAN *(in a friendly tone)*: You can tell me!

DEATH: I'm worried, Mr. Chairman.

EVERYMAN *(stands up)*: He's worried! *(to MISTRESS)*

Isn't that touching? (*to DEATH*) Henry! You don't need to worry! Not anymore. Everything's on the upswing!

(*DEATH doesn't answer.*)

EVERYMAN (*approaches DEATH*): I would never have fired you, under any circumstances. Never!

DEATH: I know.

EVERYMAN: Come join us in a little glass of champagne!

(*DEATH considers.*)

DEVIL: Well, get with it, old boy! We've got good reason to celebrate!

(*The DEVIL takes out a fourth glass, fills it, DEATH considers.*)

EVERYMAN: Today's my birthday, Henry! Are you trying to insult me?

DEATH: No, of course not, Mr. Chairman.

EVERYMAN: Well, then!

(*EVERYMAN tries to take DEATH by the arm, but DEATH avoids him almost imperceptibly. EVERYMAN is slightly irritated. The DEVIL approaches with the four glasses, hands them around. MISTRESS kisses EVERYMAN on the cheek, clinks glasses with him.*)

MISTRESS: Here's to you! Long live the king!

(*EVERYMAN smiles, clinks glasses with the DEVIL.*)

EVERYMAN: Thank you. You've done a great deal for me.

DEVIL: My pleasure! Cheers, Mr. Chairman! Here's to the company!

EVERYMAN: Yes! (*turns to face DEATH*): And to you, old friend!

(*EVERYMAN clinks glasses with DEATH. At the moment*

*when their glasses touch, EVERYMAN can feel his heart
contracting. He groans, grasps his chest, doubles up. MIS-
TRESS, terrified, reaches for his arm, the DEVIL gives
DEATH a dirty look.)*

ACT TWO

*(Evening. The blinds covering the glass front are open. Out-
side, the city lights are visible. One monitor is still on, the
market reports are running, though the sound is off. The
large conference table is set up as a buffet, with WAITERS
and WAITRESSES behind it. Other SERVANTS with
trays of drinks. Many birthday presents. All GUESTS are
wearing tuxedos, evening dress—except DEATH and
DEVIL who are still dressed as in Part One. On stage:
DEATH as OFFICE BOY, the DEVIL as TROUBLE-
SHOOTER, EVERYMAN'S MOTHER with her lapdog,
EVERYMAN's GOOD COMPANION as FEDERAL
CHANCELLOR with TWO BODYGUARDS, MISTRESS
as EVERYMAN's SECRETARY, FAT COUSIN as CARDI-
NAL, THIN COUSIN as DOCTOR, MAMMON as IN-
VESTMENT BANKER, WORKS as UNION PRESI-
DENT, MEMBERS OF THE BOARD OF DIRECTORS
with their WIVES, MANAGERS, FRIENDS. The
GUESTS are all standing, holding champagne glasses in
their hands, facing the elevator. The DEVIL is the only one
seated, he is typing on his computer in the sitting area, has
no glass. DEATH, too, has no glass; he is standing off to one
side, looking sadly over at the DEVIL. The elevator is just
ascending from the ground floor, a bell chimes, the doors
open. EVERYMAN is standing in the elevator, wearing a
tuxedo. Beside him, his dead WIFE—somewhat pale,
somewhat capricious, but young, lovely, and dressed as she
was at her death—, the dead DEBTOR, rather battered fol-*

*lowing an automobile accident, naturally with his brief-
case in hand, in addition to the STARVING CHILD (AFRI-
CAN), the AMPUTATED CHILD (ORIENTAL), and the
COUGHING CHILD (EUROPEAN). EVERYMAN ignores
his companions, pretending they don't exist. His WIFE will
accompany him throughout, but always one step removed.
The DEBTOR is furious, continuously jostling and cursing
EVERYMAN. The CHILDREN remain at EVERYMAN's
side throughout—except for short forays out among the
guests—and will beg from him silently, automatically, and
persistently.)*

DEBTOR (*shoves EVERYMAN*): Son-of-a-bitch!

STARVING CHILD (*holding an empty bowl up to EVERY-
MAN*): Food! Food!

AMPUTATED CHILD (*has no legs, holding tightly to one
of EVERYMAN's legs*): Legs! Legs!

COUGHING CHILD: Air! Air!

WIFE (*so softly that it can eventually get on one's nerves*):
I love you.

(*EVERYMAN remains standing in the elevator, staring out
at the crowd. After a while his guests become uncomfortable, GOOD COMPANION begins to sing "happy birthday," and ALL join in. EVERYMAN makes an effort to
smile, steps out of the elevator, which shakes the AMPU-
TATED CHILD from his one leg, with his companions in
tow. The elevator doors close. MISTRESS, holding two
glasses, steps up to EVERYMAN and gives him a glass.
ALL hold their glasses high in a toast to EVERYMAN who
forces a grin. The DEVIL now rises to join the others, sings
along. DEATH does not sing. DEATH and the DEVIL are
the only ones who can see EVERYMAN's companions. The
DEVIL notices them, disapproves; DEATH sees it all as a
good sign that perhaps EVERYMAN will gain some insight.)*

ALL (*singing*): Happy birthday to you, happy birthday to you, happy birthday, Mr. Chairman, happy birthday to you!

(*Cries of "Hurray!" and "Cheers!" while ALL raise their glasses to EVERYMAN and drink, except DEATH and the DEVIL. EVERYMAN gives a forced smile, also takes a sip. The DEVIL doesn't like the look on EVERYMAN's face, so he sidles over to him, to keep an eye on him. GOOD COMPANION, WORKS, MAMMON step forward.*)

ALL THREE (*simultaneously*): Mr. Chairman—

(*EVERYMAN bursts out laughing, the THREE exchange surprised glances.*)

WORKS, MAMMON (*simultaneously*): Mr. Chancellor, if you please!

GOOD COMPANION: Mr. Chairman of the Board, my friend! Today was a hot one. A bad day. For you, for me, for the entire country. We were all on the edge of the abyss. But now I feel confident in saying that we are saved, that we have done it, together we have done it, we have overcome enormous difficulties. Your company is saved, our workers' jobs— 100,000 jobs—have been preserved. This day of darkness has turned out to be a day of joy!

(*The GUESTS applaud, DEBTOR whistles shrilly through his teeth in protest, EVERYMAN looks over at him briefly, grins derisively. During the rest of GOOD COMPANION's monologue, the CHILDREN mingle a bit with the GUESTS, beg from them, finger the fine garments. The GUESTS do not notice.*)

GOOD COMPANION: This magnificent success, this grand victory over a crisis that truly affected the entire nation, we owe primarily to you, my friend: to your tireless efforts, to your spirit of self-sacrifice

for the common good, to your feeling of responsibility on behalf of all your countless workers; we also
owe a debt of gratitude for your inexhaustible opti-
mism that any and every crisis can be mastered, if
all work together in the interest of all.

(*Applause. DEBTOR grimaces, as if he had to vomit.*)

GOOD COMPANION: Most honored Chairman, my good
friend (*he makes a sign to ONE of his BODY-
GUARDS who hands GOOD COMPANION a vel-
vet-covered jewelry box and takes the champagne
glass from his hand*) . . . the Federal Government,
late this afternoon, unanimously voted to bestow
upon you on the occasion of your birthday the highest medal our nation has to give, that being the
Golden Eagle Of The Republic.

(*Applause.*)

DEBTOR: Bullshit! And a medal, too! (*to EVERYMAN*)
You, bastard!

(*GOOD COMPANION opens the box, takes out the medal,
hands the box back to the BODYGUARD.*)

WIFE (*during the above ceremony, repeating herself*): I
love you.

EVERYMAN (*turns around to face her, hisses quietly*): Yes!
I heard you!

(*A few of the GUESTS who overheard him, exchange astonished glances. MOTHER and MISTRESS have also heard
EVERYMAN's aside.*)

GOOD COMPANION (*stepping up to EVERYMAN*): One
hour ago I spoke on the telephone with our nation's
President, who is presently out of the country on a
state visit. He begs your pardon for his absence and
has authorized me to convey to you his heartfelt
wishes for a happy birthday and his deepfelt grat-

itude for your accomplishments in the service of our nation.

(*Applause.*)

DEBTOR (*clapping his hands in mockery, yelling in contempt*): Bravo! Bravo! Bravo!

GOOD COMPANION: It is with great personal pleasure, dear Thomas, honored Chairman, that I am pleased to present you with our Golden Eagle!

(*Applause. DEBTOR makes a gesture, dismissing the entire ceremony, goes over to the buffet, ravenously stuffs food in his mouth and drinks champagne, all the while observing the scene. Meanwhile, GOOD COMPANION unfolds the multi-colored ribbon, representing the national colors, and holds it up as the medal dangles from it. The CHILDREN surround EVERYMAN again.*)

EVERYMAN (*gesturing*): Get away! Get away!

(*The CHILDREN retreat a step or two. GOOD COMPANION looks irritated, EVERYMAN bows his head down to receive the medal, GOOD COMPANION places the ribbon about his neck. Continuous applause.*)

GOOD COMPANION: May the flight of this eagle carry you onward and upward, Thomas, higher and higher, and may you never fall, as seemed so dangerously near today! My heartfelt congratulations!

(*Applause.*)

DEBTOR (*yelling over from the buffet*): I hope you choke on it, you bastard!

(*GOOD COMPANION shakes EVERYMAN's hand, hugs him, kisses him on both cheeks, then steps back. ALL are now expecting EVERYMAN's response. Just as EVERYMAN prepares to reply, the CHILDREN mill around him again, he looks down at them.*)

EVERYMAN (*to the CHILDREN*): What do you want from me? I don't have anything to do with you! Get lost! Beat it!

(*The CHILDREN retreat a few steps, the GUESTS look astonished, partially believing that EVERYMAN means them. The DEVIL is upset.*)

DEVIL: A word of gratitude.

(*EVERYMAN is still looking at the CHILDREN.*)

EVERYMAN: Why don't you get lost!

(*The CHILDREN don't budge, just stare at him. The GUESTS are confused. MISTRESS is upset, worried, takes a step toward EVERYMAN, but then stops short, because she is "only" his secretary.*)

DEVIL (*louder*): A word of gratitude!

MOTHER (*steps forward*): What's wrong, Thomas? Don't you feel well?

(*EVERYMAN doesn't hear her.*)

WIFE: I love you.

(*EVERYMAN turns around to face his WIFE, looks at her in despair.*)

DEBTOR: Dumb bitch!

THIN COUSIN (*steps forward*): Thomas!—Thomas!

EVERYMAN (*notices THIN COUSIN*): Oh, Doctor! You're here too? From the morgue . . .

THIN COUSIN: What's wrong with you?

EVERYMAN (*tormented*): I don't know.

GOOD COMPANION: You're burned out. You need a break for a couple of days, you really do.

EVERYMAN: Yes . . . a break . . .

DEBTOR: You'll never get a break, I promise you that. I'll

be with you wherever you go. Even in bed. Even on
the john!

THIN COUSIN: Should I give you a little something?

EVERYMAN: What do you want to give me?

THIN COUSIN: A prescription . . . something to pep you up
. . .

EVERYMAN: Something to pep me up . . .

DEVIL: Yes!

EVERYMAN (*to THIN COUSIN*): Yes, maybe you're right.
Something to pep me up . . .

(*EVERYMAN looks at the CHILDREN who approach him
again, unnoticed by the GUESTS. EVERYMAN motions
THIN COUSIN to come over to him.*)

EVERYMAN (*softly*): Do you think you might have something for—hallucinations?

(*THIN COUSIN looks at him, pulls him aside. The DEVIL
sneaks over, nervously listens in on their conversation.*)

THIN COUSIN (*softly*) : You're having hallucinations?

(*EVERYMAN nods.*)

THIN COUSIN (*softly*): Don't say that out loud!

DEBTOR (*mimicking*): Hallucinations!

THIN COUSIN: Or else your company'll be right back in
the soup. No matter how high your eagle soars.
(*reaches into his medicine bag, pulls out some med-
ication, squeezes two pills out of their foil wrapper*)
Take this for the time being! That'll get you back up
on top! I take 'em myself when I'm feeling down.

(*EVERYMAN sticks the tablets in his mouth, washes them
down with a drink of champagne. DEBTOR approaches,
holding a plate piled high with food from the buffet.*)

DEBTOR (*grinning*): You'll have to take a hellova lot more pills than that to get rid of me! A hellova lot more! (*to EVERYMAN's WIFE*) What do you think, sweetie?

THIN COUSIN: I want to see you at the clinic tomorrow.

EVERYMAN (*lost in thought*): Tomorrow . . .

THIN COUSIN: Right, first thing tomorrow morning! Now pull yourself together!

(*THIN COUSIN steps aside, EVERYMAN looks around the circle of his GUESTS who are all staring at him.*)

EVERYMAN: I beg your pardon. It's been a hard day. Very hard. But now I'm back in the groove!

(*All the GUESTS are still waiting for his acceptance speech, but since he doesn't start, and an embarrassing silence threatens, WORKS strides over to a heavy package that is lying somewhere on the floor, picks it up, steps up to EVERYMAN. During WORKS' speech, the CHILDREN approach EVERYMAN again, surround him, beg, tug at his sleeves and pantlegs. During the following monologue, DEBTOR walks over to WORKS, mimics him, repeats WORKS' words and mocks WORKS in gesture and movement.*)

WORKS: Mr. Chairman, I'll make it short, a union boss shouldn't be making flowery speeches! We've had lots of battles, the two of us, hard-fought battles, sometimes almost brutal; but we always fought with our cards on the table, without cheating, without dirty tricks, without hitting below the belt. As the representative of the working man, I have always placed my demands on the table openly and honestly, and, following a difficult struggle we've always been able to reach consensus. Each of us has been willing to meet the other half-way, each of us has made concessions, has accepted losses, but a livable compromise has always resulted, because you are not some turn-of-the-century capitalist and I'm not some turn-of-the-century Marxist; no, here are two progressive men, two modern managers who aren't concerned about ideology, but about people. Two business leaders who both know that what's good for the company is good for the workers, and what's good for the workers is also good for the company. As Union President, I am proud, very proud that—together with the company and with the government—I was able to avert a major catastrophe and save countless thousands of workers from the threat of unemployment. With this in mind, Mr. Chairman, all the best, and keep plugging!

(*Applause. DEBTOR claps too, sarcastically. WORKS shifts the package under his left arm, can barely hold it up, shakes EVERYMAN's hand, then shoves the heavy package in his arms.*)

WORKS: A small token from your union employees!

(*EVERYMAN hefts the package onto his desk, puts down his glass, unties the ribbon, removes the wrapping paper; inside is a model of a modern field howitzer.*)

DEBTOR (*slapping WORKS on the back*): What a piece of work! Fantastic!

WORKS (*to EVERYMAN*): Our apprentices made it. In their free time, of course.

(*Applause.*)

EVERYMAN: Swell! (*to the AMPUTATED CHILD sitting at his feet*): Right?

MAMMON (*steps forward*): My dear Mr. Chairman, dear Thomas, I would like to join in with birthday greetings of my own, and, as the President of your company's bank, I want to assure you that we will always, always be right by your side. Your credit is unlimited with us!

(*Applause. MAMMON reaches into his coat pocket, pulls out an envelope.*)

MAMMON: As proof of our support and as a sign of our trust I would like to present you with this check, with our very best wishes!

(*MAMMON gives EVERYMAN the envelope. Applause. EVERYMAN opens the envelope, takes out the check, examines it. As the STARVING CHILD holds his empty bowl up, EVERYMAN waves the check in STARVING CHILD's face.*)

EVERYMAN: You could fill your damn bowl a couple of times with this, huh?

(*DEBTOR also looks at the check.*)

DEBTOR: 20 billion! 20 billion! And you ruined me for a lousy 1.3 million! (*punches EVERYMAN*) You, sonofabitch!

(*EVERYMAN pretends not to notice, looks at the check.*)

EVERYMAN: 20 billion ... (*to MAMMON*) Remember how we started out, you and me?

(*DEBTOR goes over to the buffet, piles more food on his plate, gorges himself.*)

MAMMON: Of course, Thomas! Together we pushed fixed-interest loans. Those were the good old days!

EVERYMAN: Yes, those were the good old days! I wanted to show my father that I could make it on my own. Without him. Wanted to bring money into the company, not be a drain on its finances. The way my son is. (*trying to catch a glimpse of MISTRESS*) Where is he? Why isn't he here on my birthday?

MISTRESS: Oh, you remember . . . Caracas!

EVERYMAN: Oh, of course! Caracas . . . !

MISTRESS: Everything has been taken care of. He'll be here tomorrow.

EVERYMAN: Tomorrow! Tomorrow! (*loudly*) There is no tomorrow!

(*The CHILDREN have surrounded him again, stretching out their hands to him.*)

EVERYMAN: Leave me alone! Why do you keep bothering me? And only me? Go bother the others! (*gestures toward the GUESTS*) Everyone here is responsible! Them, too!

(*The GUESTS exchange embarrassed glances.*)

MOTHER (*steps forward*): Thomas!

EVERYMAN: Oh, Mother! You here, too?

MOTHER: Of course I'm here. (*steps up close to him, softly*) Thomas! If you see something, believe in it. Maybe it's a sign. Something that could help.

EVERYMAN (*desparately*): Help . . . ! How? How?

MOTHER (*gently*): Thomas!

DEVIL: Finish her off!

EVERYMAN (*screaming at his MOTHER*): You! You were the one who drilled it into my brain. The company! The company! The company! That's the only thing in the world that matters. The only thing!

DEBTOR: And she's right, too! I really mean it! (*with a glance toward Heaven*) I still do!—Uh-oh, now I've really put my foot in my mouth!

MOTHER (*helplessly*): Father . . .

EVERYMAN: Father! Father wasn't even there! Father was always at the company. And you were his mouthpiece. At home. How could I turn out to be anything but what I am?

DEVIL (*off-handedly*): I don't have to stand here and listen to this nonsense. I only wanted what was best for you.

MOTHER (*the DEVIL has no power over her*): Yes, you're right, Thomas. I'm sorry. I'm so very sorry!

(*The DEVIL turns away, annoyed. MOTHER looks around, is trying to find someone, sees the FAT COUSIN.*)

MOTHER: Your Eminence!

FAT COUSIN (*steps forward*): Yes?

EVERYMAN (*notices him*): Why, Uncle George! Are you here to congratulate me, too?

FAT COUSIN: Naturally, Thomas! (*approaches, shakes his hand*): I wish you a happy birthday!

DEVIL: Provocation.

EVERYMAN: Thank you, your Eminence! Do I have to kiss your ring?

FAT COUSIN: No, you don't have to.

EVERYMAN (*still holding FAT COUSIN's hand*): But I really want to.

(*EVERYMAN looks at FAT COUSIN's ring, kneels on one knee, kisses the ring. FAT COUSIN, embarrassed, withdraws his hand, EVERYMAN remains kneeling. ALL— even FAT COUSIN and the DEVIL—are uncertain if EVERYMAN is serious or if he is only trying to make fun of the Cardinal.*)

EVERYMAN: Will you bless me?

FAT COUSIN: If you really want me to . . . ?

EVERYMAN: Yes, I believe I really do. Even though I have a hard time believing.

(*The DEVIL is upset again, afraid his scheme may be coming unravelled.*)

FAT COUSIN (*becoming indignant*): How am I supposed to bless you if you don't believe?

EVERYMAN (*in depair*): Because I need it! Because I need it! I need blessing, don't you understand?

FAT COUSIN: Of course! Naturally, I understand. I can see you're not doing well. You're having an existential crisis. I'm glad. Perhaps that is a path toward understanding. I will gladly help you on your quest. My confessional will always be open to you. If you still remember what that is—confession.

EVERYMAN: Man, Uncle, I'm not going to tell you my whole goddamn life story! Come on, bless me, that's all I need!

FAT COUSIN: First you must make a confession of faith, then you'll get your blessing! But it must be sincere. Not for the sake of appearances. Not out of convention! The way it was at your drunken wedding. In the cathedral. Where you accepted my blessing with an arrogant grin. Even at your confirmation you grinned at me so arrogantly. As a 12-year-old runny-nosed kid! I was really tempted to slap your face.—Do you know who am I? Who do you think I am? I am a representative of the Church. A dignitary! I demand respect! Not for myself. But for my office! For my office, you understand?

(*EVERYMAN stares straight ahead, looks at the CHILDREN who have surrounded him again, but for the time being are not begging.*)

EVERYMAN (*to the CHILDREN*): He won't give me a

chance. It's the office . . . He's worried about his office. Why don't you go and cling to him for a change? Just look at him! He's just as devoted to the good life as I am. And really ought to be taking care of you. Because of his office! Right? Oh, hell, does it really matter . . . ?

(*EVERYMAN slowly gets to his feet.*)

DEBTOR (*groans out loud*): God, do I feel horrible!

(*DEBTOR wipes the sweat from his brow, frantically tries to find the insulin needle in his briefcase, drops his pants, gives himself an injection while sitting on the floor, remains seated, breathing heavily, leaning back against a table leg.*)

GOOD COMPANION (*during the above, glancing at his watch*): I'm sorry, Thomas, but I have another appointment this evening, unfortunately I have to—

EVERYMAN: You don't have to do anything! You're staying here!

WORKS: Actually, I really should be . . .

MAMMON: Yes, the time has also come for me . . .

EVERYMAN: It's my birthday! My birthday party! And none of you are going to leave until I say so! Is that clear?

(*The DEVIL is relieved that things now seem to be going according to his plan.*)

GOOD COMPANION: Well, all right, a few more minutes . . .

EVERYMAN: You're all embarrassed, aren't you? Because I'm being myself. The Chairman has never been himself before. Not even in front of his friends. And, after all, we are all friends, aren't we?

WORKS: Well, now that you mention it, I'm afraid I have to disagree! As a representative of your employees,

I can't really be a friend of the employer. That's totally incompatible.

EVERYMAN: Well, of course not, Mr. President! Naturally, you're an exception. You and I in bed together—that would really be incompatible. That could cost you your head.

WORKS: Yes, it sure could!

EVERYMAN: Uncle George! What would you suggest I do? In my existential crisis?

FAT COUSIN: Believe!

EVERYMAN: I can't. I'm sorry.

FAT COUSIN: Well, then . . .

EVERYMAN: Is that all you've got to say?

FAT COUSIN: Go see a therapist!

EVERYMAN: A therapist! Of course! Why, you already sent my mother to a therapist. Even though she believes. Apparently. All of a sudden. (*to his MOTHER*) You never said anything to me about all this, since my childhood, since you taught me how to say my prayers, at night, just before I went to bed . . . (*to FAT COUSIN*) I can't believe, because all of a sudden I'm afraid!

(*FAT COUSIN raises his hands, helpless.*)

WIFE: I love you.

(*EVERYMAN turns around to face his WIFE, stares at her for a long time.*)

EVERYMAN: I don't know what that means—love. I liked you. And wanted you. You brought money into the company.—Why did I have to meet you when I was so young? (*somewhat aggressively*) So that it would hurt me so much more?

(*WIFE doesn't answer. EVERYMAN surveys his GUESTS.*)

EVERYMAN: Haven't any of you noticed that someone's missing?—Well? Who's missing? The 64-thousand-dollar question!

(*No one answers. EVERYMAN looks at his WIFE.*)

EVERYMAN: See, Brigitte, nobody's even noticed that you're not here. Nobody's even asked about you. That's how influential I am. How important. (*laughs*)

FAT COUSIN: What's wrong with your wife?

EVERYMAN: She killed herself. This morning.—I visited her two hours ago. (*glances at THIN COUSIN*) In the Doctor's morgue. She's lying there in a drawer. In the deep-freeze. A small, naked, dead woman. Her head is shaved. The scar from the autopsy has been sewn up with a few hasty stitches. I didn't recognize her. (*to his WIFE*) I didn't recognize you. I said to the pathologist, "There must be some mistake." No, no mistake! Beg your pardon, but that's your wife! (*shakes his head*) So strange. Totally strange. Lying there without any hair. Without any makeup on her face. She was always so proud of her hair. All of a sudden I saw her face. Saw it for the very first time. (*looks at his WIFE*) A pretty face. Completely relaxed. Her body, too. So fragile and small . . . like a child . . . (*looks at the CHILDREN*) Like you. I treated her just as badly as I've treated you. And she was always there. She was my wife.— I . . . (*can scarcely go on*) . . . loved her. As she was lying there.—(*looks at his WIFE*) I killed her.

DEVIL (*the OTHERS can't hear him*): No!

EVERYMAN: Yes! I killed her!

(WIFE steps up to EVERYMAN, looks at him.)

DEVIL *(the OTHERS can't hear him)*: She was sick. Wasn't fit to live. The weak must perish, so that the strong can survive.

THIN COUSIN: She was sick, Thomas! There's nothing you could do.

EVERYMAN: I killed her! "Drown! Go ahead and drown," I told her.

(WIFE lays her hand on EVERYMAN's cheek. In despair, he cradles his cheek in her hand.)

THIN COUSIN: Your nerves! Your nerves are shot. It's understandable. Come, now, calm down!

(WIFE slowly withdraws, then disappears unnoticed.)

EVERYMAN: I am calm. I've never been so calm. I'm just trying to figure things out.

GOOD COMPANION: Do you think you could figure things out without us? Now I really have to—

EVERYMAN *(calmly)*: You're staying. Or else I'll retract everything. I'll lay off all my workers. All of them! Then you can pack your bags! And take your government with you! *(to WORKS)* And you, too!

(EVERYMAN notices that his WIFE has disappeared, he looks around the room in search of her.)

EVERYMAN: Brigitte! Brigitte!

(GOOD COMPANION looks over to the THIN COUSIN.)

THIN COUSIN: Thomas! You're coming with me, right now! To my clinic! And you'll take an extended rest! For two weeks. I insist! As your doctor.

EVERYMAN: You won't insist on anything. Or should I tell everybody about the drug-addicted children from rich families, the ones on withdrawal you've got locked up in your basement? Incognito. In strictest confidence. And for a stiff fee! My son, too, of course. Sure! And—the alcoholic politicians too! I almost forgot about them.

THIN COUSIN (*insulted*): You know something, Thomas? I suggest you find yourself another personal physician! (*goes to the door*)

MOTHER: Thomas! You'll apologize right this minute! (*goes after the THIN COUSIN*) Sebastian! Sebastian! Please don't go! He's been through a great deal!

THIN COUSIN: I know. But that's no reason to insult me. To blackmail me. Of course I sweep everything under the rug, do it all the time. But I do it out of friendship. Out of friendship!

MOTHER: Thomas!

EVERYMAN: Yes! I'm very sorry! I apologize! I just don't want anybody dictating to me anymore, that's all. I know what I'm doing. I've never known so clearly in all my life.

THIN COUSIN: Oh, crap! You're completely beside yourself!

EVERYMAN: No. I know who I am. Finally.

THIN COUSIN: Sure, fine, whatever you say . . . (*goes to the door*).

EVERYMAN: I apologized to you, what more do you want?

THIN COUSIN: Nothing at all. I just want to go home. I've also had a very long day. (*opens the door*) Call me if you need anything!

(*THIN COUSIN exits, closes the door behind him. Silence.*)

EVERYMAN: I'm doing everything wrong. I always do everything wrong! Even now!—Today was really the worst day of my life. The worst. I was the worst. A monster.

worst day of my life. The worst. I was the worst. A monster.

DEVIL (*screams in rage, ALL understand him*): This has gone far enough, you understand? Now, pull yourself together! Please!

EVERYMAN: May I present my troubleshooter! The best consultant I ever had. I owe everything to him. I'd be nothing without him. At least that's what he thinks. (*to the DEVIL*) Am I right?

DEVIL: I saved your company!

EVERYMAN: Thank you! Thank you very much! But please don't ever yell at me like that again. Or else you'll be out on the street.

(*With great effort, the DEVIL holds his temper in check.*)

EVERYMAN: Is that clear?

DEVIL (*modestly*): Of course, Mr. Chairman! Please excuse me!

EVERYMAN: From now on I'm my own boss again. Is that clear?

DEVIL (*impudent again*): Oh, if you don't mind my saying so, you were always in charge. Don't overestimate my assistance, Mr. Chairman!

EVERYMAN: Yes, I shouldn't overestimate your assistance. You're right. I'm responsible. Me! (*looks at the CHILDREN*) That's the reason for these uninvited guests. I'm sorry, you're too far away for me. And there are too many of you. Too many. I don't know you. I knew others. (*looks at his GUESTS*) Not only did I kill my wife, today, but I killed someone else, too.

DEBTOR: Ah, now you remember, huh?

EVERYMAN: He's lying in the drawer next to my wife. I

read his name. And pulled out the drawer. A heavy man. Even in death. Had a lot of weight to carry around. An accident. I took over his firm. For 1.3 million. This morning I made him an offer he couldn't refuse. (*to the DEVIL*) Right?

DEVIL: Business is business!

EVERYMAN: Yes! Business is business!

(*DEBTOR gets up, breathing heavily, stuffs a couple more sandwiches in his pockets, approaches EVERYMAN.*)

DEBTOR: I would've done the exact same thing, if I were you.—Okay, fine, I'll beat it.—God, do I feel awful! (*starts to leave, turns around, grins*) We'll see each other again! (*turns back to the door*) What a punishment! What a punishment! (*disappears*)

EVERYMAN (*to FAT COUSIN*): Uncle George, I'm afraid. I'm really afraid. (*commanding*) Come here! Come over here, right now!

(*FAT COUSIN goes over to him.*)

EVERYMAN: Help me! Console me! Threaten me! Do something!

FAT COUSIN: If you believe, you don't need to be afraid!

EVERYMAN: Believe in what? What am I supposed to believe in? Tell me! It's all a big fat lie! A big fat lie!

FAT COUSIN: God is no lie.

EVERYMAN: People are lies. So God is a lie!

FAT COUSIN: People aren't lies either!

EVERYMAN: Oh, yes they are! All of them! All of them! Especially the highest ones, the most important ones, the most powerful ones! Like my dear Banker here. The one who manages all that money. He started his career with me. We smuggled stocks and bonds over the border. Worth millions. We tricked our business partners any way we could. Cheated them with pie-in-the-sky promises. Ruined small investors with stock in dead companies. He started his bank with the profits. And his bank is now the biggest in the whole country. With my share of the profits I joined my father in his company. God, was he proud! What a resourceful son!

(*Furious, MAMMON goes to the door.*)

EVERYMAN: You're leaving already? Why? I'm just telling everyone how resourceful you are. (*screams*) You are my money! You belong to me! You have to stay with me! Till the bitter end! If I want, my company can go broke in 10 seconds! And you along with me.

(*MAMMON reaches for the doorknob.*)

EVERYMAN: You're staying!

(*MAMMON hesitates, then takes his hand away from the doorknob.*)

EVERYMAN: That's right. Take another glass of champagne and enjoy my birthday party.

(*Embarrassed and furious, MAMMON tries to lose himself among the GUESTS. EVERYMAN looks around, he see WORKS.*)

EVERYMAN: And then there's the President of the Union! Bought and sold for a piece of leather. For a soccer ball. (*to his GUESTS*) He would have swallowed those 15,000 layoffs. He would have sold them out. For a soccer ball. Those are all lies, too.

(*Furious, WORKS goes to the door, turns around.*)

WORKS: Now the barn's on fire, I guarantee you! You can't do that to me!

(*WORKS exits, slams the door behind him.*)

GOOD COMPANION: Well, I've also had enough! (*turns toward the door*).

EVERYMAN: Mr. Chancellor! My old friend. He's also for sale. For sale for power. He's got enough money anyway. But he would do anything, betray anyone, sell anyone, even the whole country; would toss all his principles overboard—just to be able to be one thing: Chancellor!

GOOD COMPANION (*frozen in his tracks*): We are no longer on speaking terms. You'll be sorry, Mr. Chairman! You should never have started in on me. Not with me. I'll destroy you. And this attempt at blackmail, you'll pay for that, I guarantee you!

(*GOOD COMPANION goes to the door, followed by his two BODYGUARDS. The door flies open. POOR NEIGHBOR enters, dressed as earlier that morning, briefcase in hand.*)

POOR NEIGHBOR: Ah, Mr. Chancellor! You're leaving so soon?

(*GOOD COMPANION tries to get past him.*)

POOR NEIGHBOR: Wait! I've got a birthday present for our Chairman! This is something you won't want to miss!

GOOD COMPANION: Not interested.

(*POOR NEIGHBOR approaches EVERYMAN, opens his briefcase, pulls out a pistol, drops the briefcase, points the gun at EVERYMAN. GOOD COMPANION, who was just on his way out, sees it, turns around, his BODYGUARDS do the same. The GUESTS—including MISTRESS and MOTHER—all step back out of the line of fire, only the DEVIL remains standing beside EVERYMAN, looks over at DEATH with astonishment. DEATH remains impervious. The CHILDREN also remain standing by EVERYMAN, though they no longer mill around him.*)

EVERYMAN: Well, that's wonderful! Finally, somebody with convictions. Finally, somebody who can't stand all the buying and selling.—For those of you who don't know him, this is my neighbor. This morning I stole his company out from under him.

(*POOR NEIGHBOR is surprized and confused by EVERYMAN's reaction. ONE of the BODYGUARDS pulls out a pistol, quickly sneaks up behind POOR NEIGHBOR, places the pistol to his head.*)

BODYGUARD: Nice and easy! Don't get excited! (*holds out his left hand*) The gun!

(*POOR NEIGHBOR does not react.*)

EVERYMAN: Beat it! I don't need your protection!

(*The BODYGUARD is confused.*)

EVERYMAN (*screams*): Beat it! Get out!

(*The BODYGUARD looks over at GOOD COMPANION who gives him a sign. The BODYGUARD looks at POOR NEIGHBOR, puts his own pistol away, goes to the door. GOOD COMPANION has already disappeared, the SEC-OND BODYGUARD with him. The FIRST BODYGUARD looks back once more, exits, closes the door behind him. POOR NEIGHBOR still has his pistol aimed at EVERY-MAN.*)

EVERYMAN: Well, what are you waiting for, Anthony? Shoot! Go ahead and shoot! Or are you too scared? (*yells*) Come on, do it!

(*POOR NEIGHBOR takes closer aim at EVERYMAN, his finger tightens on the trigger, he starts to tremble, can't pull the trigger, starts to cry, he drops the arm holding the pistol, stands there sobbing. EVERYMAN goes over to him, puts his hand on POOR NEIGHBOR's arm.*)

EVERYMAN: Come and have a drink with me.

(EVERYMAN leads POOR NEIGHBOR over to the bar, pours two whiskys. The CHILDREN follow EVERYMAN, but are no longer insistent. The GUESTS are all relieved that nothing has happened and start to leave—except DEATH, the DEVIL, MISTRESS, MOTHER, FAT COUSIN.)

EVERYMAN: Sure, just leave! Beat it! Or else I'll expose all of you! *(sees MAMMON sneaking out)* Hey, Mr. Moneybags, stay put! I want to take you along with me.—Too bad! He's already gone!

(EVERYMAN hands POOR NEIGHBOR the glass of whisky. POOR NEIGHBOR puts away his gun, EVERYMAN clinks glasses with him.)

EVERYMAN: Cheers, Anthony! Here's to you!

(The TWO drink. Tired, DEATH sits down in a leather armchair.)

FAT COUSIN *(steps forward)*: Thomas!

EVERYMAN: Your Eminence? Another drink?

FAT COUSIN: You make me sick with your self-pity. Only a man without faith could have so much self-pity.

EVERYMAN: Leave, George! As you can see *(gestures toward POOR NEIGHBOR)*, I've got lots to do!

FAT COUSIN: May God be with you! *(goes to the door)*.

EVERYMAN: I don't need him. Take him along with you to your posh residence! That's where he belongs.

(FAT COUSIN exits.)

EVERYMAN *(to the servants)*: You can all go home now! The party's over! Thank you!

(The WAITERS and WAITRESSES leave the room. EVERYMAN, the CHILDREN, POOR NEIGHBOR, MIS-

TRESS, MOTHER, DEATH, and the DEVIL are now alone.)

MISTRESS: You fool! You've ruined everything! Everything!

EVERYMAN (*laughs*): It was already ruined. A long time ago.

MISTRESS: We were doing so well. You ruined yourself with your roundhouse punches. You idiot!

EVERYMAN: What are you talking about?

MISTRESS: The company!

DEVIL: Nothing's happened to the company! (*points to the monitor*) Look!

(*ALL look at the monitor, except the CHILDREN.*)

MISTRESS: It's going up!—It's going up!

POOR NEIGHBOR: Your stock?

EVERYMAN: Yes, my stock!

POOR NEIGHBOR (*watching the monitor*): That's unbelievable!—And I thought you were going to let me shoot you because you were ruined.

EVERYMAN (*smiling*): I *am* ruined!

POOR NEIGHBOR: But your stock's rising. And how! It's not stopping. It's not stopping! Every second you're making millions. Millions and millions!

(*EVERYMAN pours himself another glass of whisky, also refills POOR NEIGHBOR's glass. POOR NEIGHBOR doesn't notice, because in his enthusiasm he's engrossed in the monitor.*)

MISTRESS: Thomas! Just take a look at that!

(*EVERYMAN takes a disinterested glance, lights a cigarette.*)

DEVIL (*proudly*): Well, did we do a great job, or what?

EVERYMAN (*sarcastically*): Great job! Great job, Trouble-shooter!

MISTRESS: Thomas! Now nobody'll be able to touch you! Not the Chancellor, or the Union President.

EVERYMAN: No, now nobody'll be able to touch me.

POOR NEIGHBOR (*enthusiastically*): I can't believe it! I can't believe it! You're rich! Richer than anybody could ever imagine!

EVERYMAN: Do you want it?

POOR NEIGHBOR: Who? What?

EVERYMAN: The company.

DEVIL (*outraged*): No!

MISTRESS (*simultaneously*): No!

EVERYMAN (*to POOR NEIGHBOR*): You can have it.

POOR NEIGHBOR (*insulted*): Come on, don't joke around with me!

EVERYMAN: It's no joke. I don't feel like making any more jokes. Unfortunately.

POOR NEIGHBOR (*incredulously*): You want to give me your company?

EVERYMAN: Yes.

MISTRESS: You can't be serious!

POOR NEIGHBOR: Why would you want to do that?

EVERYMAN: I don't need it anymore.

MISTRESS: Have you gone completely off your rocker?

(*EVERYMAN goes over to his desk, takes out a piece of paper, writes something on it with his fountain pen.*)

DEVIL: No, goddammit!

(*EVERYMAN just looks at DEVIL with a grin, signs the piece of paper.*)

EVERYMAN (*to MISTRESS and MOTHER*): Come over here. I want you to sign as my witnesses!

(*MOTHER hesitates.*)

EVERYMAN: Come, now, mother! You'll still have your private fortune.

(*MOTHER now approaches, signs. EVERYMAN looks at MISTRESS.*)

MISTRESS: You're crazy! (*points to the paper*) I'm not signing that thing! You're not mentally stable! I'm going to call the Doctor! (*goes to the desk, picks up a phone*).

EVERYMAN: You want to have me declared incompetent, is that it?

(*MISTRESS looks at him, hangs up the phone.*)

MISTRESS (*to MOTHER*): Why are you going along with this? It's absolutely insane!

MOTHER: He must know what he has to do.

MISTRESS (*to the DEVIL*): Don't just stand there, do something! Please!

DEVIL: I'm sorry, it seems as if he doesn't want my advice anymore. Or am I mistaken, Mr. Chairman?

EVERYMAN: No, you're not mistaken, troubleshooter!

DEVIL: You're not very grateful.

EVERYMAN: Are you really that concerned about gratitude?

(*The DEVIL is furious.*)

EVERYMAN: I am grateful to you. I now see some things more clearly.

DEVIL *(bitterly)*: But that wasn't the point of the whole exercise.

EVERYMAN: What was it then?

(The DEVIL doesn't answer.)

EVERYMAN *(to MISTRESS)*: Are you going to sign, or aren't you? *(looks at DEATH)* If not, my faithful companion Henry will. Won't you?

DEATH: Yes.

MISTRESS *(in desparation)*: I don't understand!

EVERYMAN: It's really quite simple. I'm not well. Surely you've noticed that by now.

MISTRESS: I have. If you're not well, then just go to the hospital! Please!

(With a smile, EVERYMAN shakes his head at her lack of comprehension.)

MISTRESS *(breaks out in tears)*: But why not?

(EVERYMAN gets up, goes over to MISTRESS, takes her in his arms.)

EVERYMAN: Do you love me?

MISTRESS: Yes! Of course!

EVERYMAN: Even if I give the company *(pointing to POOR NEIGHBOR)* to him?

MISTRESS: Of course! I'm not some floozy who has to make it to the top.

MOTHER: I'm sorry, Rita. I must apologize to you.

MISTRESS: Not necessary! *(smiling)* I am used to the Good Life, I didn't mean that at all! But I can also get used to generic brands!

EVERYMAN: Then sign right here, please!

(MISTRESS goes to the desk, signs. EVERYMAN hands

the paper to POOR NEIGHBOR who stares at it; he simply can't believe this is happening to him.)

POOR NEIGHBOR: This isn't just some bad joke?

EVERYMAN: No, Anthony. It's just an attempt to set things right. Otherwise it wouldn't be possible. Pure sentimentality.

POOR NEIGHBOR: I've got to get home! I've got to tell my family! *(shakes EVERYMAN's hand)* Thank you, Thomas, thank you!

EVERYMAN: You ought to get rid of the weapons factories.

POOR NEIGHBOR: What?

DEVIL *(with inner rage)*: You can't be serious!

POOR NEIGHBOR: You can't be serious! We're living in a golden age! The super powers are disarming, and the other countries are re-arming! We can finally have wars without having to worry about a world war! The Islamic world is being reshaped! There's civil war in Africa! Latin America is a goldmine! This is the deal of the millenium! 'Scuse me, Thomas, when I say so, but I think you're stepping down at just the right time! Otherwise you really would have ruined the company!

(POOR NEIGHBOR looks down incredulously at the piece of paper one last time, races to the door, stumbles over his briefcase, picks it up, closes it, runs out.)

EVERYMAN *(to the DEVIL)*: Yes, Troubleshooter! The time has come! You're fired! *(pulls out his checkbook and a ballpoint pen)* Your fee?

DEVIL: I'll get it myself! When the time comes! For now, my assistance was gratis.

(The DEVIL goes over to his laptop, closes the lid and picks

it up, goes over to the elevator, presses the button. The doors open, the DEVIL gets in, presses a button, the doors close, the elevator goes down to Basement-1. EVERYMAN has been watching the DEVIL, now looks over at MISTRESS, crosses to her, looks her in the eyes.)

EVERYMAN: Tell me, would you want to go on living if I were dead?

(*MISTRESS looks at him, astonished, doesn't answer.*)

EVERYMAN: I apologize. That was just a slight relapse. I love you. You're beautiful. Maybe I can remember you just the way you are.—Now I'd really like to be alone for a little bit, if you two don't mind.

MOTHER: Yes. It's all right. (*comes over to EVERYMAN, kisses him on the cheek*) Good bye, my son!

EVERYMAN: Good bye, mother!

MOTHER (*to MISTRESS*): Well, what do you think, Rita? Shall we go have a drink, together?

MISTRESS (*is pleased that MOTHER accepts her*): Love to, Madam!

MOTHER: Well, then, come along! (*to DEATH*) Good night, Henry!

DEATH (*rising*): Good night, Madam!

(*MOTHER goes to the elevator, MISTRESS looks at EVERYMAN who is suddenly afraid. He gives her a brief hug, but doesn't overdo it, so that she won't notice. She does, however, notice some of his sorrow at parting, looks at him. EVERYMAN smiles, kisses her on the lips, then gently pushes her away. She hesitates, looks at him. The elevator arrives, a bell chimes, the doors open. MISTRESS looks over at the elevator, back at EVERYMAN; he smiles at her, she goes to the elevator. His MOTHER enters the elevator. MISTRESS follows her, looks back at EVERYMAN, sud-*

denly her heart aches, and she experiences a great loss at their separation.)

EVERYMAN: Mother!

MOTHER: Yes?

EVERYMAN: Please say hello to my son for me. Tell him I love him. He's not like me.

MOTHER: I'll tell him.

(*MOTHER presses a button, the doors close, the elevator goes down to Basement-1. EVERYMAN looks at DEATH, looks at the CHILDREN who are now sitting calmly at his feet, looks at the monitor, goes over to his desk and presses a button, the monitor goes off. He presses another button, and the lighting in the entire suite dims; the room is illuminated only by the city lights outside. EVERYMAN looks at the CHILDREN, goes over to them, sits down with them on the floor.*)

EVERYMAN: Yes . . . I didn't want to understand. I didn't want to think about it. That it was me. (*to the AMPUTATED CHILD*) My cannons shot away your legs. (*to the STARVING CHILD*) I took the bread right out of your mouth, (*to the COUGHING CHILD*) and I polluted the air, your clean air. Somehow I always felt guilty, of course, deep down inside me. And when you feel guilty, you either come to understand or you get angry. I got angry. And kept on killing you, taking your bread, your health.—What can I do now? It happened. It can't be changed. It's too late. (*looks at the CHILDREN*) I am sorry.

(*EVERYMAN stares off into space. The CHILDREN withdraw imperceptibly and finally disappear. DEATH, who has been standing by, calmly waiting, now slowly ap-*

proaches EVERYMAN, stops in front of him. EVERYMAN looks up, slowly rises.)

EVERYMAN: Is it time?

DEATH: Yes, it is time.

EVERYMAN: Would you mind if I had one last cigarette?

DEATH: No, not at all, please do.

(EVERYMAN lights a cigarette, mixes one last drink at the bar.)

EVERYMAN: That was a long day.

DEATH: Yes. A long day.

EVERYMAN: The longest one of my life.

DEATH: That's always the way it is.

EVERYMAN *(approaching)*: Really?

DEATH: Yes. Always.

EVERYMAN: Can you remember how my father died?

DEATH: Of course! I was there, or did you forget?

EVERYMAN *(smiling)*: Yes, of course!

DEATH: In the old office building. At his desk.

EVERYMAN: He passed away easily, didn't he?

DEATH: Yes, he died easily. Very quickly. Without a struggle. He was old.

EVERYMAN: He was different than I am. Not as unscrupulous. A father. Even a father to his workers.

DEATH: Those were different times.

EVERYMAN: Yes. Perhaps. This is an unscrupulous age.—He believed in God. Maybe that was it.

DEATH: Yes, maybe.

EVERYMAN: I can't believe in God.

DEATH: Maybe God believes in you, Mr. Chairman!

(EVERYMAN smiles, empties his glass and puts it down, takes a last drag on his cigarette, stubs it out in the ashtray, looks at DEATH, smiles with mild trepidation.)

EVERYMAN: If there is such a thing as justice, afterwards . . . then I'm really in for it, aren't I?

DEATH: Oh, it's not as bad as all that . . .

EVERYMAN: Well, then . . .

(THEY exchange glances, EVERYMAN is miserable from fear.)

DEATH: It'll all be over in a second. Don't be afraid.

(DEATH touches EVERYMAN very gently on the left arm. EVERYMAN has a heart attack, gasps for breath, holds his hand over his heart, collapses, lies doubled-up, groaning on the floor.)

DEATH *(softly)*: All over in a second.

(EVERYMAN dies. DEATH looks down at him for a while, then goes to the elevator, presses a button, the elevator rises from Basement-1, the doors open, DEATH gets in, presses a button, the doors close, the elevator goes down to the Ground Floor, while, simultaneously, the white triangle comes down from above, the CEO-light goes on, the elevator doors open, from inside a radiant white light. GOD THE FATHER, GOD THE SON, and GOD THE HOLY GHOST (ALL are dressed as at the beginning) step out, the elevator doors close behind them, the THREE approach EVERYMAN, look down at him.)

GOD THE FATHER: I see . . .

GOD THE SON: Just a little heap . . .

GOD THE FATHER: As always.

GOD THE SON: But it's still a touching sight. You just wouldn't understand.

GOD THE FATHER (*threateningly*): Listen, don't start that again!

GOD THE HOLY GHOST: Yes, unfortunately I can't identify with it! As far as I'm concerned, all of them are just little heaps! Even when they race around and pretend they're really important! Childish, in a way! Truly childish!

GOD THE SON: Oh, you . . . You don't have the faintest idea! You—

GOD THE HOLY GHOST (*interrupts*): Don't you dare tell me to go hover over the waters!

GOD THE SON (*grinning*): I didn't say a thing!

GOD THE HOLY GHOST: You'd better not!!

GOD THE SON: Although I'm sure that's the best place for your talents! Unfortunately, your hovering over people didn't do a whole lot of good!

GOD THE HOLY GHOST: Father! Why do I always have to put up . . .

GOD THE FATHER (*interrupts*): Quiet! Just be quiet! You two are really impossible! (*to EVERYMAN)* Rise!

(*EVERYMAN slowly rises, GOD THE SON helps him to his feet; EVERYMAN's worldly body remains lying on the floor. EVERYMAN looks at the THREE, GOD THE FATHER gestures toward the elevator. EVERYMAN smoothes out his tuxedo jacket, slowly goes to the elevator, the doors open, a hellish noise errupts, the sounds of war—the thunder of artillery, exploding bombs, machine gun fire, the clattering of helicopters, etc. The audience glimpses an endless wasteland with mushroom clouds, the glare of explosions, etc. Just then, DEATH and the DEVIL arrive (in their traditional costumes, as at the beginning), stepping out of the wasteland into the room, they look at EVERYMAN who has stopped in his tracks, then join the THREE*

GODS. Alone, EVERYMAN stares into the wasteland, turns around, looks back at the THREE GODS, becomes afraid. GOD THE FATHER impatiently waves him on. EVERYMAN follows his command, steps into the wasteland, the elevator doors close behind him, and instantly the horrendous sounds of war cease.)

GOD THE FATHER (*to DEATH*): You warned him twice, didn't you?

DEATH: Yes, my Lord and God. I took the liberty.

GOD THE FATHER: That's fine . . . He needed it, as far as we could see. (*to the DEVIL*) Thank you. You did your part.

DEVIL: I didn't succeed! Unfortunately!

GOD THE SON (*grinning*): He really put one over on you, didn't he?

DEVIL (*to GOD THE SON*): You warned him, too! Through his mother! (*to GOD THE FATHER*) That really wasn't fair!

GOD THE FATHER: No matter what, you had your chance.

GOD THE SON (*to the DEVIL*): It's your age-old problem. You go too far, with your excessive ambition. And then, at the top, at the peak of escalation, you lose your cool. That's your tough luck. You ought to be satisfied with less. Then you'd achieve more.

DEVIL: He's trying to tell me how to do my job!

GOD THE SON: I apologize! Forget it! It's better this way. I like it a lot better when your methods aren't successful.

DEVIL: Well, I guess I wasn't a total failure. Or else He wouldn't have sent him off into the wasteland!

GOD THE SON: Yes . . . (*to GOD THE FATHER*) What were you trying to prove, anyway?

GOD THE FATHER: Nothing. I'm not trying to prove anything. I don't have to prove anything!

GOD THE SON (*pointing to the elevator*): Is that necessary?

GOD THE FATHER (*gently*): Son! Can a camel pass through the eye of a needle?

GOD THE HOLY GHOST (*to GOD THE SON*): Purification! His spirit must be purified! Completely! And even if it takes an eternity! But that doesn't matter to you! You're not interested in the spirit at all! You and your body! (*raises his hands*) O Head of Blood and Wounds!

(*GOD THE SON is not even interested in responding to this provocation.*)

GOD THE SON (*looks over at the elevator, then to GOD THE FATHER*): But he'll make it, won't he? To the green meadows. He will, won't he?

(*GOD THE FATHER raises his hands, gesturing "perhaps?" GOD THE SON looks at him sullenly, goes to the elevator. GOD THE FATHER, GOD THE HOLY GHOST, DEATH and the DEVIL follow him. The elevator doors open, radiant white light streams out of the elevator. ALL enter, the doors close behind them, the white triangle races upwards, while, simultaneously, the red inverted triangle speeds downwards.*)

THE END

Abraham
a play about love

Second version

Translated by
Heidi L. Hutchinson

Felix Mitterer
Remarks on the play *Abraham*

I knew a man in a village somewhere in Austria. One day he told me, through a third party, that he was homosexual, that he had AIDS, that he would like to tell me his story, that he would like me to write a play about it. It was months later that I finally wrote him a letter, telling him I would come as soon as I could find the time. Several more months passed, and he wrote me a postcard: "I'm ready for you any time. But my own days, weeks, months (?) seem to be running out. On the other hand, I may still be around for a while." Two weeks later I called, and his mother answered the phone. "I'm sorry, Mr. Mitterer, he died a few days ago." I felt guilty, was furious with myself. And felt obligated, now more than ever, to write the play. I spoke to his parents. Since they knew of their son's wish, they answered my questions. But I could tell that they were afraid. When I went to talk to the doctors or to his friends, his parents had always been there first; they had explained that they were nervous wrecks and couldn't sleep any more, because Mitterer was writing a play about their son. So I threw away what I had written so far and assured the parents that I wasn't interested in increasing their suffering, and that neither their son nor they would be recognizable in my play.

Abraham didn't become an "AIDS play," but rather a play about a loving homosexual relationship, and about how a person must fight with himself if he believes in God and in the laws of the Church, and if he himself thinks that his sexual orientation is a sin. In addition, the play's main character lives in the country. And we know what it means when word gets around in a small town that someone is a homosexual and on top of that has AIDS. *Abra-*

ham is also a play about the love between a father and
son. In spite of this love, the father puts pressure on the
son in every way that he can. His motive is fear. The fear
of losing prestige, power and honor, of falling into dis-
grace. The play ends in a nightmare, in a Biblical apoca-
lypse. The father sacrifices the son.

Characters

PETER (35), architect
MAX (60), contractor and Peter's father
GEORGE (27), Peter's lover
VICAR (60)
ERIC (50), mason's assistant
GABY (30), prostitute
WERNER (30), biker type
CHARLY (30), junkie
JUDY (30), transvestite
6 to 10 EXTRAS ("Death," village people, boy, Filipina, subway riders)

Locations

Men's room in a tavern (Country)
Max's living room (Country)
George's apartment (City)
AIDS ward (City)
Subway station/Greek beach
Garbage dump (Country)

Prologue

Sound of ocean waves. As if carried in on the wind from afar we hear the most famous of all Greek hassapikos, "Frankosyriani" sung by Markos Vamvakaris.

WERNER: In Athens and Thessaloniki, and in the Greek neighborhoods of Smyrna and Istanbul at the turn of the century lived a group of men who called themselves Manges. They were the descendants of freedom fighters and mountain robbers. Now they were getting by as smugglers, gamblers and idlers. A Mangas is arrogant and pugnacious and will never try to avoid a knifing. He speaks softly and haltingly; only the initiated understand his jargon. He wears a dark jacket, a black or purple collarless shirt, tight striped pants, pointed shoes with heels, and a wide-brimmed hat in the style known as "Republiko." His moustache is twirled upward at the ends and a waxed curl sticks to his forehead. In his belt he carries a double-edged knife and often a pistol as well. He wears his jacket with only his left arm in the sleeve, so that he can wrap it around his arm with one quick motion, in order to ward off the knife of his opponent. His hand plays incessantly with his worry beads. A Mangas is proud like no other man. He doesn't marry, he doesn't produce children, he doesn't hold down a regular job. He lives only for the moment. In the coffee houses, in the harbor taverns and hashish bars he meets with his comrades to sing and dance. He turns the night to day. If he meets a boy who wants to be just as proud, just as courageous and free, then he adopts him as his little son. No Mangas ever grows old. One day he is killed. In hand-to-hand combat or by the police. Then his comrades throw a big party. And the little son dances.

1. Men's room in a tavern (Country)

(A poorly maintained men's restroom. Music and shouting from the direction of the dining room. A MAN dressed as Death is sitting, leaning against the wall, sleeping, and remains motionless throughout the entire scene. PETER (dressed as Batman) is pulled into the room by GEORGE (dressed as Catwoman). The viewer should not be able to tell that GEORGE is a man in costume. PETER tries to kiss GEORGE, GEORGE "shows his claws," hisses at PETER, and runs away with PETER in pursuit. GEORGE cracks his whip at PETER, who catches it on the third try and pulls GEORGE to him, kisses him. GEORGE hugs PETER. The VICAR comes in (dressed as the Archangel Michael with a flaming sword) and sees the two of them.)

VICAR: Well, beg your pardon!

(PETER backs off, startled.)

VICAR: Do that at home, if you must! (*looks at GEORGE and points with his sword in the direction of the exit*) Get out! This is the men's room!

(GEORGE jumps at him, hissing, with his claws raised threateningly. The VICAR backs away.)

VICAR: Stop it! Don't do that!

(GEORGE does not stop. The VICAR pokes his sword at him, GEORGE whacks it out of his hand with the whip. PETER is starting to laugh, since he is unrecognizable in his mask. GEORGE puts his arm around the VICAR.)

GEORGE (*in a well-faked female voice*): We have to stick together, Archangel! Together we will fight evil! Any time, any place, and especially right here, where mankind satisfies its most basic needs! The scum of humanity meets in the bathroom. Right, Batman?

PETER: Sure! But right now let's let the Archangel use the toilet. (*starts toward the exit*) Come on!

GEORGE: Just a minute! The moment has come to solve a question that has puzzled mankind since the beginning of time!

(*The VICAR tries to pull away, but GEORGE holds on to him.*)

GEORGE: Do angels have a sex, and if so, which one?

PETER: Yeah, that would be interesting!

VICAR (*fighting them off*): Let me go!

GEORGE: So, which is it, Archangel? Man, woman, both, or none? Well? No answer? Well, then I need to proceed with an examination! (*GEORGE tries to reach under the VICAR's angel costume, the VICAR pulls away, flees into a stall and locks it.*)

VICAR: You haven't heard the last of this! I'll figure out who you two are! This is obscene!

(*GEORGE walks over to the stall, lies down on the floor and looks under the door.*)

GEORGE: A woman! He's a woman! He's sitting down!

VICAR: Get lost, you stupid girl! I'll call the police!

GEORGE (*gets up off the floor*): That's not very nice, Madame Archangel! After all, Batman and I have been risking our lives to clear out the big city swamp! You, madame, have taken your flaming sword crusade only into the small towns! In the city, the center of sin . . .

PETER (*hisses*): Quit it! (*approaches GEORGE, softly*) It's the Vicar!

GEORGE (*astonished*): You're kidding!

PETER: No! Come on!

(*PETER tries to pull GEORGE to the exit, GEORGE gets free and kneels down in front of the stall door.*)

GEORGE: Vicar, reverend sir, I know it's not quite the proper moment, but I feel an uncontrollable urge to relieve myself, too, right here and now! Please hear my confession!

PETER: Stop it! (*PETER tries to pull GEORGE away, he resists and is dragged by PETER toward the door.*)

GEORGE: I confess—

VICAR: Obscenity! Blasphemy!

GEORGE: I confess that, though always on the job fighting evil, I am a sinful woman, solely motivated by unchaste thoughts and lust. All I want is men, only men—

(*The drunken MAX appears, dressed as a bear. The first one he sees is GEORGE.*)

MAX: Oh, 'scuse me! (*looks back at the door*) Am I in the ladies' room?

GEORGE (*gets up*): You're in the catbox, Sir! But bears are welcome, too! Make yourself at home!

MAX (*pushes back his mask*): Man, is it hot!

(*PETER is startled as he recognizes his father.*)

MAX (*looks at GEORGE*): What are you doing here, kitty, huh? Looking for a tomcat?

(*GEORGE meows and rubs up against MAX. MAX laughs, walks over to the sink and cools his face with water. PETER pulls GEORGE toward the door.*)

GEORGE: What's the matter with you! Let me go! Christ, are you boring!

(The drunken ERIC enters, dressed as a buxom gypsy woman. While it is easy to mistake GEORGE for a woman, this is not at all the case with ERIC.)

ERIC: Batman! Wow, am I seeing things? Hey, Batman, I'm crazy about you! Come on, let's dance!

(ERIC grabs PETER and starts to dance with him to the music from the party in the tavern. PETER tries to get away from ERIC, but the latter won't let him.)

ERIC: Holy shit, have you got a chest, Batman! I'm crazy about that kind of thing! Hey, Max, did you see his chest? Holy shit, I can hardly stand it!

MAX: You know, the kitty doesn't look so bad either!

ERIC: Then attack it! Attack it! I'll let Batman attack me! Lordy, have you ever seen a chest like this? *(punches PETER in the breastplate)*

MAX *(to GEORGE)*: May I have the pleasure?

GEORGE: Gladly, sweet teddy bear!

(MAX begins to dance with GEORGE.)

PETER *(to ERIC)*: I don't wanna dance anymore!

ERIC: But I do! I do! I'm crazy about you, Batman! Don't be prejudiced against foreigners, okay? A juicy gypsy girl like me is quite a find! Criminy, c'mon now, hold me nice and tight!

(MAX suddenly forces GEORGE against the wall and kisses him passionately. GEORGE returns the kiss. PETER see this, panics, tries to pry himself out of ERIC's grip, but ERIC holds him tight and begins to sing along with the dance music. MAX reaches between GEORGE's legs, stiffens suddenly, lets go of GEORGE, backs off, and looks at him in shock. PETER does not see this. The toilet flushes, and the VICAR comes out of the stall.)

VICAR: What's going on here? This has gone 'way beyond the silliness of Mardi Gras!

ERIC (*continuing to dance with PETER*): Vicar, I'm crazy about Batman! We're getting married tomorrow! Right, Batman? We'll have children with chests of iron! Holy shit!

VICAR: Max! You be reasonable at least! Throw that woman out!

MAX (*dully*): It's a man.

ERIC (*lets go of PETER; astonished*): Huh? Really? (*looks at GEORGE*) Can't be!

MAX: It's a man!

ERIC (*steps close to GEORGE*): No, really? Are you a man?

GEORGE (*grinning, in his normal voice*): Just like you.

ERIC: Wow, amazing! I wouldn't have though it! Everyone recognized *me* right away! No, really, that's super!

(*MAX suddenly disappears into a toilet stall and vomits. PETER retreats toward the exit, gestures madly to GEORGE to come along, but GEORGE is looking in MAX's direction.*)

ERIC (*also looks toward the toilet stall*): Oh, my, he's had a few too many this evening!

VICAR (*looks at GEORGE*): That's incredible! And in our town!

ERIC (*confused*): What?

PETER (*"casually" to GEORGE*): Listen, I have to go! You coming too?

GEORGE: Yeah, okay. Well, gentlemen, this has been quite a party! (*walks over to PETER*)

ERIC: The pleasure was all mine! Bye, Batman! (*watches*

GEORGE leave) Really, now, he did make a lovely kitty, didn't he, Vicar?

(*MAX comes out of the toilet stall, follows GEORGE hastily, grabs him, drags him back in to the men's room, takes off his mask, and looks at him.*)

ERIC (*shakes his head*): Incredible!

(*MAX rips the top of GEORGE's costume from his body; it falls to the floor, complete with the built-in breasts. GEORGE stands there with naked torso. ERIC is perplexed that MAX should be so furious. PETER wishes he could flee the scene, but he remains standing near the exit.*)

MAX (*to GEORGE*): You're not from around here, are you?

GEORGE: No.

MAX: Do you think it's funny, what you did with me just then?

(*GEORGE doesn't answer immediately. MAX slaps him.*)

ERIC: Come on now, what's the matter, Max? It's Mardi Gras! You normally have a sense of humor!

MAX (*keeps his gaze on GEORGE*): He was kissing me!

ERIC: What? (*grins*) No kidding? Really kissing?

VICAR: What's the world coming to! Good grief!

MAX (*to GEORGE*): You faggot! (*to PETER*) Are you together, you two?

(*PETER doesn't answer.*)

VICAR: Of course! I surprised them! No doubt about it!

ERIC: Well, then, let's have a look who this is!

(*PETER tries to escape. ERIC runs after him and drags him back. MAX walks over to him and tears PETER's mask off his face, then recognizes his own son. The VICAR and*

ERIC recognize PETER as well. ERIC lets go of him, baffled.)

ERIC: It's *you*?

(MAX looks at PETER in silence.)

PETER: I fell for the costume just like you, Papa!

(GEORGE now suddenly realizes that MAX is PETER's father. MAX looks at GEORGE, then at the VICAR.)

MAX: Listen, Vicar, would you mind leaving us alone here for a minute?

(The VICAR hesitates, then walks toward the exit, sees his sword lying on the floor, picks it up, and disappears. MAX looks at ERIC, ERIC gets the message, grabs GEORGE in a flash and holds him around the waist. MAX walks over to the sink, takes off his mask, lays it down, looks in the mirror, and rinses out his mouth with water.)

PETER: Come on, Papa, let him go!

(MAX doesn't answer, just washes his face.)

PETER *(to ERIC)*: Eric, please!

ERIC *(grins)*: Sorry, Batman, your father is the boss! Plus my best buddy! Right, Max? And you must admit, the tomcat is asking for a rubdown! Walks right into our peaceful community and seduces the two most respected citizens! We can't have that, now can we, Peter? Although I must admit, I do like the kitty too! I actually feel a little lesbian tonight! Damn! What say, kitty?

(GEORGE tries to defend himself and kicks ERIC in the shin, but ERIC only holds him tighter.)

ERIC *(comfortingly, as if to a skittish but harmless animal)*: Come, come, come!

(*MAX dries his face and hands with the towel and comes back. He looks first at GEORGE, then at PETER.*)

MAX: Be my guest! You go first!

PETER: What?

MAX: Hit him! Go on!

PETER: Come on, Papa! Nothing happened!

MAX: Oh, yes, something did happen. (*points to GEORGE*) Be my guest!

(*PETER turns away and starts to leave. MAX grabs him and pulls him back and pushes him toward GEORGE.*)

MAX (*yells*): Hit him! I'm telling you to hit him! Go on!

(*PETER doesn't react, MAX pushes him aside, punches GEORGE in the stomach, then kicks him in the groin.*)

(*Blackout*)

2. Max's living room (Country)

(*Old fashioned, "country style" furniture. If there are walls, they are hung with hunting trophies and oil paintings with nature subjects. On a table stands a bucket with a bottle of champagne, two champagne glasses, a crystal bowl with chips, and a candelabra with three lighted candles. After a moment, the doorbell rings.*)

VOICE OF MAX: Hazel, get the door, it's Peter! Tell him to go to the living room, I'll be right there!

(*After a further moment ERIC enters, looks around, notices first the champagne and then the candles, walks over to the table, takes some chips and stuffs them in his mouth, pulls the champagne bottle out of the bucket, looks at the label, his face shows approval and at the same time envy. He puts the bottle back in the ice. MAX enters with a bottle of beer and a glass, and looks at ERIC with surprise.*)

MAX: What are you doing here? Listen, I'm expecting company, I don't have time now!

ERIC: Is it your birthday?

MAX (*sits down and pours beer into his glass*): No, it's not. So tell me, what do you want?

ERIC: 'Scuse me, sorry if I surprised you . . .

MAX: You're in debt again.

ERIC: Yeah.

MAX: I thought all your accounts were blocked . . . ???

ERIC: Naw, not all of 'em.

(*MAX shakes his head, drinks some beer, and lights a cigarette.*)

ERIC: Listen, I was real close! I had thirty thousand in my hand! You wouldn't believe how it was going! I had to keep betting! All my problems would've been over! All at once!

MAX: You've been telling me that for twenty years now! Don't you ever learn?

ERIC: It's a passion!

MAX: Passion, smassion! You are responsible to your people!

ERIC: They're gonna take my house away if you don't help me!

MAX (*shakes his head*): I've had enough, Eric! I've advanced you enough money to last for years! I'm not your sugar daddy! Get out of here, I'm expecting company!

(*ERIC stands helpless. MAX looks at him, then sighs, gets out his checkbook and ballpoint pen, writes out a check, holds it out to ERIC. ERIC goes to him and takes the check, and looks at the amount.*)

ERIC: That's not enough.

MAX: What?

ERIC (*lays the check on the table*): It's not enough. If I don't deposit forty thousand in the bank tomorrow, they're taking my house. The furniture's already gone. My wife just sits around crying.

MAX (*gets up*): Forty thousand? Are you out of your mind? I'm not giving you forty thousand! How would you ever pay it back? On top of your other debts?

ERIC: I can't pay it back.

MAX: That's what I thought . . . (*sits back down*)

ERIC: I don't want to pay it back, either.

MAX: I beg your pardon?

ERIC (*sits down*): Sorry, Max, but I'm gonna have to tell you something. This doesn't come easy. But I don't see another way out.

MAX: What?

(*ERIC stares straight ahead.*)

MAX: Go on, talk!

ERIC: I think maybe it would be better if it wasn't widely known that your son (*hesitates a moment*) is of the other persuasion.

(*MAX stares at ERIC for a long time, then suddenly stands up and looks at ERIC threateningly. ERIC is startled and gets up, too. The doorbell rings, MAX looks toward the door, sits back down, writes a new check and holds it out to ERIC, who takes it.*)

MAX: It's not true, but I'll help you out one more time. For the last time, you got that?

ERIC (*looks at the check and beams*): Thanks! Thanks, Max!

MAX (*softly, threateningly*): And be careful! You know even I have my limits. Then you'd better watch out.

ERIC: You saved me, Max! Ill never forget it! Thanks! (*He extends his hand toward MAX, but MAX doesn't take it. PETER enters, ERIC quickly pockets the check, MAX puts the other check away.*)

ERIC: See you tomorrow, Max! (*passes PETER on the way to the door*) Hi, Junior! I was just leaving! (*turns around at the door*) Your costume was really fantastic!

(*ERIC exits, MAX drinks beer and refills his glass. PETER looks surprised at the champagne and the candles, and sits down.*)

PETER: Are we celebrating something? (*startled*) Is it your birthday?

MAX: Naw. (*lights another cigarette and holds the pack out to PETER*)

PETER: I quit smoking.

MAX: We don't see each other much lately. Every time I come to your office you're out.

PETER: Yeah, I'm out at the construction sites a lot. You know . . . If you don't keep on top of these guys . . .

MAX: You're right there. Maybe you should come back and live here with me. We'd see each other more often.

(*PETER says nothing.*)

MAX: When you get married, your place'll be too small anyway.

(*PETER says nothing. MAX looks at his watch.*)

MAX: Still haven't found the right girl . . .

PETER (*without looking at him*): Naw. You know them all. The selection isn't all that great.

MAX: But Silvia was a nice-looking girl. And a hard worker. Nature lover. I thought you had something there.

PETER: Didn't work out somehow.

MAX: You're too choosy. A woman is a woman. God knows I wasn't madly in love with your mother, either. But it was fine. Never had problems with her. Of course, after a while you need a little something on the side. Once in a while. That's just normal. I used to go into town once a month, too. (*looks at PETER*)

PETER (*nods*): I'll see.

MAX: When you get married, I'll transfer the business over to you right away. Then you'll be the boss. You can do whatever you want.

PETER: Yeah, okay . . .

MAX: It can even be someone from out of town, Peter, I don't care . . .

(*The prostitute GABY rushes in, wearing a thick fur coat.*)

GABY: Hello, hello all! Sorry, Max, I was stuck in traffic! All iced over! A huge pileup in the other direction! Musta been seven dead! Big mess!

(*MAX gets up, takes her coat and lays it over a chair back. Under the coat, GABY is in her "working clothes." PETER looks at her with astonishment, then looks questioningly at MAX. MAX picks up his glass and beer bottle.*)

MAX: Have fun.

(*MAX exits. PETER watches him leave, stunned. GABY extends her hand to PETER. He stands up.*)

GABY: Hi, Peter, I'm Gaby!

PETER: How do you do.

GABY: I've only seen a picture of you so far. In real life you're much better looking. Same with me! I tell you, I look like an absolute tramp! Always making a face! Like a total zombie! And with what I've spent on pictures! The best studios! Still doesn't help! (*flops down into an easy chair*) Right now, I really need a smoke! Totally stressed out! (*She digs for cigarettes in her purse. PETER sits back down, GABY can't find a lighter, but lights her cigarette from a candle.*)

GABY: An incredible mess, let me tell you! Explosions! Flames ten feet high! Like in a warzone, just like in a warzone! A firetruck smashed into the ambulance! On our side they stopped traffic so that the helicopter could land! Are you crazy? Aren't you gonna open the bubbly?

(*PETER gets up and opens the champagne bottle.*)

GABY: The people stuck in the cars were screaming just like in a horror movie! A couple of the injured were stumbling around covered with blood! One even climbed over the guard rail and came toward me! (*she gets up and demonstrates*) Like this! I shut my window real fast! But he just kept going, went over the other guard rail and disappeared in the woods, in the dark! The night of the living dead! Wow, gruesome! Really!

(*She takes a glass, holds it up, PETER pours her some champagne, she empties the glass in one gulp, holds it out to PETER again, he fills it again, puts the bottle back in the bucket and sits down. GABY drinks, then leans back.*)

GABY: Ah! I feel better now! And I go through this every ten days, can you imagine? (*She walks over to the stereo, selects a CD, puts on some "romantic" music, and sits back down.*) There's always something happening on this road. Really weird! I've had the head next to me twice already! Do you know the story of the cut-off head? (*doesn't wait for an answer*) On the bridge just before your exit, where the wind is always so strong that you have to hold on to the wheel with both hands, these people are driving along, and all of a sudden there's a full visor helmet next to them on the passenger seat. And in the helmet is a head! Saying, "Mother, Mother!" And beyond the bridge it's suddenly gone again. A motorcyclist was killed there a few years back. A truck with steel plates in the back. Slammed on his brakes and zip! "Mother, Mother!" he keeps saying, in his hollow voice. You miss your mother, too, don't you?

PETER: I can't remember. It's been too long.

(*GABY pours herself more champagne.*)

GABY: You don't forget your mother. Mine's been dead a long time too. But she shows up every once in a while. (*laughs*) Even in the oddest situations! (*drinks*)

PETER: You say you come here often?

GABY: Sure! Every ten days! Your Papa is lonely. He doesn't have anyone left. Except for his old aunt. And she's a little crazy, you know. He's all alone in this big ol' shack. He built it for you, Peter. For you and your family. That's his greatest wish.

PETER (*gets up, upset*): What's going on here? What sort of game are you two playing with me?

GABY: He only means well, Peter!

PETER: Well, does he think he can just play matchmaker for me, or what? Sends me a prostitute! Unbeliev-

able! But that's typical of him! He doesn't understand a thing! Absolutely nothing!

GABY: That's not true! He's a real big-hearted human
being, your Papa is! A classy human being!

PETER: Yeah, I can see how classy he is! He'd better just
leave me alone! Or I'm out of here! What an idiot!

(*PETER starts to leave, GABY gets up and walks over to
him.*)

GABY (*appeasingly*): Peter! Wait a minute!

(*PETER stops.*)

GABY: He loves you! He always talks about you whenever
I'm with him. He's proud of you! That you got
through school so fast! That you're an architect!

PETER (*exasperated*): Yeah, I know all that!

GABY: You mean everything to him!

(*PETER stands there, devastated.*)

GABY: Do him a favor. Marry someone, have a child with
her, then he'll be happy. Then he'll accept the other
thing, too.

PETER: I couldn't do that to a woman!

GABY: God, you wouldn't be the only gay man who got
married and had children. There are women who
aren't the least bit interested in sex either. You
could find one of them.

(*PETER doesn't reply.*)

GABY: At least give him a chance and try it with a woman.

PETER: I did already.

GABY: Once is not enough. Maybe she was the wrong one.

PETER: Look, I want to. But I can't. I just can't!

(*GABY steps back, takes off her top, she is dressed in a seductive teddy.*)

GABY: Look at me, Peter! Come on, look at me!

(*PETER looks at her.*)

GABY: You can have me. For the whole night. Can do what you want with me. (*She walks over to him and starts to dance with him to the music on the CD.*) You can do anything. Really, anything. Just try. Let yourself go.

(*They dance. GABY kisses PETER on the neck. He closes his eyes.*)

(*Blackout*)

3. George's Apartment (City)

(*Designer furniture. The biker type WERNER, dressed like a tough, is flopped down in an armchair, his feet up on a table, drinking whisky and smoking a cigarillo. There is a second glass of whisky on the table.*)

WERNER (*loudly*): A totally hysterical case! After months he finally visits Christian in the ward, and even then only because his wife threatened to leave him, and what happens?

(*GEORGE enters in a bathrobe, drying his wet hair with a towel.*)

WERNER (*continues*): The old man gets sentimental, hugs him, Christian starts to cry, and suddenly the father jumps up as if he'd been stung by a tarantula and wipes off his face as if a leper had spit on him, and yells for disinfectant! The nurse comes in and asks what the matter is. "His tears," the old man screams, "I'm covered with his tears!" The nurse tells him that there aren't enough viruses in the tears, completely safe, but she still had to disinfect his face.

GEORGE: What an idiot! (*picks up his whisky glass and drinks*)

WERNER: But that's not all. He leaves, but then comes back five minutes later, demands to see the doctor, and tells him that he saw a mosquito in the room, and that it will surely transmit the virus if it bites the patient and then bites him.

GEORGE: Cut it out now, I don't want to hear all this!

WERNER: Marcus has it too, did you hear?

GEORGE: Cut it out, Werner!

WERNER: Well, I dig it, it totally turns me on!

GEORGE (*in disbelief*): What turns you on?

WERNER: When a guy's sick.

GEORGE: Come on! You're full of it!

WERNER: No, I mean it! You're fucking Death! Is there anything more exciting?

GEORGE: Oh, give me a break! You must be completely out of your mind! Well, thanks a lot! I'm glad you told me!

(*GEORGE turns away. WERNER grins and pulls him down onto his lap.*)

GEORGE: Let go!

WERNER: I like 'em best in the last stages. When they're just a skeleton.

GEORGE: Let go of me! You're nuts!

WERNER: Listen, they're grateful! I see myself as a good

Samaritan. Everyone else keeps three yards distance!

(*GEORGE pulls away and stands up.*)

GEORGE: Stop it! Spare me! You're awful!

WERNER: Come on, don't act like a prude, I don't like that!

GEORGE: I'm not a prude!

WERNER: Then don't act like one!

(*GEORGE is insulted, he goes into the bathroom, the sound of the hairdryer can be heard. WERNER gets up and pours himself some whisky.*)

WERNER (*calls*): What do you want? It's going to get us all anyway! (*starts to sing a Freddy Mercury song*)

(*The hair dryer sound stops, and GEORGE comes out of the bathroom, brushing his hair.*)

WERNER: We're all going to croak! No exceptions!

GEORGE: Maybe you! Not me!

WERNER: How do you know?

(*GEORGE doesn't answer.*)

WERNER: Who knows, maybe I've been positive all along . . .

(*GEORGE sits down, drinks whisky, and stares straight ahead.*)

GEORGE: That's cruel of you. Really! Why do you have to talk like that? You know I'm scared.

WERNER: If you're scared, you just die sooner. Naw! I'm gonna live like there's no tomorrow, as long as I can! What others experience in thirty years, I'll get in ten! Then when they throw me on the heap, at least I won't have missed anything!

GEORGE: They're gonna find a cure, aren't they? I can't imagine they won't.

WERNER (*grins*): Sure. But we won't be around to see it.

GEORGE: Boy, are you inspiring today! (*after a pause*) You were just kidding, weren't you? That you like to do it best with them.

WERNER (*suddenly very sweet*): 'Course! I'm always just kidding! You know me. Come here.

(*GEORGE gets up, starts to walk over to WERNER, the doorbell rings, he stops, looks at WERNER, exits, returns, sits down, and drinks whisky. PETER follows him in, is upset to see WERNER there, and stops.*)

PETER (*to GEORGE*): Sorry. I've come at an inopportune time, haven't I?

WERNER (*mockingly*): Inopportune! Inopportune! How nobly he expresses himself, our country gentleman!

(*PETER looks at GEORGE, GEORGE looks straight ahead, PETER goes back toward the door, GEORGE watches him go, PETER turns around and comes back.*)

PETER (*to GEORGE*): I wanted to apologize. I really behaved like an ass.

GEORGE: You betrayed me! You stood by and watched while your cow farmers beat me up!

PETER (*helplessly*): It was my father.

GEORGE: Yeah, I heard. I was still conscious at first, if you recall!

PETER: What should I have done?

GEORGE (*gets up*): Admit it! Finally admit it! Defend me! I am your lover!

WERNER: A marital spat! I can barely hold back the tears!

GEORGE: You keep your big mouth shut! (*sits*)

WERNER: Next time I'll go along! I've been wanting to go to the country for a long time! (*suddenly angry*) When I'm with you, no one'd dare beat you up!

PETER (*sits down*): Look, George, I'm ruined if they find out. My father will kill himself. Try to understand that! It's different in the country!

GEORGE: Then leave there! Come live with me! You can get a job here in the city easy!

PETER: Listen, I'm practically running my father's business! That's where my job is!

WERNER: The dough is more important to him! No question! (*gets up; to GEORGE*) Tell me, what do you see in this bastard?

PETER: What are you talking about, dough? This has nothing to do with dough! It's my home!

WERNER: Oh, give me a break! I came from the country, too! The cities are full of intolerance, too! I don't know what to call those freaks out there! There is no word for them! Everything is so small! Tight, narrow-minded! It makes me choke just to drive past one of those little towns! Makes me want to puke!

PETER: My God, what a cynical asshole you are! The people there aren't monsters! They like me! I belong! I really belong! I'm in the brass band, the building commission, the soccer club, the beautification league!

WERNER (*relishing the word*): Beautification league! Beautification league! What in the world is that? What do you beautify? Boy, this guy really makes me sick! (*pours himself another glass of whisky*)

You probably even go bowling with your back-woodsmen!

PETER: Yes, I go bowling, too. (*to GEORGE*) And besides, I need the countryside, George. The meadows and the forest, the hill behind the house, our orchard, the crows, the way they fly up, flapping and screeching.

WERNER (*to GEORGE*): Wow, now even the crows are flapping! Well, then there's only one solution, Georgie-Boy, if you're so in love with him! Pad yourself with silicone, three hours at the beauty parlor, into the wedding dress and off you go to the village church! I'll be your best man!

GEORGE (*to WERNER*): Would you please leave? You're not needed here, Werner!

WERNER: So? All of a sudden I'm not needed here?

GEORGE: Actually, it's been quite a while now.

WERNER (*finishes his drink and sets down the glass*): It won't take long before you're bored with Safer Sex Johnny, don't you think?

(*GEORGE doesn't answer. WERNER steps in front of PETER and looks at him. PETER can't tell what he is going to, do and is a little apprehensive. WERNER takes PETER's resisting hand, pulls him up out of the chair, and lays PETER's hand on his leather-clad chest.*)

WERNER: You should get yourself one of these! He really goes for this stuff. Just a helpful marriage tip. (*lets go of PETER's hand, turns away, then back to PETER*) Ah, one more thing, I almost forgot! (*"whispers"*) Demand an HIV-test before you say "I do!"

GEORGE: Would you get out of here? Just get lost!

(*WERNER walks to the door, then turns*)

WERNER: Farewell, Georgie-Boy! Till we meet again! (*exits, singing the same Freddy Mercury song as before*)

(*GEORGE gets up, pours PETER a vodka, hands him the glass, picks up his own. They sit down and drink. PETER is angry and at the same time jealous of WERNER.*)

GEORGE: He's not as bad as he sounds.

PETER: Well, there must be something you see in him.

GEORGE: Tell me, why didn't you call? It's been three weeks! For three weeks I've been waiting for you to call! Or did you expect me to call you?

PETER: Listen, I was just in shock!

GEORGE (*after a while*): What shall we do, Peter? Where do we go from here?

PETER: I could never survive here. I know that.

GEORGE: Come on, you don't even know the city!

PETER: I went to school here. I know the bars, I know the parks and I know the toilets. It's degrading. Sad. I always felt wretched after one of those. The heteros have it all. We have nothing but the toilets. I want so much to be normal. Just plain stinkin' normal.

(*GEORGE walks over to PETER, sits down next to him, and lays his arm around PETER's shoulder.*)

GEORGE (*smiles*): And you are.

PETER: Yeah. Don't I wish. Don't I wish. (*looks at GEORGE*) I love you. Really. I can't help it.

GEORGE (*grins mischievously*): You don't have to help it!

PETER: I'm really awfully sorry about the incident!

GEORGE: Come on, it was my own fault! I insisted on going with you. And I figured a costume party would be the best opportunity. It was fun. They were all incredibly hot for me, weren't they?

PETER: You can say that again!

GEORGE: I went too far. But I was simply so high! I felt so secure under that mask! But your father gave it to me! Pow! (*looks at PETER*) I probably would have betrayed you too in the same situation.—Your father knows, doesn't he?

PETER: Yeah, long since. He just doesn't want to accept it.

GEORGE: My parents are the same way. But I left home young enough.—And the other two? Did they believe you?

PETER: Eric for sure, the one who was holding onto you. He's too naive. He can't even imagine it.

GEORGE: Well, you never know! After all, he was dressed as a lady, too!

PETER (*smiles*): Yes, but not as convincingly as you!

GEORGE: And the Vicar?

PETER (*smiles*): He caught me when I was a child. With another altar boy. He won't say anything.

GEORGE: May I be your altar boy tonight?

PETER (*smiles*): Sure. I'd love it.

(*Blackout*)

4. MAX's living room

(*The VICAR is eating with gusto a greasy blood sausage with sauerkraut. MAX is smoking a cigarette. BOTH are drinking beer.*)

MAX: Good?

VICAR: Wonderful! Wonderful! God, am I hungry! I never got anything to eat all day! Morning mass, wedding, then instead of the wedding banquet, a bedside visit, then a funeral, and instead of the wake, back to the terminal patient, because he'd begged me with outstretched hand!

MAX: Who is it?

VICAR: Who *was* it, you have to ask now; he finally made it. Old Wendling, a farmer. The only one I've had all year! Everyone's dying in the hospital! Boy, did he put up a fight!

MAX: Yeah, I know him. He always put up a fight, all his life. I liked him.

VICAR: Well, everyone draws his last breath someday, what's the use? It's not the end.

MAX: If it's all true.

(The VICAR looks at him sternly.)

MAX: As far as I'm concerned, I'd want it to be over. So I can have my peace and quiet. At some point everybody needs peace and quiet!

VICAR: There is a Heaven, Max!

MAX: Naw! Don't take it wrong, Vicar, but I don't believe that. That's a dream, nothing else.

VICAR: I always thought you were a believer, Max.

MAX: I only believe that we will be punished. That there is a court of punishment. And it already starts punishing us in life. Demands sacrifices. Heavy sacrifices. That's enough for me.

(The VICAR is finished eating. He lays down his knife and fork and wipes his mouth with a napkin.)

VICAR: Come on, Max! I know you're a little discouraged at the moment, but there still is faith, hope, love!

MAX: There probably is faith, but surely no hope. And love—I know myself what that is. There's lust, but there's no love.

VICAR: Come now, stop it!

MAX: I know myself. I'm talking about myself now.

VICAR: You love your son, don't you?

MAX: Yes. What's that got to do with it?

VICAR: That's love, too.

MAX: No. That's existence. That is my life after death. I am in him. And if he had produced children, I would live on in them, too. But as it is . . .

VICAR: I'm going to have to talk to him.

MAX: I already tried it with a sexy woman. A really sexy woman. I know her. She really knows her stuff. He did it with her, but—

VICAR: Please, spare me the details!

MAX: Sorry. But who else can I talk to . . .

VICAR: I'll take care of it. I've known him since he was a boy.

(*PETER and GEORGE enter. GEORGE has dressed especially neatly for the occasion. PETER did not expect to find the VICAR here. He knows what this means; it serves only to strengthen his resolve. MAX looks at the two with alarm. The VICAR turns around.*)

VICAR: Hello, Peter!

PETER: Hello, Vicar!

GEORGE: Hello!

VICAR (*to PETER*): Who have you brought along?

PETER: This is my friend. George.

VICAR: Oh, really? This is your friend?

PETER: Yes. The one from the men's room. You remember. Mardi Gras.

MAX (*gets up; there is fear in his voice*): Why'd you bring him along?

PETER: So you can meet him.

MAX: Oh? You think I care?

PETER: No. But I care.

MAX: Is he going to stay here now? And live with you?

PETER: Not exactly. He doesn't care much for the country life. But he's going to visit me from time to time.

VICAR: Please sit down! Or do you want me to dislocate my neck?

(*PETER and GEORGE sit down. GEORGE finds the situation very uncomfortable. MAX looks at GEORGE, then walks over to him, grabs him and drags him toward the door. PETER gets up, pulls GEORGE away from MAX, pushes MAX away and shakes a threatening finger at him.*)

PETER: Quit it! I'm warning you! Or I'm out of here! And you won't ever see me again!

(*MAX starts to leave. The VICAR gets up.*)

VICAR: Wait a minute, wait a minute, what's going on here? This won't do at all! Everyone sit down! You, too, Max! Come on! Otherwise I'm leaving!

(*PETER and GEORGE sit down. Then MAX comes back and sits down.*)

VICAR (*to PETER*): So you want to come out in the open with your sexual orientation?

PETER: Yes, I do.

MAX: Do you know what this means, Peter? You'll ruin our company! Not even the tiniest house builder will want to hang our sign on his property!

PETER: I don't believe that!

MAX: I've been mayor twice! I'm on the town council! I'm a member of the Chamber of Commerce! No one pays as much in taxes as I do! I've got power, influence, respect!

PETER: So? None of that will change! You are you and I am I! No one can make you responsible! Papa! People aren't as narrow-minded as you think!

MAX: I'm already being blackmailed, Peter! Blackmailed! Because of you!

PETER: Who? Who's doing that?

MAX: It doesn't matter who!

PETER: I'm sorry, Papa! But that makes it all the more important that I come out of the closet! Then no one can blackmail you ever again!

MAX: Before you move him in here, I'll kill him!

VICAR: Now give me a chance to talk, please, Max! (*turns to PETER*) Peter! You're a devout Christian, aren't you?

PETER: Yes, I am.

VICAR: Then you try to live by God's commandments, right?

PETER: Yes.

VICAR: Good. Then let's have a look at this. First: Thou shalt honor thy father and thy mother!

PETER: I do. Otherwise I wouldn't have waited this long.

VICAR: Second: Homosexuality is a sin against nature and against God. The Bible says—

(*This whole process is making GEORGE incredibly disgusted.*)

PETER: I've read the Bible, Vicar! Second Samuel, chapter

one, verse twenty-six. David grieves for Jonathan:
"Very pleasant hast thou been unto me: thy love to
me was wonderful, passing the love of women!"

VICAR: Will you look at him! Can you believe it? He's a
Bible scholar!—My dear young man, I can quote
you ten other verses, if you like!

PETER: No, thank you! You can save your breath! It always depends on the interpretation!

VICAR: The only true interpretation in this matter, my
son, comes from God!

PETER: Oh? And what does God say?

VICAR (*comes closer to PETER and says softly*): God says
AIDS! Did you understand me? (*shouts*) God says
AIDS! That is His answer to homosexuality! A tiny
little virus, the new plague, the new scourge of God,
to punish you! But not just you! God punishes us
all! You've even already infected the women! The
children! Innocent children! You homosexuals are
the cause of this new plague, which is spreading
over the entire world! Because we tolerated you for
too long! Because we wanted to be modern! Liberal!
What is God trying to say? Destroy the homosexuals, he says! If you don't, the whole world, all of
mankind, will perish from this plague!

(*GEORGE is more intimidated and frightened than
PETER. The VICAR picks up his beer glass, empties it and
puts it back down.*)

VICAR (*very calmly and objectively to PETER*): Think
about it. (*shakes MAX's hand*) Bye, Max. (*He exits.
There is a moment of silence.*)

PETER (*to MAX*): I'm not changing my mind.

MAX (*almost stuttering, almost weeping*): This is just a delusion of yours, Peter! Where did you ever get that

from? This just can't be! All of us have always been normal! Please, Son, don't do this to me!

PETER: It's who I am, Papa! It's who I am! I do feel guilty! I feel terrible! But what can I do? I can't change my skin! I'm sorry, Papa, really!

(*MAX is on the verge of tears, but tries to hide it by running his hand over his face. He gets up and leaves the room. PETER and GEORGE watch him leave, look at one another, then PETER stares straight ahead. Suddenly he looks toward the door again, appears panicky, runs outside, a rifle shot can be heard. GEORGE jumps up.*)

(*Blackout*)

5. Men's room in a tavern

(*A trumpet flourish can be heard from the direction of the banquet hall.*)

VOICE OF ERIC: I'm not a public speaker, as you all know, but just a simple mason's assistant, but I'll try anyway, and at any rate, before I've had too much beer! (*laughter and applause from the wedding guests*) Dear bridal couple, right reverend Vicar, honorable Chief of Police, venerable Mayor, beloved ladies, dear wedding guests! My speech is primarily directed at you, honorable Chairman of the Chamber of Commerce, dear Max, my boss and friend!

(*GEORGE comes out of a toilet stall, hesitates a moment, looks toward the exit, abruptly turns around, braces himself with both hands against the stall wall, struggles with himself, then turns around, walks toward the exit, doesn't have the courage to walk out after all, stands still again, listens to the speech.*)

VOICE OF ERIC (*during the above*): You came into this world a poor farm boy, you went to work at fourteen as a construction laborer, and today you are the largest building contractor in our county. You've attained almost everything you ever wanted in your life. And today, today your final and possibly greatest wish is coming true. Your son Peter is entering the bonds of matrimony and holds out the prospect—which we wish him from the bottom of our hearts—, that your company, dear Max, will be handed down from generation to generation, managed by hard-working grandchildren and great-grandchildren! This I wish you, dear Max, in all sincerity, and if in the past thirty years (*almost on the verge of tears*), I have occasionally made you angry, then I beg you to forgive me! All the best to the bridal couple!

(*Applause from the guests, the band begins to play a dance number. GEORGE is disgusted by the speech, at the same time despondent, doesn't know what to do, walks furiously up and down. PETER enters in his wedding tuxedo; he can't bear the proceedings any longer and covers his face with his hands.*)

GEORGE: Peter!

(*PETER turns around and sees GEORGE.*)

PETER: Is that you? What are you doing here?

(*GEORGE looks helpless, PETER walks over to him and puts his arms around him.*)

PETER: I can't stand it! I can't stand it! (*turns away from GEORGE in despair*) Now I'm trapped!

GEORGE (*walks over to PETER*): Come on, let's get out of here!

PETER: I can't!

GEORGE: It's my fault! Because I'm such a coward! I've always been a coward! You know what I was going to do, why I came here? I was going to force your hand. I was going to compromise you! I was going to go into the church, right up to the altar, and take you away! Like a gallant knight! (*takes out a switchblade*) I even brought a sword, in case they attacked us! (*puts the knife away*) But I didn't even dare go in! I hid in the toilet! Where we all belong! You said it yourself!

(*PETER embraces GEORGE. MAX and ERIC enter. PETER and GEORGE quickly separate.*)

MAX (*furious*): You could have spared us your speech! You damned hypocrite!

ERIC: I meant it sincerely, really! Believe me, Max! It really came from the heart!

(*The music in the dining hall stops.*)

MAX: I'm going to turn you in! For blackmail!

ERIC: Max, please! Look—

(*ERIC sees PETER and GEORGE and abruptly stops talking. MAX looks in the same direction, recognizes GEORGE, is stunned and almost collapses. ERIC does not recognize GEORGE.*)

ERIC (*looks at MAX*): What's the matter? Max! Are you okay?

MAX: I have to talk to my son. Would you please leave?

(*ERIC looks astonished and walks toward the door.*)

GEORGE: Hey! Aren't you the gypsy girl?

ERIC (*turns around*): What?

GEORGE: Aren't you the gypsy girl from the Mardi Gras party?

ERIC: Yeah. Why?

MAX (*screams*): Would you get out of here right now, please?

ERIC: Yeah, yeah, I'm going! (*exits*)

MAX (*to GEORGE*): Why did you have to come here?

(*ERIC reappears and eavesdrops.*)

MAX: Why can't you leave us in peace?

GEORGE: I love him.

MAX: But there are enough other men, if you don't mind my saying so!

GEORGE: I only love him.

MAX (*steps close to GEORGE*): Look, boy, everything has turned out okay now! Do you want to ruin it all?

(*GEORGE doesn't answer.*)

MAX (*to BOTH*): You can see each other, as far as I'm concerned! But not here! (*pleading*) Peter!

PETER (*notices MAX's tremendous fear*): Yeah, okay, Papa. (*to GEORGE*) Please go now, George!

(*GEORGE looks at PETER, nods slowly, walks toward the exit, sees ERIC standing motionless next to the door. MAX and PETER see him now too.*)

ERIC: Aha, so that's the way it is! That's what you're up to! Interesting!

(*GEORGE stops.*)

ERIC (*to GEORGE*): I wouldn't have recognized you, sonny boy. You were so beautifully made up that night. Really beautiful. Perfect!

(*GEORGE tries to pass ERIC, but ERIC blocks his way.*)

MAX: Let him go, Eric!

ERIC: Why? He's got to stay! We've got to introduce him to the bride!

(*GEORGE tries to pass again, ERIC pushes him back.*)

ERIC: You know, Max, I'm afraid I'm still in debt.

PETER: Oh, so you're the blackmailer?

ERIC (*ignores PETER*): But we don't have to talk about that today, Max, it can wait. (*steps aside; to GEORGE*) Be my guest, young man!

(*GEORGE at first starts to walk by ERIC, but then suddenly grabs him by the shirt and throws him into the room.*)

GEORGE: You rat!

(*GEORGE pulls his knife, flips the blade open, walks over to ERIC, grabs him, and holds the knife to his throat. A WEDDING GUEST enters, sees what's going on, and runs back out. The four MEN don't notice this.*)

GEORGE: Who do you think you are, huh? You piece of shit!

PETER: Come on, George, let's go! (*to MAX*) You can see it's no use, Papa! The lie isn't going to work!

(*Six MALE WEDDING GUESTS, including the one who has just been here, and the VICAR hurry in. Behind them, three WOMEN appear, among them is the BRIDE. She is a Filipina in a white wedding dress with a veil.*)

VICAR: What's going on here?

(*ERIC pushes GEORGE away and tries to regain his composure.*)

ERIC (*to ALL*): Keep calm, no need for excitement! Nothing happened!

VICAR: Nothing happened? He threatened you with a knife!

ERIC (*looks at MAX*): Oh, shucks! It looked a lot worse than it was! Max! You tell 'em! Nothing really happened, right?

MAX: No, not really.

PETER (*to MAX*): Stop! Enough! Are you going to let him blackmail you till the day you die?

(*MAX can hardly bear the situation any longer. The BRIDE forces her way in, looking confused.*)

PETER (*to ALL*): I'm homosexual! Gay! Eric was blackmailing my father because of it! Come on, George, let's go!

(*PETER takes GEORGE by the arm and walks with him toward the MEN. ERIC starts to attack GEORGE from behind, GEORGE notices, turns around quickly and points his knife at ERIC, who draws back. PETER drags GEORGE on. The MEN at the door form a wall with the VICAR in the middle. GEORGE points the knife at the MEN because he is afraid. PETER presses GEORGE's arm down.*)

PETER: Put the knife away!

(*GEORGE does not comply, but looks back at ERIC.*)

PETER (*to the MEN*): My friend and I are leaving now. Let us through!

VICAR (*over his shoulder*): Quick! Someone call the police!

(*One of the WOMEN runs away. PETER attempts to push the MEN aside, but is knocked backward. GEORGE pushes up his sleeve, makes a cut in his forearm, holds the knife up, looks first at ERIC, who is still lying in wait for him, and then at the OTHERS.*)

GEORGE: I've got AIDS!

(*ALL freeze. Suddenly GEORGE rushes toward the VICAR, who steps aside horrified. GEORGE passes him holding the knife high, and the OTHERS now also shrink back fearfully. PETER and GEORGE leave through the gap. PETER looks back at his father and stops when he gets to the BRIDE.)*

PETER *(to the BRIDE)*: I'm sorry. Be glad this happened. You'll hear from me about the divorce.

(PETER and GEORGE exit, GEORGE walking backward, holding up the knife.)

ERIC: People like that should be exterminated! Exterminated! *(to MAX)* Under Hitler they'd've long since been gassed!

(MAX falls to his knees, moaning.)

(Blackout)

6. George's apartment.

(The place is disorderly. Articles of WERNER's clothing are lying around, on table and floor are empty beer and wine bottles and full ashtrays. The doorbell rings, but no one goes to answer it. It rings again, then, after a pause, again, then a single continuous ring. WERNER comes out of the bedroom, sleepy, hung over and in his underwear, looks at his watch, feels his aching head, then goes out to the front door.)

VOICE OF WERNER: Charly, is that you?

VOICE OF MAX: I'm Peter's father.

VOICE OF WERNER: He's not here!

(WERNER comes back from the door. The continuous ringing sets in again, accompanied this time by a kicking against the door. WERNER turns around with a sigh and goes back out to the door.)

VOICE OF WERNER: Hey! Are you hard of hearing or something? I said Peter's not here!

VOICE OF MAX: Then I want to talk to his friend!

VOICE OF WERNER: He's crashed! Get lost!

(*Increased kicking against the door, WERNER opens it and comes back into the room, followed by MAX.*)

MAX: It's nearly evening! Have you guys turned time upside down, or what?

(*WERNER goes back into the bedroom.*)

MAX (*indignant*): Hey! (*looks around*) Well, good night! That's just how I imagined it!

(*MAX sits down, lights a cigarette, looks toward the bedroom door, assumes because of WERNER's presence that it is over between PETER and GEORGE, gets up, goes over to the bedroom door, raises his hand to knock, the door opens, and GEORGE comes out of the bedroom in his bathrobe. He is disheveled, drowsy, looks sick, and talks with difficulty, because he has taken a tranquilizer.*)

GEORGE: Peter isn't here, Mr. Schmiedinger.

MAX: And where is he?

GEORGE: Well, he must be at the office.

MAX: Where is that?

GEORGE (*closes the door*): Please leave us alone! We've had enough trouble on your account!

MAX: Oh yeah? You on account of me? Is that how it is?

(*GEORGE doesn't answer. MAX pointedly sits back down.*)

MAX: Do you have a new boyfriend now?

GEORGE (*comes closer*): What do you want from Peter?

MAX: I want to talk to him.

GEORGE: What's left to talk about?

MAX: That's none of your business! You've got a new boy-friend anyhow! Does Peter know that?

(*GEORGE turns away toward the bedroom.*)

MAX: Tell me, don't you have a job?

GEORGE (*turns back*): Naw. Not any more. (*walks over to the bedroom door, turns back again*) I was fired.

MAX: Why?

GEORGE: Because I'm sick.

MAX: Then it's true what you said in the men's room? 'Cause afterward I thought it was just a ploy of yours, so that they'd let you go.

GEORGE: It was. But even back then I was positive. I just didn't know it.

MAX (*gets up and walks over to GEORGE*): If you've infected my boy, I'll kill you. I swear it, by everything that's sacred to me.

GEORGE (*smiles*): I don't think that would be worth it.

(*GEORGE goes into the bedroom and closes the door behind him. MAX watches him go, thinks for a moment, then sits back down. After a while the doorbell rings. WERNER comes out of the bedroom, goes to open the door, and comes back with CHARLY. CHARLY is a long-haired, depraved heroin addict, also with AIDS. The moment CHARLY sees MAX, he tries to leave, but WERNER holds him back.*)

WERNER: He's not a cop! Just company from the country!

(*WERNER pulls CHARLY into the bedroom. CHARLY looks back at MAX apprehensively.*)

MAX: Well, good night! Boy, is this a den of thieves! (*calls in the direction of the bedroom*) You should all be eradicated!

(*After a while the front door is opened from the outside with a key, and PETER enters in suit and tie and carrying a briefcase. He sees MAX.)*

PETER *(surprised and delighted)*: Papa!

(MAX gets up, PETER sets down the briefcase and shakes MAX's hand.)

PETER: Hi! How did you ever find me?

MAX: A friend helped me out. He's with the police.

PETER *(irritated)*: What?

MAX: Now, tell me the truth, Peter! Do you like this life? Is this what you wanted?

PETER: Naw. But you don't always get just what you want—I'm awfully glad you came, Papa! Really!

MAX: Can we go somewhere and talk?

PETER: Yes. Just let me tell George.

(PETER goes into the bedroom, and reappears immediately, dragging CHARLY toward the exit.)

CHARLY: Hey, old man, stay cool, okay? *(pulls loose)* He still owes me dough!

(WERNER enters, his upper arm tied off with the belt from GEORGE's bathrobe; he has a used needle in his hand.)

CHARLY: How about it, Werner? This is the last time you get anything if you don't pay!

WERNER: I'm payin', I'm payin'! *(searches for his wallet in his leather pants, which are lying on the floor.)*

PETER *(calls)*: George! George!

WERNER *(with a bill in his hand)*: I don't have more than this, Charly!

(CHARLY walks over, takes the money, looks at it, pockets it, rips the wallet out of WERNER's hand, looks inside,

finds one more small bill, takes this as well, throws the wallet on the floor, grabs WERNER.)

CHARLY: I'll kill you! You won't play this game with me anymore!

WERNER: I'll pay the rest tomorrow! Cool it, man!

(*GEORGE appears in the door holding his bathrobe shut, since WERNER has the belt.*)

PETER (*to GEORGE*): Why do you do this to me? Why do you do this to me?

CHARLY (*to WERNER*): Okay, till tomorrow! But watch out! I'll cut you right open! Hasta la vista! (*exits*)

PETER (*to GEORGE*): Don't I do everything for you?

GEORGE: Yeah, you do.

PETER: So why do you keep getting into bed with this junkie (*points to WERNER*)?

WERNER: Because you don't give it to him anymore, Country Gent!

(*PETER looks at GEORGE.*)

GEORGE: Beat it, Werner! Go on! Put your clothes on and get out!

WERNER (*takes the belt from his upper arm and throws it at GEORGE*): I'm outa here! I hate to interfere with family reunions!

(*WERNER starts to dress. GEORGE ties the belt around his waist.*)

GEORGE: Forgive me, Peter. You're right, you know. I'm sorry. It won't happen again.

MAX: How about it? Can we go now?

GEORGE (*is afraid*): Where are you going?

PETER: To a café.

WERNER: The prodigal son returns to the bosom of his family, huh? (*to GEORGE*) One day you'll be glad you have me! He's going to abandon you yet!

(*GEORGE looks anxiously at PETER.*)

PETER: I'm not going to stand by and watch this any longer, George. If he (*points to WERNER*) shows up here one more time, I'm leaving. I don't want to share you. And if that's too much middle class morality for you, then we'll just have to go our separate ways.

GEORGE (*walks over to PETER*): It won't happen again, Peter. Forgive me.

WERNER (*to PETER*): Now don't make a scene, what's the point? He doesn't love anyone but you, don't you think I know that? I've spent the last three weeks sleeping in the train station, with the homeless guys, because I'm totally broke and can't pay my rent! That's why I'm here! I wanted a bed for a change! And a shower!

PETER: Is it our problem if you spend all your money on that heroin shit?

WERNER: Don't take the name of the divine drug in vain! Know-it-all!

GEORGE: You're killing yourself, Werner!

WERNER: I'll survive all of you. (*grins*) I'm really sorry for you. (*He has finished dressing, kisses GEORGE on the cheek and exits.*)

GEORGE (*to PETER*): Please don't leave. You can talk here. I have to go back to bed anyway. Okay?

PETER: All right.

(*PETER looks at MAX. MAX sits down again.*)

GEORGE: Good-bye, Mr. Schmiedinger. (*goes into the bedroom*)

MAX: God, this is insanity! Pure bedlam!

PETER: Like something to drink?

MAX: Yeah, give me something stiff. I need it.

(*PETER pours two vodkas, hands one glass to MAX, sits down. They drink. MAX lights a cigarette.*)

PETER: How're things at home?

MAX: Aunt Hazel died.

PETER (*nods*): Well, she was no spring chicken. Did you get someone new?

MAX: Yes. Your ex-wife. She's my housekeeper now.

PETER (*has to laugh*): Oh, really?

MAX: Yeah. And she's my girlfriend too. It works. (*after a while*) I've been thinking, Peter. Maybe it's my own fault.

PETER: What is?

MAX: That you're the way you are.

PETER: What gives you that idea?

MAX: When I was a kid, about twelve years old, I looked at a book. An art book. There were pictures in it, of Greek statues. Naked men. I liked them. Maybe this is the punishment.

PETER (*shakes his head*): Oh, Papa!

MAX: That's not all. When your mother died, all you did was cry. Because she wasn't there anymore. You couldn't sleep. For days and days, not a moment of sleep. And so I took you into my bed and laid you on my chest and talked to you and comforted you. And then you fell asleep. So that became habit with you. You would only fall asleep on my chest. From age two to age six you would only fall asleep on my chest. Hazel always said that's not normal. But what was I to do?

(*PETER walks over to his father, puts his arms around him and begins to cry. This embarrasses MAX. He doesn't know what to do with his hands, but finally puts his arms around PETER.*)

MAX: Come home. Come back home. We'll survive this. No one has the guts to say anything, at least not in the open. Behind my back of course they talk, they make cracks about me, they don't look me in the eye. But even that doesn't matter to me anymore. What's past is past.

PETER (*weeping*): Thank you, Papa! Thank you, Papa!

MAX: We'll survive this.

(*PETER lets go of MAX, steps back and looks at him.*)

PETER: I'm coming home, Papa. But not just now. I can't abandon George now. He's sick. He has no one but me.

MAX: Why? He's got that dopehead!

PETER: I can't, Papa. Not now. Later.

MAX (*gets up*): Man, let him croak, the bastard! He's worthless! Come on! There's nothing for you here in this pigsty!

PETER: Later, Papa.

MAX: This is your last chance, Peter! Either you come with me now or it's over—for all time!

PETER: I can't do it, Papa, I'm sorry.

(*MAX walks toward the exit.*)

PETER (*gets up*): Papa! I'm looking forward to it! I've been so homesick! But give me time! Please!

MAX (*comes back; in desperation*): He'll infect you! Is that what you want?

(*PETER doesn't answer.*)

MAX (*suddenly matter-of-fact*): Now or never, Peter! Him or me!

(*PETER struggles within himself, looks toward the bedroom door, looks at MAX, shakes his head. MAX turns away, walks toward the door, then turns back.*)

MAX: I should have castrated you. Back when you were a kid. With my own hands. (*Exits.*)

(*Blackout*)

7. AIDS Ward (City)

(*A three-bed room. On the first bed sits the junkie CHARLY in a robe, smoking and nervously turning the pages of a magazine. In the second bed lies GEORGE, gray and hollow-cheeked under the covers, hooked up to an intravenous drip and using an oxygen mask, which he holds over his mouth and nose whenever he is not speaking. On a chair next to the third bed sits the transvestite JUDY, completely wasted to skin and bones, with thinning hair that has fallen out in patches, his face covered with skin cancer sores (bluish-red lumps). JUDY is wearing a beautiful Japanese kimono, has in front of him on his nightstand a mirror and makeup utensils, and is making up his face with shaking hands. There is also a styrofoam head on the nightstand; next to it lies a red rose. PETER is sitting on a chair next to GEORGE, holding GEORGE's free hand.*)

GEORGE (*in a weakened voice*): I'm doing much better now. I've gained almost 24 pounds. They're going to get me back on my feet again. Then we're going to Greece. Aren't we?

PETER: Of course.

CHARLY: Aw, cut it out! You can't even get from here to the john anymore!

GEORGE (*indignant*): I'm going to Greece, and you're going to die here! You're going to see to that yourself!

CHARLY: Yeah, that's what you'd like to see, wouldn't you? My immune system is in great shape! I have five hundred T-cells in me! Per cubic. And how many do you have?

(*GEORGE doesn't answer.*)

CHARLY (*to PETER*): He has six! Six! Six T-cells!

(*PETER looks at GEORGE with concern.*)

GEORGE: They're gonna get me back on my feet again, Peter.

(*CHARLY gets up, walks to the foot of GEORGE's bed, picks up his chart and shows it to PETER.*)

CHARLY (*points to the chart*): Six T-cells, eight hundred white blood cells! You may as well order his coffin!

PETER: Listen, do you enjoy it, when someone dies?

CHARLY (*hangs the chart back*): Anyone who dies before me is all right with me! And especially when it's a gay! It's your fault that I'm here! Am I wrong?

JUDY: No smoking! No smoking! I'll call the nurse!

CHARLY (*walks over to him*): What do you want? (*grabs JUDY by the throat*) What do you want? Don't you mess with me, you fairy!

PETER (*gets up*): Leave her alone, Charly! (*threatening*) You hear me?

(*CHARLY lets go of JUDY, who falls forward, breathing hard. CHARLY walks away a few steps, stops suddenly, puts his hand to his head and thinks hard. PETER walks over to JUDY.*)

PETER (*pulls JUDY back up*): Come on, lie down, Judy.

JUDY: I have to make myself beautiful, Peter. He's coming today. I'm okay now, thanks. That bully! (*to CHARLY*) I am a star! You can't treat me like that! (*continues to apply makeup with shaking hands*) God, my skin!

(*PETER goes back to GEORGE.*)

CHARLY: What was I going to do? (*to PETER*) What was I going to do?

PETER: How should I know?

CHARLY: I was going to do something! (*looks at his watch*) Is he out there now? Did I ask him to come now? (*walks over to GEORGE*) Listen, did I ask Thomas to come now?

GEORGE: Don't ask me!

CHARLY: I am so hungry for a needle, I think I asked him to come now!

(*CHARLY pulls a pair of cowboy boots out from under his bed, puts them on and runs out.*)

PETER: Is he always this crazy?

GEORGE: Toxoplasmosis.

PETER: What?

GEORGE: A parasite in his brain.

(*PETER doesn't want to hear about this, gets up, paces up and down despondently. GEORGE puts the oxygen mask away.*)

GEORGE: Come here. Talk to me.

(*PETER sits back down.*)

GEORGE: How are you doing?

PETER: Good. I won a competition. (*laughs bitterly*) A hospital! I've designed an incredible hospital!

(*PETER sits there, depressed. GEORGE strokes him.*)

GEORGE: We had such good times. Three years. That's really a lot. Three years of happiness. How many people have that?

(*PETER doesn't answer.*)

GEORGE: That I fooled around with Werner for so long . . . I'm so incredibly sorry, please forgive me. He held a certain fascination for me. But later on it was nice, wasn't it?

PETER (*nods*): Yes, very nice. (*is fighting with tears; after a while*) I want so much to go home. I want so much to go home. Pick apples from the tree, run through the meadows, go hunting with my father. Go bowling with my workers.

(*GEORGE moves to the side, pulls PETER to him on the bed and embraces him.*)

PETER: You know what? I'm taking you with me!

GEORGE: Where?

PETER (*sits up*): Home. To my house. In the country. I still have my apartment there. I'll care for you. I'll watch out for you.

GEORGE: Really? Would you do that?

PETER: Yes, of course!

GEORGE (*hugs him*): We have to wait a little, till I get my strength back.

PETER: How long will that be?

GEORGE: A couple of weeks. Then I'm sure I can walk out of here.

PETER (*sits up again*): I couldn't stand it here even for three days.

GEORGE: You know, it's not so bad. We're completely sheltered here. They take really good care of us. Some guys don't ever want to leave.

PETER: I'm talking about him! (*points to CHARLY's bed*) I think it's too much to ask, putting you in with a junkie like that. I'm going to complain!

JUDY: Yes, please, do that! His behavior is unbearable, the doper!

GEORGE: That'll be over soon. In a couple of days he'll go into his next phase. Then he'll be a baby.

JUDY: Well, I'm looking forward to that! What an unbearable macho man! And he never washes, either, did you notice that? (*looks in the mirror, sees that he has smeared his makeup, because his hand is shaking so, begins to cry*) Oh, God, look at me! He won't love me any more! (*looks at GEORGE and PETER*) He won't love me any more!

GEORGE: Sure he will! You're still beautiful!

JUDY (*looks in the mirror*): An ugly mug is what I've got! A deaths-head is what I've got! Repulsive! Disgusting! You know, he was always such an aesthete! He never stayed over night. So that he wouldn't have to look me in the face in the morning. But he treated me like a queen in the evening. Like a queen. A real gentleman. If only you knew who he is! A famous man! On TV every day! I'm proud of that. I sit in front of the TV, millions of people see him, and I know he loves me! I am the only person in the whole world that he loves. Isn't that marvelous? God, did it spark between us! I walk on stage, the band starts to play, and suddenly we see each other! Clark Gable, Robert Redford, Harrison Ford all rolled into one! Crazy! I almost missed my cue! I was singing just for him. Just for him. And tonight he's coming for me. For the big banquet. Tonight you'll see me in the news! At his side! (*looks at his watch, which is lying on the nightstand*) Oh, God, I have to hurry! (*continues to apply makeup, then drops the lipstick in despair*) I can't do it!

PETER: Here, let me help you.

(*PETER walks over to JUDY, takes a tissue, wipes the makeup from JUDY's lips, he stands up and PETER starts to apply his makeup over again.*)

GEORGE: Sing us your song, Judy, Please! It's so beautiful!

JUDY: Sorry, George, I have to save my voice. But when he comes, I'll be singing it anyway. As my greeting.

PETER (*is finished with the makeup job*): How's that?

JUDY: Thanks, Peter!

(*PETER goes back to GEORGE, JUDY searches for his wig in the nightstand, CHARLY comes back in.*)

CHARLY: The bastard didn't come! I'll kill him! Did I say in the park or in the visitors' john? George!

GEORGE: Don't you remember, Thomas is dead!

CHARLY: What? He's dead?

GEORGE: Well, of course he's dead!

JUDY: My wig! Where's my wig? Did you see my wig?

GEORGE: Nope, not a clue, Judy.

JUDY: I can't see him without my wig! Look at me! (*He

looks in the bed for his wig, finds it under the pillow,
sets it on the styrofoam head and styles the hair.)

CHARLY (*to GEORGE*): No, seriously, is Thomas dead?

GEORGE: You were at his funeral.

(*CHARLY looks at GEORGE with astonishment, thinks
hard; as he realizes what is happening to him, he groans in
despair and begins to bang his head against the wall.
PETER gets up and pulls CHARLY away from the wall.*)

CHARLY: Get lost! Don't touch me! (*without transition*)
I've got to call whats-her-name, uh . . . (*he can't remember the name*), uh . . . she has to get me something.

(*CHARLY walks over to his nightstand, searches through
it frantically, throwing things out. PETER sits back down.
CHARLY turns to GEORGE.*)

CHARLY: Did you take my methadone?

GEORGE: Nope!

CHARLY: You better not let me catch you! 'Cause I'll kill
you!

GEORGE: I'm no addict! I don't need your methadone!

CHARLY: But your biker needs it! He stole a whole bottle
from me before!

GEORGE: Go on, that's crazy! You're paranoid!

CHARLY (*threateningly*): Don't tell me I'm paranoid! Don't
you say that! Okay?

GEORGE: All right, all right!

(*JUDY puts on his wig, straightens it, plucks at it. PETER
is staring straight ahead. GEORGE notices this.*)

GEORGE: There's nothing between us, Peter! Werner just
comes to visit me! Honest!

(*CHARLY walks over to JUDY.*)

CHARLY: Come on, gimme a couple of Rohypnols!

JUDY: I need them myself.

CHARLY: Please! I'll pay you! Really! I'm getting some
cash soon! I've got a deal going!

JUDY: You're not very nice to me. I don't see why . . .

CHARLY (*screams at him*): Give it to me, man! I need it!

(*JUDY gets three tablets out of his nightstand and gives
them to CHARLY.*)

CHARLY: Only three? You got more, don't you?

JUDY: I need my sleep, too! Go on, get lost!

(*CHARLY goes back to his bed, puts the three pills in his
mouth, pulls from his nightstand a liquor bottle wrapped
in a paper bag, drinks from it and takes the pills, puts the
bottle back, lies down on his bed. JUDY suddenly looks at
the door, gets up, picks up the red rose, and walks toward
the door.*)

JUDY: You've come? You've finally come? I'm so happy! I've
been waiting so long for you!

(*PETER and GEORGE look toward the door with astonishment, for no one is there, then look at JUDY. CHARLY is
spaced-out.*)

JUDY: Do you remember our song? (*starts to sing "Over the
Rainbow" in a weak voice*)

(*PETER and GEORGE listen to JUDY, CHARLY is not
aware of the singing. Suddenly CHARLY sits upright,
pushes back his sleeve and rubs his forearm.*)

CHARLY: I need a needle, I'm going crazy!

(*He gets up, searches frantically in his belongings again, looks at GEORGE, walks over, tears the intravenous needle out of GEORGE's arm and out of the drip tube.)*

GEORGE: Hey!

(CHARLY sits on the edge of his bed, pushes back his sleeve, jabs the needle into his vein, makes a fist, and begins to pump.)

CHARLY *(flatly)*: I need a hit! I need a hit! I need a hit!

(PETER walks angrily to the door to call for help. JUDY collapses. PETER turns to JUDY, frightened.)

PETER: Judy!

(Blackout)

8. George's apartment.

(A sickly PETER sits with GABY at the table. GABY is not wearing her "working clothes" today; she is drinking whisky and smoking a cigarette.)

GABY: And his vacation acquaintance gives him a package, beautifully wrapped, and says, this is a goodbye present, because we had such a good time, but he's not supposed to open it till he gets home, it's supposed to be a surprise. He flies home, and in the terminal he opens the package. What do think was inside?

PETER: Haven't a clue.

GABY: A dead rat and a note! The note said, "Welcome to the AIDS Club!" Can you imagine? Welcome to the AIDS Club! Gosh, that's mean! Boy, was that a shock! Of course he immediately had a test done—and what was it? Positive! Actually positive!

PETER (*smiles*): You still go for those horror stories, don't you?

GABY: They aren't horror stories! Really! Listen, you'd be surprised how many people infect other people on purpose! Y'know, I won't do anything without a rubber anymore! Haven't for a long time now! They can pay what they want! I'm not crazy! In two more years I'm gonna quit anyway! I'm going to get a snack stand. The owner is a customer of mine. He's retiring and has no children. You won't believe it, but he got rich with it! A super location! During the day my partner mans it and at night I'll be there myself. I'm a night person. I can't do a thing during the day. Days upset me! Everything's 'way too hectic! I get my color in a tanning bed. 'Cause you do need a tan in this business. The one I'm in now, I mean. It's not good to look unhealthy. Except for a few perverted ones. I have my own tanning bed at home, you know. I have the greatest hallucinations when I'm in it! Usually end up out in space, and then—

PETER (*interrupts her*): Gaby!

GABY: Yes?

PETER: Did you talk to my father?

GABY: Oh, yeah, sorry! Yeah, I talked to him. Just over the phone. He doesn't want me to come anymore. I understand that. He doesn't need me anymore.—He married the Filipina, did you know?

PETER: No. He didn't invite me. And what do the people in town think about that?

GABY: Well, nothing. They understand that he needs someone. Especially now that he doesn't have you anymore. She never goes out into the town anyway. She's been so loyal to your father, you can't even imagine. Waits on him hand and foot. As if he were a pasha. A woman from around here wouldn't do that anymore. The perfect slave, I tell you! No wonder it suits him! And now she's even pregnant.

(*PETER nods slowly.*)

GABY (*laughs*): Of course he hopes the kid will look more like him than his wife!

PETER: And what did he say?

GABY: What? Oh, yeah! Listen, it's a little touchy at the moment.

PETER: Come on, don't beat around the bush, please! I want to know!

GABY: He has disowned you, Peter. "I crawled to him on my knees, all the way to the city," he said. "But he snubbed me, preferred his life with the gays and the junkies to a return home to his father's house. So he can just croak, for all I care. I won't shed a tear for him." Now you know.

(*PETER nods slowly.*)

GABY: Peter, I'm sorry I don't have better news. But, my God, there are plenty of kids who never return to their parents' house. I don't think that's such a tragedy. You don't need your father, you have your own life.

PETER: No, I don't. Not me. I'm nothing without him.—I am so scared, you can't imagine!

GABY: Why? (*looks at him, notices his poor condition for the first time*) Are you sick?

PETER: Yes.

GABY: The same as your friend?

PETER: Yes.

GABY: Oh, God! You poor thing! Are you getting treatment?

PETER: No.

GABY: Well, why not?

PETER: I have to go through this now. This is my penance.

GABY: No, Peter!

PETER: I'm shaking with fear. George was so brave, so courageous. When it came down to it, he was stronger than all the others. Even when he was dying, he was comforting me. I'm not courageous. For me this is hell.

GABY: Let me tell you something, Peter. Your father can say what he wants. I know him. He loves you. Still. I mean, do you really think the Filipino straggler can ever replace you?

PETER: I love him, too.

(*WERNER and a YOUNG MAN emerge from the bedroom. GABY looks surprised, then looks at PETER. WERNER puts on his leather jacket, walks over to PETER, reaches into the inside pocket of his sportscoat, takes out PETER's wallet, opens it, takes out several bills, puts the wallet back, claps PETER on the shoulder, exits with his arm around the YOUNG MAN. PETER has let all this happen without resisting. GABY watches in amazement as the two leave.*)

GABY: Well, I better . . .

PETER: Stay a while longer. Please.

GABY: Sure. Do you have a little more? (*lifts her glass*)

(*PETER gets up, pours some more whisky in her glass, sits back down, she raises her glass to him, drinks, and lights another cigarette.*)

GABY: Well, yesterday, let me tell you! I had another one of those country guys—a chicken breeder, totally smashed. Soon as it was over, he starts to cuss at me, pulls out a knife—an incredibly huge thing—right out of his briefcase and gets ready to carve me into pieces! Wow, did I ever give it to him! Reinhard—my boyfriend—had to sweep up the remains! There are guys out there, let me tell you! At home they're all responsible and straitlaced up to here, y'know, and then with us they go hog-wild. The ones that appear most normal are the most disturbed, believe me! An exterior as smooth as polyester and a mind like an outhouse! You really shouldn't torment yourself, Peter! Not many men are as normal as you! Why, just two weeks ago, there was a . . .

(*During GABY's last few sentences, PETER has started to breathe hard, he then has an asthma attack and begins to gasp for air. GABY is frightened when she notices this, and she stops talking.*)

(*Blackout*)

9. Subway station/Greek beach

(*Night. PETER sits on the ground, looking seedy, but still in his business suit. Next to him is a box containing a few coins. Against the box leans a large hand-lettered sign, saying HAVE AIDS. A man hurries by in the direction of the subway, followed by a pair of giggling girls, then a boy, then ERIC, who is following the boy [for what reason, we'll find out at the end of the play]. They all ignore PETER. The sound of an arriving, then a departing train can be heard.*)

PETER (*cries out suddenly in despair*): Father! Father!

(*The scene is transformed into a Greek beach at sunrise.*)

The sound of the waves can be heard. WERNER and GEORGE approach. WERNER is dressed in a black T-shirt, black pants and pointed shoes, his black jacket in his hand. GEORGE (very white in the face) is wearing a white linen suit and is barefoot. They have obviously been quarreling, for GEORGE is walking away hastily. WERNER runs after him and catches him by the sleeve.)

WERNER *(comfortingly)*: Έ, Ψυχογιέ; Έλα, έλα τώρα, μή κάνεις έτσι. Σ' αγαπώ βρε Γιώργο!(Hey, Sonny Boy! Come, come now, don't be that way! I love you, George!)

(GEORGE pulls away, runs ahead, spots PETER.)

GEORGE *(delighted)*: Πέτρο! (Peter!)

(PETER gets up; he is no longer sick.)

GEORGE: Πέτρο! *(Peter!)*

(GEORGE walks over to PETER and hugs him passionately.)

GEORGE: Το ξέρεις, οτι ήθελα πάντα εσένα, μόνο εσένα! (You know I always wanted you, only you!)

(WERNER slips his arm into the left sleeve of his jacket, wraps the jacket around his arm, pulls a switchblade, and flips it open. GEORGE hears this sound, looks at WERNER, lets go of PETER, steps back, looks at WERNER, then looks at PETER.)

WERNER *(to PETER)*:Έλα βρε αδερφέ, αν έισαι άντρας και έχεις κουράγιο, έλα εδώ να αναμετριθούμε! (Come on then, Brother, if you're a man and have courage, come here and fight!)

(PETER also pulls a knife and flips it open. PETER and WERNER begin to circle one another and to fight. Eventually WERNER forces PETER's knife out of his hand and prepares to stab PETER.)

GEORGE: Μή, μή σε παρακαλώ! Μή το κάνεις αυτό! (No, no, I beg you! Don't do it!)

(WERNER looks at GEORGE and then stabs PETER without ever taking his eyes off GEORGE. PETER sinks to the ground, dead. GEORGE looks at PETER, horrified. WERNER wipes his knife off on PETER and puts it back in his pocket. As if carried in on the wind from afar comes the music of the most famous of all Greek Hassapikos, "Frankosyriani," sung by Markos Vamvakaris. Because he must, GEORGE begins to dance the Hassapiko [Butcher's Dance], circling the dead PETER. Tears run down GEORGE's face.)

GEORGE (*after a while, to WERNER*): Έλα, έλα να χο ρέψεις μαζύ μου!   (Come, come, dance with me!)

(*WERNER stands next to GEORGE, each lays an arm on the other's shoulder, and they dance together. But before the song is over, GEORGE suddenly screams out in agony and runs away.*)

WERNER (*calls after him, grinning*): Γειά σου ψυχογιέ μου, στο καλό και καλή αντάμωση σύντομα! (Good bye, Sonny Boy, farewell, till we meet again!)

(*WERNER turns to PETER and looks down at him. The song is over. The scene changes back to the subway station. PETER is alive, and sick.*)

WERNER (*furious*): What are you lying around here for, you bastard? Begging for sympathy, huh? For alms?

(*WERNER jerks PETER to his feet.*)

WERNER: All we have left is our pride, you understand? (*shakes PETER*) Pride! Pride! The world doesn't need us! The world spits on us! The world lets us croak and then laughs at us! But we don't need the

world either! We spit on the world, too, and laugh!
We have each other! Each other, you understand?
We don't need any father, any mother, any brother!
Any president, any administration, any health de-
partment! We have each other and Death! Whoso-
ever loves Death, will not die! Whosoever loves
Death will live forever!

(*PETER cries out in despair. WERNER puts his arms
around him and kisses him. At first PETER yields and
goes along with him, but then he pushes WERNER away.*)

PETER (*screams*): Father!

(*Blackout*)

10. Men's room in a tavern

(*Where in the opening scene the man dressed as Death
leaned against the wall, now PETER sits, still dressed in
his business suit as in the previous scene, staring into
space. ERIC enters, drunk and looking for PETER; he sees
him.*)

ERIC: Hey, why're you blocking the bathroom? You can't
    block the bathroom for days on end! Folks gotta
    pee!

(*PETER looks at him, but says nothing.*)

ERIC: What are you doing here? Leave us alone once and
    for all! The owner's gonna call the police if you don't
    leave!

PETER: Where am I supposed to go?

ERIC: We don't care! Back to the city!

(*PETER doesn't reply.*)

414 *Abraham*

ERIC (*points toward the dining room*): Listen, a couple of
   guys are waiting out there with two-by-fours!

PETER: Well, let them come in!

ERIC: Your father is out there, too.

PETER (*despondent*): Why doesn't he come? Why doesn't
   he come?

ERIC: You hurt him too much!

PETER: Yes!

ERIC: He has no friends left. Except for me. I'm the only
   one.

(*ERIC walks over to PETER and kicks him in the stomach.
PETER doubles over in pain. ERIC steps back immediately, out of fear of infection.*)

ERIC: Did you think I was going to go to jail, huh? You
   asshole! He didn't even report me! Because he
   knows that I understand him! I'm standing by him!
   Like a rock! Every weekend a drinking spree! That
   bonds! (*walks over closer to PETER, bends toward
   him, but always with what he feels is the necessary
   distance*) You know, he's afraid his Filipino bastard
   will turn gay someday too! You see that in the Filipino men. It's perfectly normal with them. With the
   Greeks too. There you're only called gay if you dress
   like a woman. Anything else goes.

(*The VICAR enters, looks around for PETER, and walks
over to him. ERIC steps aside immediately.*)

VICAR: Peter! You can't do this! Don't make such a scene!
   Come on!

(*The VICAR tries to help PETER get up, but PETER fights
him off.*)

VICAR: Be reasonable, Peter! (*looks at him*) My God, you

look terrible! Come on now, I'll take you to the hospital.

PETER: Why? I have to die anyway.

ERIC: But not here in our shithouse! You're contaminating everything! Do us a favor and go croak somewhere else!

VICAR (*to ERIC*): Just keep your filthy mouth shut, would you?

PETER: Well, I think this is the perfect place for me, Eric.

VICAR (*to ERIC*): Please leave now, I want to speak to Peter alone!

ERIC: All right, Vicar. (*exits hastily*)

VICAR (*to PETER*): Would you like to confess?

PETER: No.

VICAR: This is your last chance, Peter.

PETER: My last chance has long since come and gone, Vicar.

VICAR: Why do you say such things? That's not true! I'm giving you the chance! God is giving you the chance!

PETER: No. I am guilty. I must do penance. That is right and fitting.

VICAR: I'm glad, Peter. Really. That you see the error of your ways, I'm glad! (*kneels down next to PETER*) Come, give me your confession. Then I will grant you absolution.

(*PETER gets up with difficulty and stands unsteadily.*)

PETER: But God says: "Destroy the homosexuals!" Right, Vicar?

VICAR (*he regrets what he said back then*): Yes! And you

are destroyed! But not for all eternity! If you repent, you will be forgiven!

PETER: I am guilty, Vicar, and I take the destruction upon myself. But I do not repent.

(*The VICAR is exasperated. MAX enters, drunk. The VICAR stands up. ERIC appears behind MAX, but remains standing at the door.*)

MAX (*shouts at PETER*): You just won't stop disgracing me! Why don't you stop disgracing me?

(*PETER sinks to his knees.*)

PETER (*imploring*): Father! Take me home! Please! Please! Take me home!

MAX: So that you can infect us all, huh? My wife and child and me? Why do you want to kill us all? Tell me that!

(*ERIC withdraws again.*)

PETER: I don't want to kill you! I just want to be with you! Father!

MAX: You've already killed me! You've already killed me!

(*ERIC returns with six MEN. Four of them are carrying various forms of wooden clubs. They approach PETER. ERIC remains in the background.*)

VICAR (*steps in front of PETER protectively*): If you beat him, you'll have to beat me, too!

(*The MEN stop.*)

MAX (*to PETER*): Go! Get out of my sight! My greatest wish! I'm begging you!

(*PETER looks at MAX and stands up.*)

PETER: Forgive me, father. You're right.

(*PETER walks out slowly. The MEN make room for him.*)

MAX (*after PETER has gone*): So this is how it is, huh? Coming after me with clubs?

ERIC: Not after you, Max!

MAX: Is this your thanks, huh? Is this how you thank me for giving you all work? (*screams*) You lived off me all your life! I was like a father to you men! And now you're coming after me with clubs!

(*MAX yanks the board out of the hands of the MAN standing nearest him and starts beating the MEN, driving them out of the men's room. ALL run away. ERIC withdraws frightened into one corner. The VICAR watches the scene with satisfaction. MAX throws the club at the last retreating MAN and stands there, breathing hard.*)

(*Blackout*)

11. Garbage dump (Country)

(*Lights up.*)

A.) (*ERIC approaches, carrying in his hand a full plastic bag with the logo of a supermarket chain printed on it. He looks around, searches the dump, discovers a sort of cave in the garbage. Its entry is covered by a dirty, torn sheet of plastic. ERIC approaches the cave.*)

ERIC: Are you in there, Peter?

VOICE OF PETER (*strangely different*): Yes!

ERIC: It's me, Eric!

VOICE OF PETER: What do you want?

(*ERIC sits down next to the entry and sets the plastic bag down.*)

ERIC: I want to ask your forgiveness!

VOICE OF PETER: For what?

ERIC: I blackmailed your father. I condemned you. I hated you.

VOICE OF PETER: Yeah, so what?

ERIC: I shouldn't have done that!

VOICE OF PETER: Why not?

ERIC: Whenever I went to the city, I didn't just go to the casino, but also to the parks and the men's rooms. I like women. But I like men, too. I just wanted to tell you that.

PETER: Fine. I heard it.

ERIC: Do you forgive me?

VOICE OF PETER: Yes, I forgive you!

(*ERIC gets up, leaves the plastic bag of groceries behind, and leaves.*)

(*Lights down.*)

(*Lights up.*)

B.) (*The VICAR approaches, looks around, sees the shelter, and walks toward it.*)

VICAR: Peter!

VOICE OF PETER: Yes?

VICAR: It's me, the Vicar!

VOICE OF PETER: Yes?

VICAR: I'm coming to confess!

VOICE OF PETER: Not to me, you don't!

VICAR: Of course! Only to you! To whom else?

VOICE OF PETER: I don't want to hear anything!

VICAR: You've got to listen to me, I beg you! When you were a child, when you were an altar boy, I watched you, you and the other boys. (*sits down next to the entry*) I enjoyed it. How I would have liked to join you! Do you hear me, Peter?

VOICE OF PETER: Yes, I hear you!

VICAR: I'm like you. I'm one of your kind. That's why I became a priest. So that no one would force me to marry, like your father forced you. And so that I have protection from temptation. I succumbed a couple of times nonetheless. I'll hate myself for it to the end of my days. Do you forgive me?

VOICE OF PETER: Yeah, I do! God won't!

VICAR: I know. God won't.

(*The VICAR gets up and walks away.*)

(*Lights down.*)

(*Lights up.*)

C.) (*Dusk. A column of smoke rises from the garbage heap. Some distance away, a rifle shot can be heard, and following that, the fluttering and cawing of crows as they fly up. After a while, MAX approaches. He is dressed in hunting clothes and carries a hunting rifle with a sight attached. He looks around, searches the dump, and discovers the shelter. MAX walks over, looks at the plastic cover, extends his hand, pulls it back, takes down the rifle, sets it down, sits down next to the shelter, lights a cigarette, takes out a pocket flask, drinks out of it, puts it away again.*)

MAX: Are you in there? Are you in there, Peter?

(*After some time, the sheet of plastic is pushed aside and PETER crawls out. He is covered with dirt and skin cancer sores, paralyzed on one side and blind. He is wearing rags from the garbage dump, and is barefoot. MAX looks with horror at his son.*)

PETER (*has difficulty speaking*): Where are you? Where are you, Father?

(*MAX falls to his knees in front of his son, puts his arms around him, pulls him to his breast, and starts to cry.*)

MAX: Oh, God! Oh, God!

PETER: Don't cry! Don't cry! God doesn't like it! The old werewolf doesn't like it!

MAX: Come with me! Come with me, Peter! I'm taking you away! We're going home!

PETER: No! Not home! Not home!

MAX: You've done your penance! It's enough! It's really enough, Peter!

PETER (*tormented*): No! Not yet! It's not enough yet! I was waiting for you!

MAX: I'm here now! I'm here now! Come with me, let's go home!

PETER: Were you shooting, Father?

MAX: Yes. I was after the old twelve pointer, you know him. Today I almost shot him. But the light was failing.

PETER: Shoot me, Father!

MAX: What?

PETER: Me! Shoot me! (*crying*) Abraham! Abraham!

MAX (*shrinks back in horror*): What are you saying?

PETER: Take now thy son, thy only son, whom thou lovest, and offer him for a burnt offering upon one of the mountains!

(*MAX stands up and backs away.*)

PETER (*sits up, weeps and cries out*): Abraham! Do it! Do it!

(*MAX looks at his son, walks over to his rifle, picks it up, cocks it, looks at PETER. PETER has heard the sound of the hammer being cocked, sinks to his knees and raises his upper body.*)

PETER (*turns his eyes heavenward*): I loved you, Father!

(*MAX takes aim at PETER. Suddenly JUDY appears at the top of the garbage heap in a radiant light. Beautiful, in a glittering dress, he looks like an angel of God.*)

JUDY (*calls out*): No! Don't do it!

(*MAX and PETER look at JUDY. MAX looks at PETER, then back at JUDY, then shoots PETER. PETER falls back, dead. The flapping of the crows' wings and their cries can be heard again as they fly up. MAX looks at his dead son, shoulders his rifle and walks offstage. The song "Over the Rainbow" sung by Judy Garland is played. Slowly JUDY comes down toward PETER, looks down at him smiling gently, sinks to his knees, pulls PETER onto his lap and lays PETER's head against his breast.*)

(*During the playing of the song, the lights go down slowly.*)

THE END

AFTERWORD

Felix Mitterer's Victims

Felix Mitterer's plays are frequently mentioned in the same breath with the Austrian popular play or *Volksstück*. To summarize here the long and distinguished history of this traditional genre (and Mitterer's place therein) would be a daunting task.[1] Suffice it to say that Mitterer's plays can be considered "popular" for several universal reasons. First, though they frequently deal with middle- or lower-class Austrians, the plays are accessible to all classes, and to non-Austrians as well. They portray problematic situations and characters, generally society's victims, whether in medieval or modern garb.

Secondly, Felix Mitterer's plays are popular in the sense that they are well received. People "like" his plays, though perhaps not in the sense that they enjoy the event; experiencing a Mitterer play, whether as a theater-goer or as a reader, can be singularly unpleasant. There are often strong doses of sex and violence, generally perpetrated against innocent victims within society. Mitterer is a sensitive witness to such crimes within our midst, and he vividly depicts the weaker, gentler beings among us who are most vulnerable to the physical and psychological cruelties inflicted upon them.

In many ways, Mitterer is a product of the late 1960s, and especially of the political activism of that era. He speaks of "solidarity" and political engagement with the clear intent that social problems not be ignored.[2] Indeed, the form and content of Mitterer's scripts may remind us of traditional morality plays, either because they are drawn from that genre, or because they provide their own mythical situations as moral reference points. *Everyman* and *Abraham* are, from their very titles, direct references to traditional moralistic themes. Similarly, Mitterer also frequently appends an introductory reference to some character or situation of Biblical or mythic proportion: an introduction to *Home* quotes the Bible's recitation of the Prodigal Son, while *The Wild Woman* has an initial explanation of the phenomenon concerning these legendary women, accompanied by a passage from Homer's *Odyssey*.

In addition, Mitterer has the amazing ability to create characters with a single gesture, characters that surprise and often touch us with their humanity and thus their vulnerability. In *Abraham*, for example, the bullying father, a true "heavy," reveals that he would take his baby son on his chest to soothe the infant. In the same play the pathetic transvestite Judy, who can no longer even put on "her" make-up, is consequently depicted as a faithful and loving person who maintains her dignity throughout the ordeal; at the play's conclusion Judy is unambiguously seen as an angel.

Another instance of surprising character development occurs in *Children of the Devil*. The scribe—a writer like Mitterer!—, an insignificant "player," turns out to be the only person who is repulsed by the interrogations and tortures, the only one who questions the validity and justice of the trial and thus feels he cannot continue. And in a departure from the traditional popular play, Mitterer devotes great care to the presentation of his female characters: they possess attributes that evoke our interest, our sympathy, and frequently our tears. Because the women are often strong, loving, caring, supportive, and giving to the point of self-sacrifice, they are thus vulnerable to the whims of a male-dominated society. For this reason they are often the innocent victims of masculine authority and cruelty.

The five plays presented here are a retrospective of Mitterer's work from 1986 to 1993 and are to be seen as a complement to the five works which appeared in the first

Ariadne volume, *Siberia and other Plays.*[3] There, too, Mitterer examines pressing social issues, as seen in the lives of several of society's victims: from the retiree who has been relegated to a nursing home by his unfeeling relatives in *Siberia,* to the various "patients" awaiting human and humane contact in *Visiting Hours.* In a historical vein, Mitterer depicted the exploitation of farm workers in nineteenth-century Austria in *Stigma,* while *There's Not a Finer Country* shows the betrayal of a Jew in a small Alpine village during the Third Reich. Even the fanciful *Dragonthirst,* a direct descendent of Mozart's *Magic Flute,* portrays the universal struggle between good and evil.

The Wild Woman (1986)

The myth of the "Wild Women"[4] is a brilliant symbol of male-female dynamics: the introductory quote from the *Odyssey* already posits an archetypal brave man, attempting to outwit a duo of dangerous women, the original *femmes fatales* of the ancient world! This timeless competition requires a victor and a vanquished, for it is a struggle to the death—as witnessed by the pile of rotting skeletons from earlier visitors. However, the theme is subtly refined in Mitterer's play: the Wild Women come, they mate, but do they conquer? No, instead they bring happiness and good fortune. But, the males in the audience ask, at what price? They require only decent treatment as human beings, with respect and love, and the freedom to be themselves. The injunction not to reveal their names or heritage is simply a reminder to accept the woman for herself, not to be distracted by her origins or her family's status. She should not be abused nor required to do anything to which she does not consent. Is this too much to ask for earthly bliss? Apparently it is, if we are to judge from Mitterer's play.

Irrespective of their socio-economic backgrounds

as woodcutters, the male characters represent several different types of men: Elias is an aged sage, Jock a family man, Les a criminal, Mutt a proud but not-so-bright farmer (and musician!), while Wendl is an innocent and modest youth. Their interactions, first as woodcutters and then as competing suitors, produce mounting tension. For these hired laborers, physical strength is an important attribute. However, as men—as human beings—, they must learn that strength alone will not solve all problems nor bring them happiness. They blunder on, under the delusion that physical strength prevails over mortal strength, or, as Elias says: "The rougher you are, the stronger you are. The stronger you are, the more you win!" As their brutal treatment of each other and of the woman accelerates, they quickly destroy each other. The woman, and her potential blessing, is freed and will now be available to other, possibly more worthy men.

At the conclusion of the play, Lex's dying words to the woman are: "You win! You've destroyed us all! Damned whore! Damned whore!" He couldn't be more wrong. The woman has not "won," though the men have indeed "lost." They have destroyed themselves, both literally and figuratively. Their (and especially Lex's) strong-arm tactics to prolong happiness through bondage, by keeping it as a trophy—like the deer nailed to the wall—is self-defeating under any circumstance. Were Elias still alive, he would certainly have reminded the men "not to look a gift horse in the mouth."

Home (1987)

Having outgrown his narrow upbringing, a young man escapes to the wide world beyond, to learn more about life and to fulfill his dreams. This age-old plot recalls the legend of Parzival who, after years of struggle, of wandering and discovery, attains the throne of the Grail Castle, the epitome of the best of both worlds, the sacred and the profane. Yet even the exemplary Parzival, revered knight of the Round Table, does not attempt to return to his humble beginnings in the forest. However, we mortals who do remember our roots, our family, friends, neighbors, are always tempted to return, to rekindle old memories as well as to be admired by awed family and friends.

In *Home* this theme forms the backdrop for Mike's adventures. Clearly, the young man has neither sought nor attained any sort of success on his journey out into the world; he is disenchanted, a drop-out, aimlessly roaming the countryside on his motorcycle—the perfect vehicle for itinerant vagabonds and trouble seekers. With him rides a "modern" woman, independent and emancipated, "in" to the point of being "far out"—a non-conformist and free-spirited traveling companion with no goals, no rules. Anything goes.

But why is a bright, idealistic young man traveling about with this "druggie" whore? To "save" her? And where are they bound? Just "south," to the beaches, so that she can more pleasantly kick her drug addiction? It becomes evident that Mike is, in fact, going nowhere ... just home. But the intriguing question arises: Why? To flaunt his new, sophisticated girlfriend? To relive fond memories of home and friends? To recapture his youth, his innocence, or his ideals? Or perhaps to repair the wounds which caused his departure.

As the play progresses, we learn more of his motives, his childhood, and the people who played significant roles in his youth: His father and mother, his boyhood friend and girlfriend (now pregnant and engaged to the arrogant and vindictive Ossi). It becomes evident that Mike could not and will not fulfill their expectations of him, for that would mean compromising his ideals. Conversely, they could not and will not change either—so all are destined to clash, to quarrel, to grow ever farther apart. Is this the inevitability of growing up, an immutable natural law viewed under Mitterer's microscope?

Mitterer has made this problematic situation even more urgent through his development of characters. While we may react with ambivalence to the young anti-hero, other male figures fare even worse, when seen as unbending rivals rather than supportive friends. Our sympathies ultimately lie with female characters, each of whom is victimized through the males' power struggle. The mother, despite all attempts to do "right" by her son, has been destroyed by her domineering husband. The hard-bitten, self-confessed whore, Nina, who has "seen it all," is reduced to a vulnerable, frightened little girl when confronted with Ossi's brutality. Mike's former girlfriend, Monika, is shown to be a loving, sensitive woman who was forced to settle for second-best; though pregnant, she is the only one who can still muster the honesty and strength to walk away from a destructive relationship when she must.

Clearly, none thrive under such relationships, and none, whether they remain at home or flee to a far-away glamor spot, can find happiness in their respective lives. There is no room for honesty, sensitivity, love, and mutual nurturing. Power and its brutal enforcement predominate. Here nothing can thrive, nothing can survive. Here we glimpse the killing fields of modern society, where parents and children alike suffer in isolation.

Perhaps the most trenchant symbol for this situation is Mitterer's suggested stage-setting: a rubble-strewn site, though it is purposely ambiguous whether the project at hand is construction or demolition, whether this chosen background represents inevitable progress or the decimation of human relationships, indeed of humanity itself.

Children of the Devil (1989)

Among all of Mitterer's plays about man's cruelty to man, this play is all the more heart-wrenching, both because it is based on historical fact[5] and because the helpless victims are children, poor children who are simply trying to survive in a hostile world. They are homeless, without family or friends other than their fellow orphans and cast-offs.

From the very first (unstaged) scene, announcing Barbara Koller's burning at the stake, the audience can relate this dusty historical event to current issues, such as the relevance of public executions and the death penalty. Granted, the children in this play may not be entirely " innocent"; after all, they have had to survive in an inhospitable environment. But neither do they deserve to suffer to this degree at the hands of the law. Are these children truly such a threat to the state or to the local communities that they must be eliminated if they cannot be exiled? The play also confronts the issue of corporal punishment—when is it *not* torture? Even the implied threat of torture is, in itself, a form of torture. The violence awaiting the children, as sanctioned by the state, is represented by the Executioner, a truly frightening figure, both through his imposing physical presence and through his sadistic delight in inflicting pain; his master stroke was the idea of attaching a bag of gun powder around the neck of those to be burned at the stake, so that the exploding powder would blow off the victim's head, thereby achieving a desired deterrent effect on the assembled audience.

Society's representative for justice, the Commissioner, goes about his required duties conscientiously and circumspectly, attempting to carry out his assigned duties in a fair and impartial manner, until he is taunted into personal spite by Magdalena Pichler with her provocations and insults. From this point on, we can see how imposing institutionalized brutality can be, especially when contrasted with the sensitivity and common sense of an impartial witness—the court scribe. He is clearly the most "normal" of all, the one person most like the decent citizens in the theater audience, and thus the one who must speak for us all. He grows weary and is on the verge of a breakdown as a result of the testimony and torture he has witnessed. He is a thoroughly decent human being, but one powerless to stop the wheels of justice as they roll over the vulnerable children.

Mitterer's final bomb is reserved for the play's conclusion, when the Commissioner is confronted with the possibility that the entire trial has been a farce, and thus a miscarriage of justice. In the seventeenth-century "Catch 22," the trial would have to begin all over again. The older "suspects" would have to be interrogated anew and would have to suffer further bouts of the Executioner's wrath. Still worse, some of the youths have now "come of age" and would themselves be eligible for torture, bringing yet more pain and suffering to the helpless children.

One Everyman (1991)

For Austrians, the mere mention of an *Everyman* play immediately calls to mind that country's classic rendition by Hugo von Hofmannsthal at the turn of this century.[6] For today's audience *Everyman* is less a drama than a traditional spectacle where the story (and its ending) is a known commodity. To a certain degree Felix Mitterer offers here old wine in new casks, an old chestnut that the audience can immediately recognize and appreciate. Mitterer's version, however, is considerably more than just a unique adaptation for the twenty-first century.

The traditional Everyman, dating back to his ancient ancestor Job in the Old Testament, is anything but a representative "every man." He is always an affluent, powerful individual, a man who has everything. And it is obvious why such an exalted character would be chosen to play this role. A person of wealth and influence has so much more to lose: a life of leisure, featuring all those earthly delights the rest of us can only dream of; a life of beauty, surrounded by fabulous treasures, both human and artistic; a life of adulation, with a fawning crowd of envious supplicants acceeding to one's every whim. To lose all this provides a dramatic "fall" from the heights of earthly abundance. The lessons learned on this grand scale have exemplary meaning for all lesser mortals, whereas the opposite would not be true: Who would even notice (or care) if a peasant fell from grace? A poor man has only his life, his miserable existence to lose through death; whether he goes to Heaven or Hell is inconsequential—he would, at best, be free of his earthly drudgery. Viewed in this light, we come to realize that the play should more aptly be titled "Everything," for that is what the main character must lose, along with his soul. Ironically, Everyman has "Everything," yet "Nothing," since he does not have salvation.

Yet how is Everyman to attain salvation in a culture cluttered with the latest conveniences, sealed off from the real world (and his soul) by the walls of wealth and power? As far as Mitterer is concerned, there will be no Reformation-related quarrel about the predominance of faith versus works; if *either* were present, it would confirm the possibility of the other, and Everyman's soul could be saved. In a traditional morality play, the role of the Cardinal would also assume immense significance. As the representative of God on earth, he would lay claim to being the arbiter, the mediator between a man and his God. Yet here we find him to be just another camp follower, first advising Everyman to see a psychiatrist, then insisting he "just" believe, if he wishes to attain salvation.

Throughout Mitterer's cast of characters we encounter other stunning innovations. Like the traditional morality play, the roles here are patently symbolic; we are familiar with the parts played by Beauty, Wisdom, Generosity, etc. By going one step further and portraying each character doubly, that is Mammon=Investment Banker, Mitterer is able to point out comparable roles in contemporary society, both as a didactic example and as a satiric target for our scorn. From the quarreling Trinity to the Wall Street Devil and a workaholic Everyman, we find familiar, traditional characters that have been around for ages, yet are refreshingly new. God the Father, God the Son, and God the Holy Ghost remind us of yet another of life's many committees, a spiritual board meeting which includes the petty bickering and personal agendas of the various participants. Here, too, the PC-toting Devil strikes a familiar chord. He is the ultimate wheeler-dealer, an amoral manipulator whose goal is not just to win the game, but to destroy the other players at all costs. His is the most fascinating and yet frightening role of all, precisely because he is so realistic, so true to type. On the other hand, the three-dimensional female characters are especially appealing; they are modern women, complete with their own psychiatrists, yet ultimately loving, caring, redeeming; they are less obsessed with the trappings of power than the men, and thus more readily willing to forsake overabundance for a merely "comfortable" life.

Yet it is the three suffering Children—Mitterer's own invention—who capture Everyman's attention and his conscience. Unlike his own generation, they are the youngest, the hope for the future. We must realize that, like Everyman in every generation, we leave a legacy with which later generations will have to live. This is a global concern in the broadest sense of the word. While we destroy those around us, those with whom we work and live, those who love us and deserve our love—it is still the helpless children of the world who represent Everyman's opposite: they have nothing and are maimed or crippled for life in our thoughtless quest for Everything.

Abraham (1993)

In many respects, *Abraham*[7] is a typical Mitterer play: a conflict between cosmopolitan and provincial values as represented by two separate individuals, a son and his father, with the threatening figure of the macho Greek gangster or *Mangas* as ominous backdrop. The explosive topic—homosexuality and the AIDS epidemic with all its moral and social implications—can be seen as a crucible for human relationships: between a son and his father, between a man (Peter) and his God, between an individual and his society. While these points can be discussed in the abstract, Mitterer does a masterful job personifying the various conflicts, destroying impersonal stereotypes, and eliciting understanding for the victims and their suffering.

A successful young architect named Peter has "designed" his life to accommodate his personality; he conducts his professional and personal (homosexual) lives in the anonymity of the city, while treasuring memories of his distant rural origins. Like Mike in *Home*, Peter is irresistibly drawn to his hometown. Though we might question the premise for the first scene—why would Peter, who is discretely hiding his homosexuality, bring his lover to his hometown Mardi Gras, risking exposure and censure?—it introduces the most brutal moment in the play. Any audience which survives this initial scene must realize the potential for an escalation of the violence and thus of the danger to which Peter and his homosexual companions are exposed.

Though his love both for his father and for his homosexual lover complicate life, Peter's compassion and love are evident in his relationships with both men. This humane and decent young son is to be seen in stark contrast to his father, Max, a former construction worker and now a hugely successful contractor. Max is a veritable bulldozer, insensitive and crude, flattening all opposition in his path. His companion Eric (and in similar respects Wer-

ner, the symbolic *Mangas*) are also cruel exploiters, he-
men who play by their own selfish rules and thus dominate
society's innocents. Intimidation, brutalization, even murder are trademarks by which they assert their will.

In one sense, the father (as such, a representative
of the elder generation) is the most important and contro-
versial character here, one who plays the pivotal role in
this relationship. He cannot be lightly dismissed as a brut-
ish and unfeeling father, as in most father-son conflicts; we
are given insight into his finer qualities, as mentioned earlier. His repeated (albeit clumsy) attempts to coax his son
into a "normal" lifestyle, from providing a skilled prostitute and later a Filipino bride to threats of disinheriting
the son, are frustrated at every turn; in desperation, he
even blames himself for his son's homosexual traits. It is
obvious that he loves his son, while abhorring Peter's sexual preference. And although Mitterer in his "Anmerkungen"[8] insists that the father has sacrificed his son on
the altar of social convention (and literally sacrifices him
at the play's conclusion), we cannot ignore the son's own insistent request for this bizarre execution. Here we could
imagine the father granting his son's death wish out of pa-
triarchal devotion to Peter, despite the fact that the
father's own bloodline will die out with the fulfillment of
the wish. This, then, is indeed the stuff of Greek tragedy—
at least for the father.

While several scenes are set in the dismal homosexual atmosphere of men's lavatories (reflecting Peter's
own feelings of guilt toward his chosen lifestyle), Mitterer
casts the concluding scene—literally—in a favorable light.
As the transvestite/angel Judy cradles the dead Peter in
an obvious allusion to the traditional Christian pietà, the
Biblical symbolism is now expanded to the Christ-like
image of a martyr, sacrificed for his cause—love. Seen in
this "light," who can not help but weep for the sacrificial
victim, Peter, and all that he represents.

To concentrate too heavily on Mitterer's victims would be an over-simplification of his artistry.[9] Nonetheless, these plays do attempt to sensitize us to the everyday cruelties committed unto the least of us, unto society's outcasts. We must not overlook the fact that those who perpetrate these cruelties, some consciously, some unconsciously, are just like ourselves, people of some affluence and influence for whom a worthwhile end often justifies an inhumane means. We are no longer just innocent bystanders in a theater of illusion, but active participants in the life of a larger community. And, like Mitterer's antagonists, we too may be victims of our own crimes—society's victims are, ironically, both those characters who are tortured and those who torture, those who suffer pain and those who inflict it. Like Lex in *The Wild Woman*, we may blindly blame others for the destruction we have wrought, while not realizing the diminishment of our own lives as well as those of our victims. Thus, in a larger sense, Mitterer purposely " victimizes" his audience. In almost every play we find one or two victims (generally a young man and/or woman) with whom we can identify. Through them, Mitterer allows us to share the frustration of being powerless, the feeling of vulnerability, and often the pain of physical abuse. Through them we learn what it is like to be one of society's many victims. And, as we leave the theater or close the covers of this book, we may never again be able to commit such acts or to walk past such brutality without raising our voices in protest. Only someone who has been a victim has a strong stake in eliminating future abuses.

Todd C. Hanlin

Notes

1. For a cogent insight into the type and role of the *Volksstück*, see Hans Eichner's "Afterword," in *Felix Mitterer: Siberia and Other Plays* (Riverside, CA: Ariadne Press, 1994), pp. 367-368.

2. Mitterer frequently repeats his personal commitment to social and political justice, for example, in the interview "Felix Mitterer im Gespräch mit Ursula Hassel und Deirdre McMahon," *Modern Austrian Literature*, XXV (1992), 19-39. See especially page 28.

3. Felix Mitterer, *Siberia and other Plays*.

4. According to Mitterer's own account in *Stücke I* (Innsbruck: Haymon Verlag, 1992, p.259), he first wrote a movie script in 1977 on this topic, but it languished for lack of interest. Then, in 1985, he rediscovered the manuscript, re-wrote it as a playscript, and produced it in 1986 in Innsbruck. Austrian Television (ORF) contracted to film the play, so in January 1987, the entire ensemble retired to an isolated woodcutters' cabin in a forest in the Zillertal, where they filmed the play in twelve days of gruelling work.

5. Through an acquaintance, Mitterer was made aware of the enormous amount of documentary evidence surrounding this, the biggest "trial" in seventeenth-century Europe. His archival research in Munich and Salzburg provided actual testimony from the trial, the basis for the composite figures he created here.

6. Hofmannsthal revised several medieval morality plays (*Death and the Fool, The Salzburg Great World Theater, Everyman*) in an attempt to bring some semblance of continuity into a modern age conspicuously lack-

ing values which could guide twentieth-century men and women to an understanding of life, its responsibilities and consequences.

7. The genesis of *Abraham* provides an interesting insight into Mitterer's inspiration for and commitment to his material. Mitterer was contacted by a friend who related that a third party had contracted AIDS and wished to tell Mitterer his story. After an inexcusable delay, Mitterer finally attempted to contact the man, only to learn that he had died days before. Stung by a guilty conscience, Mitterer felt obliged to write a play about the man's story; however, due to the parents' reluctance to cooperate, the playwright decided to write a different story, still about AIDS, but also delving into related issues, such as the son's guilty conscience and love for his estranged father. See the "Anmerkungen zum Stück 'Abraham,'" in Felix Mitterer, *Abraham: Stück über eine Liebe* (Innsbruck: Haymon Verlag, 1993), pp.77-78.

8. Ibid., p.78.

9. One astute observer points out Mitterer's own ambiguous feelings toward the authority figures in his plays. While the exploiters—the land holders, the clergy, and the politicians—attempt to retain the status quo and thus their power base at any cost, they are nevertheless part and parcel of the "old" Austria, an immutable cornerstone of its provincial tradition. They themselves are threatened today by even more destructive forces, such as development to accommodate tourism and the accompanying despoilation of the rural environment which make the lives of the "victims" even worse. See Karl E. Webb, "The Configuration of Power in Felix Mitterer's Works," in *Modern Austrian Literature*, XXVI (1993), 143-152.

Translators' Note

Any translator worth his or her salt would welcome the opportunity to translate the works of one of Europe's leading playwrights. Works of substance, written by a skilled dramatist, with provocative plots and unforgettable characters, are a translator's dream. Moreover, just the thought that these plays could (and should) actually be staged in English, that audiences will hear our translations, and that, in fact, our labor may introduce a new talent to the American stage, is an additional incentive.

But here the glory ends, and the hard work begins. Felix Mitterer poses substantial problems for the translator. His profound interest in the "little people" of this world invariably leads him to provincial settings where the characters speak a non-standard variant of the language, thus requiring a local or regional dialect on the part of the cast of characters. In some instances Mitterer himself has advised that the play be performed in the dialect of the local theater where it is to be staged, all the better to create an immediate and powerful effect on the live theater audience. Since the play's language is therefore not standard German, the problem is always: what comparable "voice" would these characters have in English? The various German dialects, whether in Austria, Germany, or Switzerland, do not correspond to regional speech patterns in America: one cannot simply impose the language of a cowboy from Texas, a surfer from California, or a cab driver from New York. Numerous questions must first be answered: Are we dealing with myth or historical reality? And what historical period is represented here, the 18th century or contemporary life? Is the speaker from a particular social class, from an urban or rural area, well educated or illiterate? Does he or she use slang or other speech peculiarities? (Does he or she swear, and if so, how vigorously?) Does the speaker have any particular speech idiosyncracies, such as short, choppy sentences, interjections, or the habitual repetition of a favorite phrase? And finally, does he or she use colloquial expressions, quote scripture, speak jargon related to a particular profession or social sub-culture? And, consequently, should the play be located in its original Austrian (or Tyrolian) setting, or, like the language, should it be adapted to present a *universal* human dilemma and not simply a local one? In fact, all of the above-mentioned situations do occur (and with frightening regularity) in Mitterer's plays.

We have tried, as accurately as possible, to address these issues, to provide translations that are faithful to Mitterer's genial originals, yet natural to the English tongue. If you, the reader or theater-goer, find these plays exciting and yet discomforting, then we have done our job.

ARIADNE PRESS
Translation Series

Lerida
By Alexander Giese
Translation and Afterword
by Lowell A. Bangerter

Three Flute Notes
By Jeannie Ebner
Translation and Afterword
by Lowell A. Bangerter

Siberia and Other Plays
By Felix Mitterer

The Sphere of Glass
By Marianne Gruber
Translation and Afterword
by Alexandra Strelka

The Convent School
By Barbara Frischmuth
Translated by
G. Chapple and J.B. Lawson

The Green Face
By Gustav Meyrink
Translated by Michael Mitchell

*The Ariadne Book of Austrian
Fantasy: The Meyrink Years
1890-1930*
Ed. & trans. by Michael Mitchell

Walpurgisnacht
By Gustav Meyrink
Translated by Michael Mitchell

The Cassowary
By Matthias Mander
Translation and Afterword
by Michael Mitchell

Plague in Siena
By Erich Wolfgang Skwara
Foreword by Joseph P. Strelka
Translation by Michael Roloff

Memories with Trees
By Ilse Tielsch
Translation and Afterword
by David Scrase

Aphorisms
By Marie von Ebner-Eschenbach
Translated by David Scrase and
Wolfgang Mieder

Conversations with Peter Rosei
By Wilhelm Schwarz
Translated by Christine and
Thomas Tessier

*Anthology of Contemporary
Austrian Folk Plays*
By V. Canetti, Preses/Becher,
Mitterer, Szyszkowitz, Turrini
Translation and Afterword
by Richard Dixon

Try Your Luck!
By Peter Rosei
Translated by Kathleen Thorpe

ARIADNE PRESS
Translation Series

ARIADNE PRESS
Studies in Austrian Literature, Culture and Thought